OSKAR KOKOSCHKA

A LIFE

OSKAR KOKOSCHKA

A LIFE

FRANK WHITFORD

WEIDENFELD AND NICOLSON

LONDON

First published in Great Britain in 1986 by
Weidenfeld & Nicolson Limited
91 Clapham High Street
London SW4 7TA

ISBN 0 297 78718 7

Photoset by Deltatype, Ellesmere Port
Printed in Great Britain by
Butler & Tanner Ltd
Frome and London

For J. G. Mosher

CONTENTS

ILLVSTRATIONS

CHAPTER HEADINGS

ONE

Oskar Kokoschka was born on the first day of March 1886 in Pöchlarn, a small town on the Danube due west of Vienna and not far from the magnificent Benedictine monastery of Melk. Since the previous May Kokoschka's parents had been living in a flat in Pöchlarn where a relative owned or managed a sawmill.

In Kokoschka's imagination the circumstances of his birth became significant. His mother later told him that a fire had broken out in Pöchlarn not long after the delivery. It rapidly became a conflagration which illuminated the night sky and threatened to destroy the entire town. As the flames approached, Oskar, his mother and older brother were rescued and driven to safety in the back of a haycart. Almost certainly, however, the fire never happened; but Kokoschka wanted it to be true and it assumed dramatic significance in his mind, providing evidence for his belief in portents. The fire held some mysterious meaning and was part of a pattern of strange, inexplicable events which punctuated and seemed to give significance to his entire life. Kokoschka fervently wished to believe in portents.

He also wished to believe he was gifted with second sight and that he had inherited the gift from his mother as she had from hers. Not for nothing did he call the first public lecture he gave 'On the Consciousness of Visions'.

Fire, said Kokoschka's mother, Maria Romana, had also accompanied her birth in 1861. The daughter of Ignaz and Barbara Loidl, she was one of a large family; some accounts say there were ten Loidl children, others eleven or twelve. Her father was a forester in the imperial service and the family lived an isolated existence in a small house surrounded by deep woods high up in the mountains of Styria, one of the least populated provinces in the Austro-Hungarian empire.

All Romana's brothers became assistants to their father as soon as they were old enough, planting and felling trees, rearing game birds, distributing fodder for the deer and wild boar and acting as beaters and loaders for aristocratic hunting parties in the summer and autumn. In the winter the house was usually cut off by deep snow and even when the paths were clear the nearest village, Hollenstein, was several hours away by foot. The female members of the family became accustomed to solitude and silence and the absence of men. Romana's father and brothers were often away about their business for days at a time, sleeping in huts placed at strategic points throughout the vast area of forest and high pasture for which they were responsible.

It was a beautiful and wild place and because of its isolation not without its dangers. Gypsies were common in the region and they occasionally left their camps to scavenge. Just before Kokoschka's mother was born, she later told her son, a group of them approached the house in search of food, terrifying the pregnant Barbara Loidl who retreated indoors with her young children and barred the door. The gypsies angrily set fire to the winter fodder stacked under the eaves and tried to smoke the family out. As the flames began to take hold of the timber house Ignaz Loidl and his sons appeared and put the gypsies to flight. Almost immediately after that Romana was born.

We do not know how or where Romana Loidl met Gustav Kokoschka, Oskar's father, but it was an unpromising match. She was eighteen when they married, unsophisticated and superstitious.

He was already over forty, reasonably well-educated, highly skilled, used only to city life and with a solid if unsatisfactory background in business.

Born in 1840, Gustav Josef Kokoschka had been brought up in Prague and spoke both Czech and German with equal facility. He had trained as a goldsmith in the family business which had been established several generations before and enjoyed royal patronage. Handsome profits enabled the Kokoschka family to live very comfortably in one of the better streets of the Bohemian capital.

When Gustav Kokoschka met Romana Loidl his family's affluence was a thing of the past however. The economic crisis of the 1880s ruined many small businesses throughout the Habsburg empire, especially those engaged in luxury trades. Gustav Kokoschka, by then head of his family and senior partner in the firm, was forced to cease trading and sell the imposing house in Prague. He moved to Vienna in 1864 where, because of the presence of the Imperial Court, he believed he would find new and richer clients and fulfil the kind of social ambitions possible only in the capital. But goldsmithery, like every other highly skilled craft threatened by industrialization, had ceased to be profitable even in Vienna and Gustav grew increasingly desperate in his search for work. He even went briefly to Paris in the forlorn hope that he might be able to start a new life there. Then he moved with his wife to Pöchlarn and returned to Vienna in 1886 where he managed to survive by repairing watches and acting as a travelling representative for a relative who sold jewelry, but his predicament worsened further when he was cheated out of most of the money he possessed. In 1889 he moved with his family again, this time to Aussig where they stayed until 1892. Then they returned finally to the capital. There seems to have been something feckless about Gustav Kokoschka.

When he married Romana Loidl in 1884 his prospects did not look good. Her love for him proved stronger than her common sense. Not only the difference in their ages, less unusual in a marriage then than now, should have made her pause. Even allowing for the harsh economic climate, it ought to have been clear that Gustav was already a disillusioned and bitter man, his pride and ambition destroyed by the reduction in his circumstances. He might once have been a business-man with members of the royal family among his clients; now he had difficulty coping even with the housekeeping account. But Romana was no doubt impressed by his urban sophistication, believed physical maturity to be synonymous with wisdom and had faith in his ability to earn a good living once conditions improved. She seems never to have regretted her decision to marry Gustav Kokoschka. She bore the debts, the moves from place to place, his unreliability and inconsistent behaviour with fortitude, but when, in 1923, he died, she seems soon to have forgotten him. When she herself died eleven years later she was buried elsewhere.

Oskar was the Kokoschkas' second child. He had an older brother, named Gustav after his father, who died in infancy in Vienna in 1887. Kokoschka thought he could remember something of the dreadful mood at home caused by his brother's death and an image of a horse-drawn hearse was etched on his memory. In 1889 his sister Berta was born in Aussig and in 1892 the Kokoschkas had another son, Bohuslav. The birth of one of these children, presumably of the brother, proved traumatic for the young Oskar. In a letter to a friend written in 1908 he revealed that his mother had 'through a dreadful accident, given birth beside me . . . the blood made me faint. Ever since then I have been unable to get along properly with people.'

Life was not easy. Kokoschka's father, despairing of ever earning his living with his craft again, became a clerk. His employers paid poor wages and treated the staff badly. To avoid giving the statutory annual bonus, the firm usually sacked all its employees just before Christmas every year and hired them again just after the New Year holiday. Oskar Kokoschka never forgot the disappointment he experienced as a child whenever Christmas arrived, for there were few presents and the family had little to celebrate. When he was older he usually did everything he could to avoid Christmas completely, preferring to use the holiday for uninterrupted work, a habit which once caught him out when, years later and alone in Switzerland, he was without food for two days because he had forgotten that the shops and restaurants would be closed.

Gustav Kokoschka was not cruel to his family. He did not drink to excess; he did not seek consolation with women; he was never violent. But his inability to earn adequate wages created enough difficulties for his family and their plight grew steadily worse. As possessions were pawned never to be redeemed, as unpaid bills mounted, the Kokoschkas were obliged to move to smaller flats increasingly distant from the centre of Vienna. By the time Oskar was old enough to begin school they had ended up in a second floor apartment on the outskirts of the city.

Gustav Kokoschka was often depressed, frequently moody and always proud. He had several influential relatives in Vienna, one of them in the imperial service, another a school headmaster and a third no less a personage than the director of the state library. But Gustav kept his distance: pride prevented him from asking for aid or seeking their company.

Oskar Kokoschka came to regard his father as inadequate and that drew him closer to his mother. From an early age he saw himself as the virtual head of the family, as the only person reliable enough to protect the interests of his mother, sister and brother. That explains why he continued to live at home long after most people of his age set themselves up on their own and why he was so ambitious for both wealth and fame. It also explains why, once success was his, great wealth always eluded him. Much of what he earned he gave to his family. Most of his letters home were to his mother and were largely about financial matters. Eventually he was able to buy his family a house and then regularly exhausted his funds paying the interest on the mortgage. When his sister married it was he who paid for the wedding. Even when his brother had reached manhood Kokoschka persisted in treating him like an adolescent. After both his parents had died he constantly worried about the well-being of his sister and brother.

His concern for his family was matched only by his mother's possessive attitude to her children. She did everything she could to discourage permanent liaisons for her sons. Significantly, both Bohuslav and Oskar only got married during the Second World War after their mother had died and when they were isolated from each other.

When Oskar Kokoschka was born the Austro-Hungarian empire was one of the greatest powers on earth. It extended from Galicia and Transylvania in the east to Lombardy in the west. It ruled Bosnia, Herzogovina and Dalmatia in the south, Bohemia and Moravia in the north. It had a population of around forty-six million which was racially, linguistically and culturally diverse. Since 1866 when it had lost a war against Prussia and Italy, the empire had remained at peace, ruled in relatively enlightened fashion by the ageing emperor Franz Josef. In spite of the strident demands for self-determination from every corner of the empire, it appeared to be as secure as ever, in the age of nationalism, an anachronism perhaps, but an anachronism that worked.

The atmosphere of Austro-Hungary in those years is memorably evoked by Stefan Zweig in the volume of memoirs called *Die Welt von*

Gestern – The World of Yesterday.

Everything in our almost one-thousand-year-old Austrian monarchy seemed to be permanent. . . . Our currency . . . circulated in gold coin and thus guaranteed its immutability. Everyone knew how much he earned or how much he was entitled to, what was permitted and what forbidden. Everything had its norm, its particular size and weight. . . . No one believed in war, revolution or subversion. Everything radical, everything violent seemed impossible in an age of reason.

This sense of security, of the immutability of all things, was enhanced by a belief in progress:

On the streets at night electric lamps shone . . . thanks to the telephone, person could already speak to person far away; he could already fly there with new speed in the horseless carriage; he already swung upward into the air in the dream of Icarus made real. . . . Water no longer needed to be fetched from the well or passage . . . hygiene spread; dirt disappeared.

Vienna was the hub of this sprawling and apparently secure empire and contained the empire in miniature within it. All of the bewildering number of languages spoken by Franz Josef's subjects could be heard in its streets: Hungarian, Croatian, Italian, Polish, Yiddish and even Romany. With a population of almost a million and a half it was one of Europe's most cosmopolitan and exciting capitals, the diversity of its inhabitants reflected in its cuisine, entertainments and newspapers. Its opera, theatres and orchestras were the envy of the world. Its cafés were a byword for civilized relaxation and stimulating conversation. Its women were celebrated for their beauty and taste. Vienna seemed effortlessly to combine the best of northern and southern Europe: German efficiency humanized by Latin hedonism; logic tempered by flair and imagination. Vienna was more than the capital of the Habsburg empire: it was the cultural capital of all German-speaking Europe.

Yet the glittering image of Vienna as the city in which every night was danced away to the music of Strauss waltzes, where the Danube was always blue and the woods echoed to the sound of happy laughter, was as false as the conviction that the empire itself would never change. Harsh reality lay beneath the pleasant dream. Out beyond the Ringstrasse, the new, impressive boulevard encircling the ancient city centre, the fashionable spectacle gave way at first to genteel and then to grinding poverty. In the districts which, like Ottakring and Leopoldstadt, had sprung up in the wake of industrialization to accommodate the influx of immigrants looking for a better life, Magyars, Czechs, Serbs, Jews, Poles and other Slavs were condemned to a miserable existence in insanitary slums.

The largest number of immigrants to Vienna were Czechs, and Gustav Kokoschka was one of them. In spite of its difficulties his family might have fared worse: by the time Oskar Kokoschka went to school they were living not in one of the grimmest city districts but on the edge of Vienna where the urban sprawl began to look almost rural. Property was cheap there but the living conditions were more healthy than in the slums closer to the centre. Kokoschka remembered it as a 'world which . . . consisted of a labyrinth of gardens. Farther away the fields and meadows began, the vineyards, woods and forests, the bluish hills which grew in height up to the . . . horizon.'

It is not easy to gain a clear idea of what Kokoschka was like as a child. Formal photographs of him dressed in his best clothes tell nothing. In his autobiographical writings he says little about the actual circumstances of his life, preferring to concentrate either on the strange visionary experiences which he claimed visited him at intervals until his death, or on mundane details of the daily round: 'Drinking water was brought into the house in barrels. I looked out for the man to come and for this received a copper coin worth four kreuzer. Water for washing was driven up in carts that looked like today's beer drays.'

In 1892 Kokoschka was enrolled in the local primary school. During his first years at school he sometimes played in the Galitzinberg park close to his home. There he got to know two little girls who were taken regularly to the park by their snobbish mother who was alarmed by the attentions of the boy who looked little better than a street urchin. Oskar liked the girls very much, not least because, as he discovered to his delight, one of them attracted him physically.

He tried to capture the girls' interest by showing off. One day he sought to impress them by blowing up an ants' nest with some gunpowder he had manufactured at home by following instructions received at school. The explosion was much bigger than expected; one of the girls fell in a faint from a swing and her shocked and outraged mother forbade Oskar to have anything to do with her daughters again. She told the park keeper to make sure he never entered the grounds again and 'the childhood Eden of my dreams was lost behind a locked park gate'.

Determined to regain his paradise, Kokoschka tried to climb into the park over the iron railings. He lost his footing and fell 'on a heap of filth, a midden full of broken crocks, crawling with unimaginable, insatiable life. A stinking yellow liquid spurted up. There was a long-dead, putrefying pig, from whose swollen carcass rose a cloud of flies.' Unconscious, Oskar was carried home, where he fell ill, unable to open his eyes or close his mouth: 'At the root of my tongue sat a fly, which constantly turned round and round, laying its grubs in a circle.' The doctor could do nothing to help. Only the prayers of a priest who came to the bedside effected a cure.

Although Kokoschka reports this story as though it were the literal truth, parts of it are too fantastic to believe. Perhaps dwelling later on a childhood prank in his memory, he transformed it into an allegory of sexual awakening: the expulsion from the garden followed by retribution and then salvation at the hands of a Catholic priest.

It seems clear that Oskar Kokoschka was a normal boy, physically fit, intelligent but not unusually gifted. In spite of his early awareness of the shortcomings of his father, he also seems to have been a happy child. He was also adventurous and boisterous – as the episode in the park demonstrates. By the time he was twelve years old and had transferred to secondary school, electric trams had replaced horse-drawn buses in the outlying districts of Vienna and he travelled on them to school.

The schoolboys, unobserved by the conductor, used to hang on the back of the driver's cab and travel part of the way for nothing. But I had not reckoned on the speed of progress as I tried the new means of transport. My strength soon failed me but I could not jump free as I used to be able to do when I had had enough. I was thrown off and brought home with my head bleeding.

The school to which Kokoschka was travelling so recklessly was at Währing in the XVIIIth district in the west of the city. It was a *Realschule*, a secondary school specializing in modern and practical subjects. Unlike the *Humanistisches Gymnasium* where the emphasis was on the study of philosophy and the classics, Kokoschka's school was more concerned with the natural sciences and modern languages. Kokoschka later regretted not having attended the *Gymnasium* largely because he would have been taught Latin and Greek there. But scholarships were available only to the *Realschule*, so he had no choice apart from forgoing a secondary education completely.

At the *Realschule* he seems not to have enjoyed his lessons very much and to have been good only at art and languages. He was not idle, however, even if his behaviour in class might have given that impression to his teachers. Bored by the instruction, he sat through most lessons reading books under his desk, educating himself, it transpired, more broadly and effectively than his teachers could have done. He gradually worked his way through most of the classics of world literature in the small, closely printed and exceedingly cheap editions published by Reclam, the Leipzig publishing house which, years before the introduction of the paperback in Britain, helped widen the horizons of several generations of German-speakers.

Kokoschka's education nevertheless contained many gaps, 'because the teachers used to interrupt' while he was struggling to read under his desk, and what they did tell him was not nearly as valuable as what the books revealed. 'We never even heard of Byron at school. But why not, for he was a kind of genius . . . instead, we were always taught about Anastasius Grün. Who on earth was Anastasius Grün?' Even had Kokoschka learned that Grün was the pseudonym of a Count Auersperg who, around the middle of the nineteenth century, wrote such epic ballad cycles as 'Robin Hood', it is doubtful whether the poet would have exercised such a hold on the young man's imagination as the exciting and notorious Byron.

Kokoschka's private studies were augmented by his father's habit of reading aloud from the works of Goethe, Schiller, Herder and Lessing whenever he was at home in the evening. It was probably only on such occasions that Oskar felt particularly close to his father, and he was later grateful to him for having kindled his interest in literature. From a relatively early age Oskar was equipped with a close knowledge of the novel and the drama that was equal to that of most under-graduates. That knowledge helped him to become a writer himself and contributed to the wealth of allusion which distinguishes so many of his paintings and prints. His wide reading also made him intellectually inquisitive and interested in a remarkably large number of fields. The extent of his knowledge of history, languages and economics was unusual for a man formally more educated than he, let alone for an artist. Kokoschka came to read all the major European languages and was fluent in at least three of them – English and French as well as German. More of his writing is devoted to a consideration of history than to art and he had no time for fellow artists who pretended to be proud of the narrowness of their interests.

Of all the books which Kokoschka read as a child and young man one made an especially deep impression on him. It was a polyglot edition of Jan Amos Comenius's *Orbis Pictus*, a richly illustrated book for children which Gustav Kokoschka gave his son even before Oskar could read. 'Comenius was a humanist, and from the *Orbis Pictus* I learned not only what the world is, but how it should be in order to become fit for human beings to live in.' Kokoschka often said that the book and Comenius himself influenced his entire life. He often referred to it in speeches and writings and when he was middle-aged and in exile in Prague he began to work on a play about the life and teachings of Comenius.

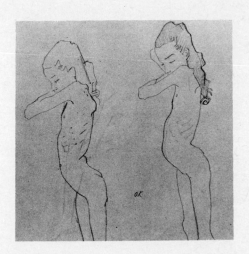

TWO

When recollecting the early life of a famous artist, his family, friends and former teachers usually stress the precociousness of his talent. Mothers remember hours spent before the fire filling sheet after sheet with astonishingly life-like sketches; schoolmates smilingly recall wicked caricatures of teachers in the margins of exercise books. Curiously there are almost no reports of Kokoschka's youthful artistic abilities.

Oskar's brother Bohuslav did remember a holiday with their uncle, Anton Loidl, in the country at Lassing in the summer of 1900 during which Oskar, then fourteen, produced some brilliant set designs for a local theatrical production. Such accounts are exceedingly rare and are supported only by very few surviving examples of juvenilia: there are photographs of some portraits and sketches of Anton Loidl from that same holiday, but nothing else is known. In spite of the obvious talent on the paternal side of the family (the Kokoschkas designed much of what they made in gold and silver), Oskar, at least as an artist, was a late developer.

Two teachers at the *Realschule* did discern some talent however. One, Leon Kellner, taught English and the other, a man called Schober, was the art master. It was he who suggested that Oskar might consider an artistic career.

For whatever reason, Oskar found Schober's suggestion attractive and, when he brought up the subject at home, his father's reaction may be imagined. Gustav was no doubt already looking forward to the time when his son would be the family bread-winner and probably entertained fond hopes that Oskar would become a chemist, a doctor or lawyer. Most of the artists he had heard of seemed permanently poor. According to his sister, Gustav was broad-minded enough to accept a compromise however: Oskar was obviously artistically inclined and it would do no good to smother his enthusiasm. He should give up his silly ideas about becoming an artist and study the history of art instead. Even though he might never earn much money as a scholar and teacher, at least there would be a *Herr Doktor* in the family. In any case he would only be able to go to university if he won a scholarship and the prospects for that seemed slim.

Encouraged by his mother, Oskar (in any case more ambitious than his father realized) decided to ignore the proposed compromise and apply for a place at an art school without telling Gustav. He chose the School of Arts and Crafts in Vienna, the *Kunstgewerbeschule*. The entrance examination was stiff and consisted in the presentation of a portfolio of work and a lengthy interview.

Kokoschka's sister Berta remembered that on the appointed day their mother waited anxiously outside the main entrance to the school for the entire time her son was being examined. She stood there from 8 in the morning until 12.30. 'Then Oskar rushed beaming out of the school. Accepted! They had taken only three of the 153 candidates, he shouted. . . . But it was months before father learned that Oskar was not a student at university but at the School of Arts and Crafts.'

Schober, the art teacher at the *Realschule*, then set about finding some kind of grant to enable Kokoschka to take up the offer of a place. He knew two sisters in Vienna, spinster ladies called Fröhlich, who had set some of their fortune aside to assist young artists. They gave

Kokoschka his scholarship. He officially enrolled at the School of Arts and Crafts on 1 October 1904.

The *Kunstgewerbeschule* was not the only art school in Vienna nor was it by any means the oldest. There was also the Academy of Fine Art which had a much longer tradition and more prestige. It produced only painters and sculptors, artists trained to respond to the promptings of their muse and to be disdainful of any creative activity that was craft-based or frankly commercial. In spite of its status the Academy was already regarded as moribund in some circles. The 1892 Baedeker guide to Vienna suggested that 'no one could have expected' the artistic significance acquired by the city during the last few decades in view of the Academy's lack of distinction: 'Although Vienna has had an Art Academy since the end of the seventeenth century it has made not the slightest contribution to the splendid renaissance in our art.'

The renaissance in Viennese art claimed by Baedeker in 1892 was more imagined than real; but his opinion of the Academy was accurate enough. The *Kunstgewerbeschule* on the other hand was progressive. A child of the nineteenth century, it taught more craft than fine art and had been founded largely in the belief that improvements in the design of manufactured goods might best be achieved through specialized education. Teaching at the Academy on the other hand was traditional and consisted in requiring the students to draw from plaster casts of classical sculpture and from live models before moving on to painting conventional subjects. It provided an education that was prescriptive, and discouraged experimentation and originality.

The *Kunstgewerbeschule* was founded in 1867 as the educational wing of the *Museum für Kunst und Gewerbe*, the Museum of Arts and Crafts, which pre-dated it by three years and was inspired by the English example of the South Kensington, now the Victoria and Albert Museum in London. That museum had grown out of the 1862 'Exhibition of the Works of All Nations' and had also spawned a school, now the Royal College of Art.

Although life drawing formed an important part of the curriculum at the Vienna School of Arts and Crafts (as did painting and printmaking) the emphasis fell on the design and the manufacture of objects for use and on vocational training. The younger institution was therefore broader in its approach and in closer touch with the real world than was the Academy.

Partly in response to the rapid growth of industrialization, schools of arts and crafts had been founded throughout Europe and especially in Britain, Germany and Austria during the second half of the nineteenth century and everywhere they had to fight for respectability. The belief that painting and sculpture were naturally superior to the crafts because they were untainted by practical considerations proved tenacious, and most ambitious students regarded an education at a school of arts and crafts as second best, more of an apprenticeship than a training for a profession.

In Vienna, however, purely local developments had produced an atmosphere in which, for a few years at least, the artist–craftsman was given his due.

In 1898 a group of artists, architects and designers had resigned from the official artists' organization (the *Künstlerhaus*) and founded their own, considerably less conservative group with the aim of injecting some vitality into what they regarded as the moribund body of Viennese art. Taking their lead from a similar dissenting group in Munich, the Viennese called their organization the 'Secession', but unlike their German colleagues, the Austrians were not primarily concerned with painting and sculpture but with architecture and the crafts. Among its founders were two architects critical of historicist ornament and eclectic styles then prevailing throughout Europe, Josef Hoffmann and Josef-Maria Olbrich. Its first president was Gustav Klimt who, although trained as a painter at the Academy, at that time regarded himself chiefly as a muralist and decorator. Most of the Secession's other members prided themselves on their versatility: they were as able to design a carpet as a canteen of cutlery.

The Vienna Secession was remarkable for the speed with which it was accepted by the public. A year after its foundation it had become rich enough to finance its own exhibition building and it quickly eclipsed all other artists' organizations in the city. For the wealthy and cultivated the word Secession became synonymous with high fashion, discriminating taste and modernity.

Although the group's many members worked in every imaginable medium they together created an unmistakable, common style which by comparison with what preceded it was simple, stressed geometry and used strong contrasts of form and colour. Whether applied to buildings or furniture by Hoffmann, book illustrations by Koloman Moser or posters by Alfred Roller, the Secession style was direct and straightforward and, although not devoid of ornament, anticipated the functionalism of the art and design of the later 1920s.

The Secession was instrumental in stimulating intense interest in the visual arts in Vienna, not merely among specialists but also among the general public. It also introduced the public to a wide range of contemporary art from almost every country in Europe. As a result of its activities all the important daily newspapers appointed new art critics and most of them were well-disposed towards modernist art. They also perceived their role as being to educate and inform, to act as the interpreters of difficult ideas.

The Secession was of great importance for the School of Arts and Crafts. While professors at the Academy were instructing their pupils not to visit Secession exhibitions lest they be contaminated by what they saw, the *Kunstgewerbeschule* was appointing Secession members as teachers. They soon dominated the school.

The close connections between the Secession and the School of Arts and Crafts were established by Baron Felician von Myrbach, himself a Secession member and the director of the school. Before he was appointed, the main aim of the *Kunstgewerbeschule* had been to provide students with a close knowledge of historical styles and traditional decorative motifs which they were expected to apply to everything they designed. The designers and artists whom Myrbach appointed reformed the school's teaching. They included Hoffmann, Roller, Moser and Carl Otto Czeschka who was to be especially important for the young Kokoschka. There was also Franz Cizek, a pedagogue with a consuming interest in the art of children who was convinced that it was much more than the inept attempt to imitate what adults did and that the natural talent of children should be encouraged with as little interference from the teacher as possible.

When Kokoschka applied for a place at the *Kunstgewerbeschule* he probably knew little of its reputation and teaching methods. He later claimed that he knew nothing of the Secession at that time either and had never seen any exhibitions of contemporary art, preferring to visit the ethnographic museum. What attracted him to that school in particular were practical considerations. If Gustav Kokoschka believed that an artistic training could not lead directly to a respectable career his son knew better. Unlike the Art Academy, the *Kunstgewer-beschule* offered a professional course for the training of art teachers. It led to a diploma which was recognized as an excellent qualification by schools throughout Austria. Kokoschka decided he would become an art teacher.

The course began with an introduction to a wide variety of media and skills. It lasted for two years. Students were expected to draw a great deal, especially from life, and there were classes in anatomy. Kokoschka greatly enjoyed working from live models, but death was something with which he sometimes found it difficult to cope. He remembered 'being sick when the professor demonstrated on a corpse; the air had entered the knee-joint with a hissing sound, and I had caught sight of the severed head, lying open-eyed in a pail under the marble slab'.

Kokoschka was at first not very happy at the school. Letters to Leon Kellner his former English teacher criticize the prescriptive teaching methods and reveal that the young artist was happier with the work he produced at home than with school exercises. They also reveal that the student was already thinking about exhibiting but intended to 'make my début only with my own notable works. . . . I prefer to wait for my maturity.'

After two years in the 'General Department' Kokoschka could have opted either to remain in it for a third or change to one of the two specialist departments open to candidates for the teaching diploma. One of them, that for graphics and printmaking, was directed by Carl Otto Czeschka. The other, that for painting, was in the charge of Koloman Moser. Kokoschka wished to study painting but Moser was not impressed by what the student had produced thus far. He did not want him in his class, 'because there was not a trace of personality' evident in the work Kokoschka had shown him which was full of 'borrowings from Böcklin, Calame and such people'. In the absence of any of the work Kokoschka had produced during his first two years of study we must assume that there were grounds for Moser's harsh opinion.

Czeschka was extraordinarily versatile, adept at a wide variety of crafts as well as a master printmaker. He was to become famous for his sparkling illustrations for the *Nibelungenlied* published in 1909. He was also better disposed towards Kokoschka than Moser and prepared to accept him in his class, even though he knew almost nothing of his work. He 'neither saw' the young man nor could 'any of my young people tell me anything about him. But then . . . his father sought me out' and accused Czeschka 'of supporting his son's change of direction from an assured job with a salary to something like art that would earn him nothing'. Czeschka patiently explained that he was doing no such thing, had not yet even met his son, and that Gustav Kokoschka should have his argument at home. He appears not to have explained that the change of direction would not disqualify Kokoschka from taking the teaching diploma.

After the unpleasant confrontation with Gustav Kokoschka, Czeschka was surprised when the son appeared in his class at the beginning of the next term. Presumably the argument had indeed taken place at home and Oskar, supported by his mother, had persuaded his father to allow him to enrol. It seems, however, that Gustav Kokoschka had perceived something of which his son might at that time not even have been aware: a desire to abandon thoughts of becoming a teacher and make a career for himself as an artist.

When Kokoschka began to work in Czeschka's class, his teacher soon realized that Moser had been right to criticize the student's work for a lack of personality. He was too easily influenced, not confident enough to develop a personal style. As Czeschka remembered:

In October I gave Kokoschka a place at a large table – by the window. His neighbour was Kalvach the Croatian, the son of a likeable, honest engine-driver. He possessed strong artistic individuality, was very gifted and also poor. – Soon Kokoschka was doing things like Kalvach! God! I had slowly to teach this tender plant Kokoschka that he was on quite the wrong path – that he shouldn't do such things – but ought to find his own inner self. Since he had seen very little art, he had to look at a lot of things and try to get to the bottom of the problem: translation – the shorthand simplification of what was to be represented – was something he couldn't fathom! He found himself very slowly; without his noticing, I was able to bring him on to produce work which he is still showing in his exhibitions today.

Kalvach was the star student at that time, for whom a brilliant future was prophesied. Czeschka was, as he suggests, eventually successful in persuading Kokoschka to go his own way, although the student's work clearly reflected a number of obvious influences for some time. A poster he designed for an art exhibition as late as 1908 is strikingly similar in format, colour, subject-matter and style to a poster designed for the same exhibition by none other than Kalvach. It was at about that time, however, that the influences on Kokoschka's work gave way to something more individual and unique.

Czeschka's teaching was an inspiration and if Kokoschka had not entered the class with the conscious intention of abandoning his teaching ambitions, he soon began to think of himself as an artist. From then on, no matter what his father might have said, there was no more talk of a safe career. It took years before his parents were happy about the decision and even when Kokoschka was successful he never failed to point out in letters home that he was earning large amounts of money and enjoying the benefits of fame.

In Czeschka's class Kokoschka designed a wide range of graphics: posters, illustrations, bookplates and even typefaces. He also learned printmaking, concentrating on lithography. But it was at life drawing that he excelled. Czeschka taught it in more or less the traditional way: students painstakingly drew posed nude models who were expected to remain motionless for long periods of time. In his own time Kokoschka preferred to make rapid sketches not of professional models but of young children, some of them from circus families, whom he encountered in the street and persuaded to pose for him. These drawings had a freshness and immediacy which impressed Czeschka who then introduced quick poses into his own life classes. Before long Kokoschka was allowed to bring his own scruffy models into the class and then Czeschka proposed that he teach life drawing to an evening class.

With the benefit of hindsight these drawings not only appear to be the most important things Kokoschka produced as a student, but also the most influential. Egon Schiele would soon make street urchins a major subject, portraying them in a similarly linear and robust style. Unlike Schiele, however, Kokoschka was not interested in the perversely erotic implications of his pre-pubescent models. His children are gawky, cadaverous and self-conscious.

Also important for Kokoschka's development is the small number of oil paintings he produced probably in 1907, although there is much uncertainty about their dating. Kokoschka received no formal training in painting at the *Kunstgewerbeschule*. Self-taught, he was therefore unencumbered by notions of what was acceptable and felt free to experiment. In 1906 an exhibition of Van Gogh's work at the Galerie Miethke (which also had connections with the Secession) received enthusiastic attention and Kokoschka may have seen it. The energetic and free handling of the paint and the bright and glowing colours of his first oils suggest that he did. Most of these pictures are portraits, but there is one still life (*Still Life with Pineapple*) in which an apparently haphazard arrangement of fruit sits uneasily on a cloth-covered table.

That painting and the portraits (most notably the one of an old man, *Father Hirsch*) appear clumsy, but their very naïve appearance gives them power. Father Hirsch (illustration 7), with his unnerving, rictus-like grin and hands frozen into an arthritic gesture, is less the portrait of an individual than a study of the mental and physical decline of old age in general. The exaggerated form of the head approaches caricature and the roughness of the paint commands attention. With the exception of Gerstl in Vienna no one was producing portraits like this anywhere in Europe at this time. In *Father Hirsch* we see the beginnings of the modern portrait in which the pursuit of physical likeness yields to an interest in character and mood.

In 1907 Czeschka left Vienna for a post at the School of Arts and Crafts in Hamburg and his class was taken over by Bertold Löffler. Kokoschka had learned a great deal from Czeschka and was already on the threshold of artistic maturity. Löffler encouraged him still further and began to put paying commissions in his way.

One of the most remarkable aspects of the *Kunstgewerbeschule* was the way in which its teachers encouraged their students to earn money and created opportunities for them to do so. Most of these opportunities were provided by an organization called the *Wiener Werkstätte* – Viennese Workshops.

In 1903 the Secession founded a company which commissioned and sold work in order to exploit commercially the ideas of its members and create a public for their products. Since the connections between the Secession and *Kunstgewerbeschule* were so close it is not surprising that Kokoschka and his fellow students were often given commissions by the *Werkstätte*. In 1907 and 1908 no fewer than nine students from Löffler's class worked for the *Werkstätte* in various ways. Some of them were involved with the cabaret which the *Werkstätte* opened in October 1907 and which was called the *Fledermaus*. Kokoschka contributed to the cabaret as we shall see later, but his earliest *Werkstätte* commissions were for postcards and sheets of brightly coloured illustrations for children. He also wrote and illustrated a little book which the *Werkstätte* published. Kokoschka never forgot his debt to the *Wiener Werkstätte*. In his ninetieth year he said that it had given him 'the basis of [his] artistic training'.

THREE

The book commissioned by the *Werkstätte* and written and illustrated by Kokoschka was *Die träumenden Knaben* – The Dreaming Youths. Although the book may have begun as a school project, it was Fritz Waerndorfer – the commercial director of the *Werkstätte* – who suggested publication of what he envisaged as a fairy-tale for children. The *Werkstätte* were already selling brightly coloured prints intended for nurseries. Kokoschka began work on the book towards the end of November 1907 and finished it at the end of March or April 1908. Copies were available for sale at the first exhibition in which Kokoschka ever participated, the *Kunstschau* in the summer of that year.

It is by no means only the immediately attractive illustrations which make *The Dreaming Youths* interesting. The book also marked Kokoschka's début as a writer. As the work of an unpractised author, the text is uncommonly original and remarkably assured. If the illustrations owe much in both style and subject-matter to the manner introduced and refined by the Secession, the text bears little resemblance to anything Kokoschka might have come across in his wide reading.

We do not know whether Kokoschka suggested to Waerndorfer that he write as well as illustrate a book, but it seems likely that he did because no one knew of his literary ambitions. Nor do we know whether Kokoschka had written anything before *The Dreaming Youths*, although its obvious command of language would be doubly surprising if he had not. A natural and impressive literary gift is made plain by this little book which proved to be the first in a series of plays, poems, stories and essays which Kokoschka produced intermittently throughout his life. Indeed, if he had not painted a single picture his reputation as a writer would be assured.

Several of Kokoschka's contemporaries were unusually versatile, possessing talents which demanded expression in two or more media. The composer Schoenberg also painted. Another Austrian artist, Alfred Kubin, wrote a strange and haunting novel, *Die andere Seite* – The Other Side. Albert Paris von Gütersloh, a Viennese actor and painter, wrote several novels, the best known of which is *Die tanzende Törin* – The Dancing Fool. In Germany the sculptor Ernst Barlach was the author of several influential plays; but even his stature as a writer cannot be compared with that which Kokoschka achieved.

Waerndorfer expected and was clearly promised a book for children and the title page and the eight brightly coloured illustrations were eminently suitable for the purpose. Using heavy black contours and generous areas of a single colour (a style more appropriate to the woodcut than lithography, the technique actually used) Kokoschka evokes an enchanted world populated by blonde girls, curiously robed male figures and naked adolescents, inhabited by stags, foxes, birds and strange fish, a world luxuriant with trees, exotic plants and wild flowers.

But the text, a mixture of rhyming and free verse, makes it immediately clear that the charming fantasy described by the pictures is visited by pain and savagery. Nor is the language accessible to young readers. Although memorable it is difficult even for adults. The imagery is couched in terms so oblique, exploits a body of symbols so personal and obscure, that its meaning is never easy to grasp.

Carl E. Schorske is surely right to see the poem as the projection 'in archetypal symbols' of Kokoschka's 'tormented experience of puberty', as a transformation of 'the childish dreams of fairyland . . . into adolescent nightmares'. These nightmares include an image of the author as a werewolf stealing into a garden and breaking into an enclosure occupied by sexually aroused women:

> My unbridled body
> my body brightened with blood and paint
> creeps into your arbours
> swarms through your villages
> creeps into your souls
> festers in your bodies.

But by the end of the story the nightmare has become a healing dream in which a young virgin satisfies the author's sexual longings without reawakening his feelings of guilt and shame:

> and i reeled
> when i recognized my flesh
> and was in love with everything
> when i spoke to a girl.

The colourful, sometimes awkward and declamatory language of *The Dreaming Youths* anticipates much of the style of literary Expressionism. The liberties with syntax, the alternating wilful obscurity and graphic sharpness of the imagery, by turns bizarre and violent, convey the sense of a message too urgent in its demand for expression to be constrained by conventions. There is a significant contrast between the intentional awkwardness of the text and the decorative charm of the illustrations. It is a contrast which reveals that Kokoschka was standing at an artistic crossroads: in one direction lay the pursuit of ornament derived both from the Secession and from folk art; in the other lay the stripping away not merely of the surface but of several layers beneath to reveal what Schoenberg, working in Vienna at that time, called the 'emancipation of dissonance'.

The inspiration for *The Dreaming Youths* was autobiographical. The sexual torments of adolescence it so vividly expresses had been inflicted on the author by a specific woman. Kokoschka described the book as his 'first love letter', and he obviously wrote it in an attempt to ease the pain and to understand the mental confusion inflicted on him by a fellow student at the *Kunstgewerbeschule* with whom he had fallen in love. He later repeatedly described her as a Swede; but she was

Austrian, the sister of one of Kokoschka's closest friends also studying at the school, Erwin Lang (who later married the famous dancer Greta Wiesenthal). Lang's sister's name was Lilith and, to judge from a contemporary photograph, she was a strikingly attractive, vivacious girl. She was five years younger than Kokoschka and often wore a bright red dress which seems to have aroused his interest as much as the sound of her name. Red, indeed, seems to have possessed a powerful erotic charge for Kokoschka, then as later. The fantasy that Lilith Lang was from Scandinavia is also significant. Kokoschka was indulging in a Nordic dream of the fair-skinned, blonde, blue-eyed girl which exercised the imaginations of many of his contemporaries.

Lilith Lang later recalled that Kokoschka had asked her to marry him. She was certainly his first serious girl-friend although their relationship did not last long and was in all important ways unsatisfactory. She could not reciprocate his feelings, was probably alarmed by his directness and frightened by the extent of his ardour. Then as later, Kokoschka had no time for patience and took no pleasure in the pursuit. He saw no point in masking his true feelings or playing elaborate games. If he felt something strongly enough, he had to express it as forcefully as he could. He could not dissemble even if rejection and frustration resulted from his attentions.

By the time Kokoschka began work on *The Dreaming Youths* Lilith Lang had indeed rejected him. He was actively avoiding her, partly suffering and no doubt partly relishing the pain she had caused him. He cursed himself for his maladroit pursuit and for being self-conscious about his background. She came from a relatively wealthy family, was well-spoken and self-assured. He was very poor, lacked social grace, was uneasy in company and although undeniably handsome, looked as awkward as he felt. She had a different circle of friends who, Kokoschka suspected, looked down on him. This emerges from a letter Kokoschka wrote to Erwin Lang towards the end of 1907: he was seeing almost nothing of her 'because I haven't got a dinner jacket and manners yet'.

Kokoschka's frustration was so great that he thought seriously for a time of leaving Vienna altogether; and those thoughts too reveal that he was still essentially an adolescent. Erwin Lang was in Berlin at the time, enjoying an extended leave from his studies at the *Kunstgewerbeschule* and Kokoschka now told him that he wanted to get away too. 'Dear God, I want so much to be happy and to travel anywhere with 100 negroes. . . . My psyche, as can be seen from the book of fairy-tales, is becoming more industrious and complicated, and this pleases the *Werkstätte* people.' And again, in the same letter: 'If I could get away from the shipwrecked people here at school and go to the negroes, or to England or anywhere, that would be my salvation.' But Kokoschka was clearly not entirely serious. He stayed at school and finished his 'book of fairy-tales'.

When Kokoschka delivered the illustrations and text, Waerndorfer was happy enough with the former but disappointed by the latter which, with its references to rape and other kinds of violence, was not at all what he had had in mind. In a letter to Czeschka he ironically observed that Kokoschka, still officially working towards a diploma in education, might very well become 'the teacher of my children'. The pictures, he added, 'are brilliant' and were enough to persuade him to go ahead with the project without demanding any changes in the text.

In another letter to Czeschka Waerndorfer revealed that he was having enormous difficulties with the printing. He revealed that one firm had agreed 'to print it at [their] expense' because the owner had

told us that he would like to work with us and wants to produce things with us at his own risk, but when he saw the Kokoschkas the beast emerged and he wrote that current trends made the sale of this kind of book quite hopeless. . . . But the things by Kokoschka are so interesting that we are nevertheless printing 500 copies, although, God knows, we do not have the money. Perhaps we shall sell them at the exhibition.

That exhibition, in which Kokoschka participated, was the *Kunstschau* of 1908 and we shall consider it in some detail later. Some copies of *The Dreaming Youths* were indeed sold there, but not enough to cover the production costs. The remainder of the edition was later purchased by the Leipzig publisher Kurt Wolff who distributed it under his own imprint. *The Dreaming Youths* was the most important piece of work which Kokoschka produced under *Werkstätte* auspices.

While he was writing it, Kokoschka was also involved in another and more unusual activity for the *Werkstätte*. He contributed to its cabaret, the *Fledermaus*, which was Josef Hoffmann's idea. He was an architect, a leading member of the Secession and a director of the *Werkstätte*. Cabarets, already popular for some time in Central Europe, were much more than places of popular and cheap entertainment. In Berlin, Munich, Prague and Vienna they provided food and drink in an informal atmosphere accompanied by songs and sketches which were often satirical, politically critical, and of marked literary quality. Some of the best writers and musicians of the day, among them Peter Altenberg and Frank Wedekind, regularly worked for the cabarets. In 1907 Hoffmann found premises for the *Fledermaus* in the basement of a house on the corner of the Kärntnerstrasse and the Johannesgasse in the centre of Vienna and set about designing the interiors along *Werkstätte* lines. The result was striking and elegant. The walls were covered with rich mosaic decorations, the floor was tiled in a black and white chequerboard pattern and the furniture and fittings, supplied, of course, by the *Werkstätte*, provided the final touch to the consciously modern and sophisticated atmosphere. There was also a stage.

The opening night, attended by a distinguished gathering, was described by Berta Zuckerkandl, the art critic of the *Wiener Allegemeine Zeitung* and one of the *Werkstätte's* staunchest supporters: 'Here is the most perfect mastery of the language proper to every kind of material . . . this formal concord crystallized out of the purpose in hand.' A sketch had been written by Peter Altenberg, and the English Barrison Sisters danced. A prologue, written by Altenberg, was spoken by Lina Vetter, the first wife of the architect Adolf Loos who – this an intriguing example of the almost incestuous closeness of Viennese cultural life – was soon to take one of the Barrison Sisters as his mistress and to offer Kokoschka his advice and support.

Hoffmann prided himself on the quality of the amenities and not least on the plumbing, which inspired the satirist Karl Kraus, a man who often poked fun at what he regarded as the pretensions of the *Werkstätte* (and who was soon to be closely associated with Kokoschka) to remark that

there has long been a debate about whether the [need to use the lavatory] is better served by the paper on which Zuckerkandl's art reviews are printed or by a costume for the lady lavatory attendant which Professor Hoffmann ought to design. In the end, however, it was agreed that the cistern was to be painted white and a chequerboard pattern printed on it.

Kraus also criticized the knives which 'no Viennese snob can, with the best will in the world, put into his mouth, and the spoons which nobody can put into his pocket'.

The *Fledermaus* cabaret was an instant success none the less and became a fashionable place to be seen, although some criticism was directed at the entertainment which was thought inferior to the amenities. Even high literary quality could not compete with modern plumbing.

About a week after the opening one of the performances given was of '*The Speckled Egg*, a short fairy-tale by O. Kokoschka'. This was a shadow play performed with the aid of puppets made of thin metal sheeting and covered with painted paper. They had movable limbs and were projected on to a screen, presumably in the Balinese manner. According to a member of the audience

Only a few people came; the apparatus, worked by the trembling fingers of the artist himself, functioned only intermittently and the people who wanted to enjoy themselves began to laugh, make jokes and complain. It was therefore a failure and there was no repeat performance. But it would not have required much good will to recognise the value of the pictures: there was compulsive poetry in them. In their bright colours and style the figures recalled oriental miniatures and the simplicity of old woodcuts.

Some of those figures have been preserved and have, not surprisingly, something of the illustrations to *The Dreaming Youths* about them. The text of *The Speckled Egg* (if there ever was one) has disappeared, however; we can only speculate about the story it told and the kind of language it employed.

The *Wiener Werkstätte* were the creation of the Secession but were by no means subservient to it. In 1905, while Kokoschka was in his first year at the School of Arts and Crafts, the Secession experienced an upheaval from which it never recovered. Its president, Gustav Klimt, left the association and took most of its outstanding members with him, including all those who taught at the *Kunstgewerbeschule*. Their leaving simultaneously broke the ties between the Secession and the *Werkstätte*. Although the reasons for their departure were complicated, the major motive can be simply explained: Klimt felt that the Secession had become too conservative and too commercially minded; in some ways the Secession had become too successful for its own good.

The dissenters, inevitably known as 'The Klimt Group', were suddenly left without anywhere to exhibit their work and it took three years before they were able to find appropriate premises. They eventually found a plot of land on the Schubertring near the Schwarzenbergplatz (where the Konzerthaus now stands). Hoffmann designed some buildings which, although temporary, provided an ideal space, and in 1908 the Klimt Group staged an exhibition there together with the *Wiener Werkstätte* and the School of Arts and Crafts. It was modestly called the *Kunstschau/Wien* – Art Show/Vienna – and its success marked the end of the Secession as a vital force in Viennese art. From then on it was Klimt and the architects and designers associated with him who dominated Austrian modernism.

179 artists participated, including, of course, Klimt and the thirteen who had left the Secession with him. Their work filled fifty-four rooms. There were separate sections for painting, graphics, posters, crafts and architecture. Garden design and art for churches were included. There was even a theatre, situated in the garden adjoining the exhibition halls. The focal point of the entire exhibition was a room, designed by Moser, devoted to the work of Klimt. It was intended as an earthly apotheosis and set standards by which all the other paintings in the exhibition were judged.

The *Kunstschau* also marked the first public appearance of Kokoschka's work. The invitation to participate was not a signal honour uniquely conferred on the student Kokoschka in recognition of his outstanding talent. No fewer than eleven members of Löffler's class also showed their work. Kokoschka was, however, given a prominent space and was fully aware of the importance of the occasion. Long afterwards he regularly referred to it as a milestone in his career. So it was.

Much of what has been written about the *Kunstschau* is misleading. Kokoschka claimed, for example, that Czeschka had arranged for him to be given a special room at the exhibition; but Czeschka was teaching in Hamburg and could not have been involved with the organization. According to Kokoschka, Czeschka thought it prudent to isolate Kokoschka's work from that of the other exhibitors because it was so different from everything else on show. Kokoschka also said that he was so apprehensive about the public response to his work that he locked his room immediately after arranging its contents and refused to allow even Klimt and the organizing committee to see his work until the exhibition had opened, until it was too late for them to object and attempt to have his work removed.

The facts are rather different. Klimt, to whom Kokoschka had already dedicated *The Dreaming Youths* ('Gustav Klimt in admiration'), recognized the talent of the younger artist. He ensured that his work was shown in one of the more important rooms of the exhibition (room 14) and defended him against colleagues and critics.

The critic Ludwig Hevesi, discussing the *Kunstschau* with Klimt, admitted that Kokoschka was very gifted but added: 'He lacks the most important thing: taste. He hasn't got a penn'orth of taste.' To which Klimt is said to have replied: 'But a pound's worth of talent. . . . Taste is good for a wine expert, for a cook. Art, however, has nothing to do with taste.'

According to Berta Zuckerkandl, Klimt also defended Kokoschka against his colleagues who feared that his work gave critics an opportunity to attack the *Kunstschau* in general. Klimt is reputed to have said,

We have the responsibility of giving a great talent the opportunity to express himself. Oskar Kokoschka is the greatest talent of the younger generation. And even if we run the risk of having your *Kunstschau* taken down, then we just go down. But we shall have done our duty.

Kokoschka's account of what happened both before and after the exhibition opened exaggerates the facts in order to dramatize the course of his early career and to present his reception at the *Kunstschau* as the beginning of a long and bitter battle with the Viennese press and public. In fact Kokoschka's contribution to the exhibition was not as dramatically unlike that of the other younger artists represented there as he would have us believe and there is not a shred of evidence for the story of the locked room.

In his opening speech Klimt described the *Kunstschau* as 'a review of the strength and aims of Austrian art, a faithful record of the present state of culture in our empire'. The work, in every imaginable medium, of 179 artists was on show, but the centre point of the exhibition was the work of Klimt himself which, since the departure from the Secession, had matured in dramatic fashion. Between 1905 and 1908 Klimt's richly ornate and sensuous style of portraiture achieved its definitive form and in his mosaics for the Palais Stoclet Klimt revealed himself as the outstanding decorator of the age.

A few days after the opening of the *Kunstschau* Waerndorfer wrote to Czeschka in Hamburg with news of Kokoschka's success.

I am finally able to write to you. You know all about the final week prior to the opening of an exhibition so you won't complain about my long silence. . . . Well then, my friend: the drudgery before the opening was enormous. Right up to the very last moment Witzmann, Prag-Rudniker and Löffler with his gallery of posters were not ready. . . . Klimt has many new things. . . . It is Kokoschka who is the great success of the *Kunstschau* . . . we bought [three pictures] from him for 200 crowns cash with the guarantee that we shall have them made into tapestries when we get the money. Orlik, Kolo [Moser] and Metzner bought his drawings and you can imagine the effect when, on the day of the opening, a Sold label appeared by all his works. The exhibition is most exciting, in its achievement the most amazing thing one can imagine. Naturally there is no other city on earth today that could stage such an exhibition.

The three pictures by Kokoschka to which Waerndorfer refers were the centrepiece of the artist's contribution to the *Kunstschau*. They were huge, called *Die Traumtragenden* – The Bearers of Dreams – and have since disappeared. They must, however, have been related to the illustrations for *The Dreaming Youths*, and were probably designed for the ladies' drawing-room of the Palais Stoclet in Brussels, the luxurious house designed by Hoffmann, decorated partly by Klimt and furnished by the *Wiener Werkstätte*. Baron Stoclet, who had commissioned Hoffmann, rejected Kokoschka's tapestry designs. He also rejected a design for a window by another young Viennese artist who had been asked to collaborate by Hoffmann. His name was Egon Schiele. The drawings Kokoschka exhibited at the *Kunstschau* and which were bought by Orlik and others were presumably the kind of angular studies of skinny children which Kokoschka had been producing for some time in school. He also showed one sculpture, entitled *The Girl*. This may well have been a portrait of Lilith Lang.

Waerndorfer's account is in sharp contrast to what Kokoschka later wrote about his reception at the *Kunstschau*. Instead of provoking a series of intemperate reactions from everyone who saw his work, it met with enthusiasm at least from Waerndorfer and several of Kokoschka's fellow exhibitors. Not only did Kokoschka manage to sell everything on the opening day, the press reviews were by no means entirely negative either.

Kokoschka remembered that the critics were hostile to a man and strikingly resourceful in their use of wounding language. But while it is true that the critic whom Kokoschka most resented, Ludwig Hevesi, did describe the artist as 'the chief savage', the *Oberwildling*, he went on to say that Kokoschka possessed obvious talent.

One of the most perceptive reviews was written for the newspaper *Die Zeit* by Richard Muther.

The *enfant terrible* here is Kokoschka. Since precocious success has already damaged many a young man it is pedagogically correct to apply the brakes. Therefore, Herr Kokoschka, your tapestry designs are dreadful: *Oktoberfest* fun-fair, raw Indian art, ethnographic museum, Gauguin gone mad – for all I know. And yet I can't help myself: I have not experienced a more interesting début for years. This *enfant terrible* is in truth really a child, certainly not a poseur, no, a decent young man. He personally explained the point of his pictures to me with a naïvety uncommon today. And while I listened to him, while he explained his childlike words with the aid of awkward gestures, I told myself quietly: here is something genuine and fresh, something elemental that demands expression . . . I must remember the name Kokoschka. For anyone who acts so much like a cannibal at the age of twenty-two might possibly be a very original, serious artist by the time he is thirty.

The review lacks sensitivity to Kokoschka's models: there was little of Gauguin and even less of primitive (apart from folk) art in his work. Yet Richard Muther's guardedly complimentary words evoke a picture of the personality and appearance of the young artist which, although sketchy, is convincing. He was still young and still a student, anxious to make a name for himself but uncertain about how to do it. He was gawky, inarticulate, uneasy in the presence of those with more formal education or of social standing, and unsure about whether his interests would best be served by social compliance or by exaggerating his lack of social skills so as to appear wild and untameable. He was about to opt firmly for the second course, no doubt encouraged by the example of Van Gogh, an artist whose unconventional life was even then being transformed into myth.

It should not be forgotten that Kokoschka, young and unknown, was remarkably lucky to find himself mentioned in the reviews at all, let alone in terms as friendly as Muther's. He was but one of scores of artists represented, many of whom had reputations almost as great as that of Klimt himself and many of whom were not discussed in the press at all.

Kokoschka also claimed that what he showed at the *Kunstschau* was radically unlike everything else in the exhibition. In fact the tapestry designs must have been very like the illustrations for *The Dreaming Youths* which, with their bright, flat colours, strong contours and carefully balanced compositions clearly follow *Werkstätte* conventions. They may, like the drawings of skinny children exhibited with them, have also possessed an unfashionable awkwardness, a slight rawness of outline and directness of execution, but they could not be said to have marked a radical departure, in any sense. Kokoschka's work was certainly on the verge of such a departure, but this could not have been anticipated from what he showed at the *Kunstschau*.

There is yet another aspect of Kokoschka's memory of the *Kunstschau* which does not survive close examination: the meeting with the man who was to prove so important to him during the next few years – the architect Adolf Loos.

According to Kokoschka they first met at the 1908 *Kunstschau* where Loos bought one of the artist's works, a self-portrait bust in clay. Loos, by that time an opponent of the Secession and the *Wiener Werkstätte*, immediately persuaded the young artist to sever his ties with Waerndorfer and Hoffmann and became his patron, adviser and agent.

In 1931 Loos recalled that first meeting in a way which adds to the confusion.

He had made the poster for the Vienna *Kunstschau*. I was told that he was employed by the *Wiener Werkstätte* and was occupied with the painting of fans, drawing picture postcards and similar things in the German fashion – art in the service of the businessman. It was immediately clear to me that one of the greatest crimes against the Holy Spirit was being committed here. I had Kokoschka summoned. He came. What was he doing at present? He was modelling a bust. (It was complete only in his head.) I bought it. What did it cost? A cigarette. Done: I never bargain. But we finally agreed on a price of 50 crowns.

For the *Kunstschau* he had made a full-sized drawing for a tapestry. It was the best thing in the exhibition and the Viennese went in to laugh themselves silly at it. I should have liked to buy it very much, but it already belonged to the *Wiener Werkstätte*. It ended up in the rubbish from the exhibition, in the garbage.

I promised Kokoschka that he would have the same income if he left the *Wiener Werkstätte* and I sought commissions for him.

Confused by the time that had elapsed between the events and his recording of them, Loos plainly made mistakes. The bust bought by Loos was yet nothing more than an idea and was not exhibited until the second *Kunstschau* in 1909. The tapestry designs for which Waerndorfer paid 200 crowns, although now lost, did not end up 'in the rubbish from the exhibition'. Although Loos may well have first seen Kokoschka's work and first met the artist in 1908, he did not begin to help him until 1909: for the time being Kokoschka continued to work happily and productively for the *Werkstätte*.

Kokoschka's memories of the 1908 *Kunstschau* and the one that followed it a year later were more imagined than real. They were also crucial to the way he saw himself. Forgetting the complimentary reviews and allowing the criticisms to play on his mind, he fostered an image of himself and of his native city in which he was the tormented victim of incomprehension and jealousy. The deep affection for Vienna which never entirely left him was now tainted by loathing. Until the end of his life he was torn between these two emotions whenever he thought about Austria and its capital. In this he was similar to so many other Austrian artists and intellectuals: Kraus, Mahler, Schoenberg, Schiele, Freud and, indeed, to that failed painter Adolf Hitler. In a way the negative feelings proved useful: they eased the pain when the old Austria passed away for ever and when Kokoschka found himself in exile.

Adolf Loos began to work on Kokoschka's behalf in 1909 but Kokoschka may have been in regular contact with him during 1908. Although Kokoschka's work continued broadly to follow fashionable *Werkstätte* conventions, Loos's ideas and those of the people to whom he introduced the young artist confronted Kokoschka with an entirely new, intellectually rigorous world which he found irresistible. Content though he had been to earn a modest living from *Werkstätte* commissions, Kokoschka had not been much stimulated by the ideas behind the organization or by the personalities which dominated it. Loos and his friends were to prove very exciting and they gave the artist the will to move in a truly new direction. The second *Kunstschau* of 1909 demonstrated that such a move could be accomplished only gradually and that the *Werkstätte* style was tenacious.

The *Wiener Werkstätte* on the one hand, Loos on the other: between them was a chasm that was no longer bridgeable. 1908 marked a turning-point in Viennese cultural history. It was the year in which the first unambiguous signs appeared in every branch of artistic and cultural life that a sea-change was taking place. In 1908 Freud published his *Character and Anal Eroticism*, which announced a new kind of depth psychology, and Loos wrote *Ornament and Crime*, a key work in modern architectural theory. The premières of Schoenberg's first two string quartets also took place in 1908.

Yet these events were little more than ripples on the surface of a pool in which a familiar and reassuring world continued to be reflected. 1908 was also the year in which the empire celebrated the sixtieth anniversary of the Emperor Franz Josef's accession. Together with the *Werkstätte* and the *Kunstgewerbeschule* Kokoschka was involved in designing posters, costumes and floats for the spectacular pageant presented in the streets of Vienna.

It was, according to Werner Hofmann, 'the last apotheosis of the monarchy', and the festivities were 'the last in the series that had gone on for decades in which the theatrical consciousness found free expression'.

But the moment of self-proclaimed triumph and faith in the future was soon followed by the annexation of Bosnia and Herzegovina with which 'Austria arrogantly took the step into the abyss which was to become its grave. In its role as the keeper of order (i.e. the police force of the Balkans) it laid the fuse which was lit on 28 June 1914 by the assassination at Sarajevo.'

In art and literature it was precisely the question of the 'theatrical consciousness', of the sharp contrast between appearance and reality which inspired the most vigorous debate. In July 1908 a criticism of the *Kunstschau* appeared in a journal called *Die Fackel*. The author was Otto Stoessl who attacked the preciosity of the style introduced by the Secession and the delight in superfluous ornament exhibited by the work of the *Werkstätte*, Klimt and his followers.

This taste [Stoessel wrote] peers through every window, looks into every jar, puts its nose into everything; no object is too negligible to be reshaped and allegedly spiritualized. . . . The dignity of the craftsman formed these objects with unpretentious simplicity and modest precision. Today taste has noisily taken over these things and has placed its own purpose above theirs . . . an imagination . . . which disturbs the primitive, natural style of private life . . . so that not even eating and drinking are permitted to be the unassuming activities which they properly are. Craft is infected by . . . the monkey of art: taste.

This was the issue on which artists and architects were most obviously divided: put simply, ornament versus function; and in 1908 the majority was on the side of ornament. But it was already clear that what had begun with the foundation of the Secession as a move towards necessary reform had since lost sight of its original aims and had degenerated into superficiality. It is tempting to perceive a connection between the state of art in Austria and the condition of the country itself: both were undergoing a process of dissolution, and both sought to erect ornate façades to cover a collapsing edifice.

In 1908 Emil Klager sought to reveal the truth about an aspect of Viennese life which showed up the state of Austria in general. In lectures and an illustrated book he looked beyond the impressive buildings of the city to reveal the 'districts of misery and crime', the slums and hidden corners frequented by the homeless which were often hard by the most expensive areas, one of them indeed in the drainage system alongside the Secession building itself. Klager wanted to unmask 'the vainglorious high culture of the metropolis' that was 'intoxicated by ideas of progress'.

Klager was provoked by the hypocrisy which he saw around him. The pretence of Secessionist architecture, the vacuous ornament of Klimt's painting, were both equally and unwittingly expressive of the pretence which had infected society with a terminal disease. Vienna was a city in which the most celebrated personalities were actors.

FOVR

For Kokoschka the second *Kunstschau* of 1909 was as important as the first. It was more international in scope than the one in 1908 and showed Van Gogh, Gauguin, Vuillard, Bonnard, Vallotton and Matisse from France, Minne and Toorop from Belgium, Munch from Norway, Liebermann and Corinth from Germany and Shannon, Gordon Craig and Bone from Britain. As might be expected, Klimt once again dominated the Viennese contribution.

Kokoschka, who shared a prominent position in the exhibition with Egon Schiele, showed a group of life drawings, some coloured illustrations, a portrait and one sculpture, *The Warrior*, which Loos claimed to have bought for a single cigarette before it was made. That sculpture and the portrait *(The Trance Player)* were markedly different from anything Kokoschka had exhibited at the previous *Kunstschau*.

Once again the young artist's contribution received wide press coverage. Berta Zuckerkandl described Kokoschka as 'certainly the strongest talent among the young at the *Kunstschau*' but, echoing Muther's opinion of the year before, added that Kokoschka's 'supporters would do well to remove him from the confusing influence of the public, to take him far away from too exclusive a stylistic tendency, from too enthusiastic friends and put him in another artistic milieu'.

Another critic referred to Kokoschka's 'undeniable gifts' but also thought they were being misdirected.

It would be wrong, however, to create the impression that Kokoschka's contribution provoked no extreme reactions. It did, and Kokoschka was deeply and irreparably wounded by them. Josef Strzygowsky, for example, wrote of the portraits: 'This Oskar Kokoschka who uses his Koko-rays on people who have the misfortune to fall under his brush, is qualified to decorate the brothels with frightening pictures of syphilis and paralysis.'

He also compared the paintings to 'disgusting plague sores' and 'puddles full of foul stench'.

The life drawings on show were similar to those shown (and sold) at the previous year's exhibition; the coloured illustrations were gouache and ink illustrations to a new prose poem by the artist called *Der weisse Tiertöter* – The White Animal Slayer; the fan was a commission from the *Wiener Werkstätte*; one of the portraits was of a friend (the actor who called himself Ernst Reinhold) and later entitled 'The Trance Player'; the sculpture was a painted clay bust forty centimetres high which, although described as a self-portrait, has the beginnings of a beard and is not much like the artist in other ways either.

Although the fan and the illustrations for *Der weisse Tiertöter* were roughly similar in style to what Kokoschka showed at the first *Kunstschau*, the sculpture and the oil portrait of Reinhold revealed a significant shift in direction. In the former, an energetic manipulation of the clay and the addition of paint produced a highly expressive grimace, and in the latter, robust brushwork and the direct gaze of the sitter achieve an unnerving effect.

The Trance Player may have been the first portrait Kokoschka painted and was almost certainly executed before 1909, perhaps at about the same time as the portrait *Father Hirsch*, in fact a likeness of

Reinhold's father. Both betray the influence of Van Gogh and confront the viewer with a powerful and disturbing personality. The mesmeric stare of the blue eyes in *The Trance Player*, their pupils half obscured by heavy eyelids, the dramatic gesture of the left hand and the bluish-white glow which seems to flicker around the head convey the impression of a young man with supernatural powers.

Kokoschka's contribution to the *Kunstschau* went beyond the exhibition itself. Hoffmann's design for the exhibition site included an open-air theatre in a garden where, during the *Kunstschau's* run, a variety of plays were performed, one of which was a kind of ballet, with music by Franz Schreker, based on Oscar Wilde's story 'The Birthday of the Infanta'. Two plays by Kokoschka were also staged.

We do not know whether the artist suggested putting on his plays or whether he was invited to present something as a consolation for the disappointment caused by the failure of *The Speckled Egg*. Perhaps, since there was no money for professional performances of any kind, the organizers were delighted to have the programme filled by plays which, like Kokoschka's, were staged by students working for nothing.

Inclement weather repeatedly forced Kokoschka's plays to be postponed and they were eventually performed to a full house on 4 July 1909. One of the reasons for the large audience may well have been the striking poster which Kokoschka designed and which shows a kind of pagan *pietà*, a white-faced woman embracing a male corpse which is blood-red, as though flayed. As soon as the performance began everyone present must have realized that they were participating in a highly unusual event. Kokoschka had promised the *Kunstschau* committee that his plays could be staged with no financial outlay and consequently the appearance of the sets and costumes was rudimentary. The actors, all of them students, were dressed in rags. Kokoschka had painted the simple backdrop and was responsible for the make-up which was very stylized, transforming the actors' faces into masks frozen in expressions of extreme emotion. Nerves, veins and muscles were painted in bright colours on to their limbs. The play was directed by Ernst Reinhold.

Although several versions of the first play that was staged that evening were later published, it no longer survives in its original form. This is not surprising, since Kokoschka had only written it the day before the première and then merely handed each actor his lines scribbled down on separate scraps of paper.

The play was called *Mörder, Hoffnung der Frauen* – Murderer, the

Hope of Women. It is very short and consists of a single scene acted by two main characters ('Man' and 'Woman') accompanied by a chorus of 'Warriors' and 'Maidens'. Music was specially composed for the première and played by a band of drums, pipes, clarinets and cymbals.

Like *The Dreaming Youths, Murderer, the Hope of Women* is about sexual longing and frustration. Its imagery is considerably more violent and explicit than that of the poem however. The woman, lusting after the man, is branded on the breast by the male chorus and she then stabs the man who almost dies. The woman is killed, however, and in some mysterious way her death gives the man strength and he leaves the stage at dawn having first slaughtered everyone in the chorus.

The words spoken by the actors do little to aid an understanding of the action. For the most part they are an incoherent mixture of incomplete sentences, exclamations and screams. The essential theme of the play is nevertheless reasonably clear: the male, threatened by the woman's sexual desire, regains his strength by killing her.

Murderer, the Hope of Women is thus like the projection of an adolescent nightmare and reveals much of Kokoschka's state of mind at the time. Significantly, the woman was dressed for the first performance in a bright red costume and red was Lilith Lang's favourite colour. Kokoschka, still confused and depressed by his failure to win her love, eased his frustration by dreams of sadistic blood-letting, of the slaughter of what was causing him pain.

The theme of the play was not suggested entirely by Kokoschka's own unhappy love affair, however. The battle of the sexes, the idea that the female of the species gains dominance over the man by enslaving him through sex, was central to Schopenhauer's philosophy, informs much Viennese literature of the time and was one of the major aspects of a book by Otto Weininger published in 1903. Called *Geschlecht und Charakter* – Sex and Character – it argued that the female element, the libido, was in continuous struggle against the male, intellectual and reasoning element. Weininger, who committed suicide in despair after his book received scant attention, was not unknown to Kokoschka. He may also have influenced Freud.

The first performance of *Murderer, the Hope of Women* is, like much else about Kokoschka's life at this time, surrounded by myth. There are reports not merely of cat-calls and boos from the audience but of a full-scale riot. It is said that Bosnian soldiers fought in the aisles while the play proceeded and that the police were called in to restore order. It is also alleged that Kokoschka was saved from arrest by the intervention of Adolf Loos and Karl Kraus who were in the audience, and that, as a result of the scandal, Kokoschka was immediately expelled from the *Kunstgewerbeschule*.

Tempting though it is to accept such entertaining reports at face value, there is, alas, no reliable evidence for their veracity. The reviews in the press were few in number and unanimous in their bewilderment, but they nowhere refer to riots, police or Bosnian soldiers. While it is true that Kokoschka left the School of Arts and Crafts, apparently without taking an examination, in the summer of 1909, there is no proof that he was dismissed. Indeed, his teacher Roller recalled that his leaving was accompanied by a prize for outstanding achievement, and within three years Kokoschka was himself teaching at the school.

That evening in June 1909 another play by Kokoschka was performed at the *Kunstschau* open-air theatre. This was *Sphinx und Strohmann* which had already been presented at the *Fledermaus* cabaret in March together with *The Speckled Egg* and readings from two of Kokoschka's poems by Ernst Reinhold.

Sphinx und Strohmann – Sphinx and Strawman – is even more curious than *Murderer, the Hope of Women*. It is also short, also consists of a single scene, and also concerns the battle of the sexes, although on this occasion it is the man (Herr Firdusi, the strawman) who dies, having been betrayed by his adulterous wife.

If the work Kokoschka exhibited at the 1909 *Kunstschau* revealed that his art had taken a new direction, the plays and especially *Murderer, the Hope of Women* did nothing less than announce the arrival of a new style of drama which would quickly influence an entire generation of avant-garde playwrights throughout the German-speaking world. Indeed, it was as dramatist rather than artist that Kokoschka first established his reputation in some quarters.

After the *Kunstschau* of 1909 Adolf Loos began to work energetically on Kokoschka's behalf. He had promised the young painter that he would have an income at least as large as that provided by the *Wiener Werkstätte* if he were to cut his ties with that organization and rely on Loos entirely for support. Kokoschka did so and never regretted it, although the break with the *Werkstätte* was not as clear as he made out.

A letter of 14 September 1909 from Fritz Waerndorfer to Czeschka provides a tantalizingly incomplete glimpse of the circumstance of the artist's break with the *Werkstätte*. Waerndorfer reported:

a dreadful row with poor Kokoschka. Yesterday he came into my office like a madman and was utterly unpleasant. Finally I threw him out – literally – and I am sorry about it today but he has now become truly unbearable. . . . He is now completely finished. But at the same time I believe that only an insane fear of a winter without work which is now facing him drives him to play these stupid games. Peppo [Hoffmann, the architect] believes quite rightly that he has only two choices. If he wants to be the solitary genius, then he must go to ruin like the genius. If he wants to make a living, then he must make concessions.

From this letter we may infer that Kokoschka had gone to Waerndorfer to make large demands, almost certainly before committing himself finally to Loos. One of those demands was for a teaching post at the *Kunstgewerbeschule*, but, as Waerndorfer continued in his letter to Czeschka: 'Naturally Kokoschka's hopes of getting a professorship . . . are completely futile.'

Loos was an architect and his writings reveal the extent of the change that took place in Viennese cultural life during the years between the foundation of the Secession and the outbreak of the First World War.

Born in December 1870 in Brünn (now Brno) and the son of a stonemason, Loos became a master mason himself before studying architecture in Dresden. He then spent three years with relatives in the United States, an experience which left him convinced of the absolute superiority of Anglo-Saxon culture and the dull provincialism of Austrian life. According to Loos, countries which followed the British or American example (like Japan) had become rich and powerful while others which did not (like China) were cultural colonies.

In 1898, two years after returning from America, Loos wrote that 'Philippole [now Plovdiv, a small town in Bulgaria] is to Vienna what Vienna is to New York'. In 1903 Loos wrote and published two slim issues of a journal called *Das Andere* – The Other – which he ironically described as 'a journal for the introduction of western civilization into Austria'. As an aphorist he was invariably witty and cutting. Referring to one of the leading architects and designers of the age, he announced that 'the time will come, when the furnishing of a prison cell by Professor van de Velde will be regarded as an aggravation of the sentence'.

What Loos hated most was every kind of sham and hypocrisy. Sham was almost all he saw when he contemplated Austria. Whether in sexual morality, attitudes to the monarchy or in the political system, Austria was dishonest and pretentious. Since Loos believed that buildings provide the clearest indication of the moral condition of the society which erects them, he reserved his greatest scorn for the pompous villas, theatres, churches, museums and other public buildings on the Ringstrasse in Vienna.

Although all erected in the second half of the nineteenth century, these buildings pretended to be old. They used a variety of historical styles to create the appearance of the Classical, the Gothic or the Renaissance and their façades were a riot of decoration. Since historicism was the dominant style throughout Europe at the time the buildings on the Ringstrasse were typical of their period, but Loos regarded the degree of sham as peculiarly Viennese. In an essay published in 1898 in *Ver Sacrum*, the Secession journal, Loos described Vienna as a 'Potemkin city', comparing the hypocrisy of its monuments to the cardboard villages erected in the Crimea by Field Marshal Potemkin to impress Catherine the Great with the splendid living conditions of the peasants there.

Loos was allied to the Secession for a time because the association was dedicated to artistic reform, but he soon turned against the Secession, since the preciosity and predilection for ornament revealed in most of its members' work proved too much for his rigorous taste. In artistic matters he was a kind of Puritan moralist who was out of place in an Austria that was Catholic and Baroque. As he wrote in his satirical story *Vom armen reichen Mann* – Concerning the Poor Rich Man – Loos accused the architect (and he was thinking of Hoffmann) of making the man's apartment 'very hard work' to live in in the manner prescribed. 'The architect therefore supervised the mode of occupation during the early weeks to ensure that no mistakes should creep in,' Loos indeed turned against almost everyone. He had few friends and saw himself as a lone, embattled prophet crying in an architectural and cultural wilderness.

In 1909 one of his supporters described him as

a young architect with the narrow greyhound head of the English sort and eyes full of innocence which appear to see everything for the first time; the entire man vibrating like a steel razor-blade; an Austrian, no, a European, no, an American, no: an entirely new type, a cosmopolitan and, especially in Vienna, the ambassador of a new, clamouring epoch: Adolf Loos.

The writer went on to ask,

What has become of the man?

and ironically to speculate:

Did he develop into a teacher, a civilizer in the grand manner? Did he build cities? Or did he die, was he ruined, did he sink back into darkness? Did he bleed to death on the great tasks or did he grow shallow?

The answer was:

Neither the one nor the other. He lives in semi-darkness, in the shadow of his thoughts which have been honoured more than he has himself.

The essay continues:

Adolf Loos dedicates his life's work to the proposition that a chair should be a chair, a fork a fork, a house a house. A thing should be a thing. Out of this amazing triviality in which not a trace of intellect can be perceived, he builds monumental thoughts. With such childlike demands he is making a revolution. Napoleon's statement is proved: everything of genius is simple, but simplicity is difficult.

Although it is true that Loos failed to win widespread admiration, he was by no means unemployed. Adventurous wealthy clients commissioned designs for villas and even for shops. The most famous of the latter was a store on the Michaelerplatz opposite one of the main entrances to the Imperial Palace in Vienna. Because of its lack of cornices it quickly became known as 'the house without eyebrows' and inspired a campaign for its destruction. Emperor Franz Josef hated it so much that he turned his head and closed his eyes whenever he was being driven past it. Loos was also responsible for the equally striking American Bar on the Kärntnerstrasse.

Loos's buildings make impressive use of marble, exotic hardwoods and other luxurious materials, but by the standards of the time they were unacceptably simple in plan and elevation and worryingly devoid of decoration. Loos hated ornament which he castigated in his writing. In his most celebrated essay, written in 1908 and significantly called *Ornament und Verbrechen* – Ornament and Crime – he argued that decoration was the outward sign of decadence, a lack of civilization and even of evil: savage tribes delight in extravagant pattern-making; criminals love to have themselves tattooed.

How was such a man attracted to Kokoschka's art which was anything but spare and simple? Loos's taste in painting was quite different from his taste in architecture and design. He saw them quite differently: 'The aim of a work of art is to shake you out of your comfortable existence. The purpose of a house is to serve your comfort. The work of art is revolutionary, the house is conservative.'

Adolf Loos was not the only Viennese critic of sham and hypocrisy.

Better known and more influential was Karl Kraus, the journalist who had founded the literary and satirical magazine, *Die Fackel*, which waged an unrelenting campaign against fellow journalists, sexual mores and politicians. For Loos, society was clearly mirrored in its buildings; for Kraus it was the use of language which revealed all. He therefore castigated those who wrote for effect, were mealy-mouthed or who otherwise failed to treat the language with the respect it demanded.

Kraus's aim was nothing less than the purging of the German language itself which, according to him, had long since become corrupted by the dishonesty of those who used it. In order to illustrate his point he ran a regular series of articles in which the convoluted and flowery prose of the Berlin journalist Maximilian Harden appeared beside Kraus's own 'translations' which were invariably pithy, clear and made Harden look stupid.

In the foreword to the first issue of *Die Fackel* (April 1899) Kraus described the period as one in which 'Austria . . . is threatening to perish from acute boredom'. He described himself as 'a publicist who, even in political questions, takes the "wild men" to be the better people'. Referring to the lack of a political programme in his journal, Kraus employed a brilliant play on words to describe the aim of *Die Fackel* as consisting not in what it provides (*bringen*) but in what it destroys (*umbringen*). The foreword concludes with the hope: 'May *Die Fackel* therefore illuminate a land in which – in contrast to that of Charles v – the sun never rises.'

Loos came to despise the Secession and everything it represented; Kraus abhorred the literary movement associated with it – Impressionism – and its leading apologist Hermann Bahr. Loos and Kraus were friends and admired each other greatly. Both were moralists of such passion and conviction that, if born some three centuries earlier, they would happily have served the Inquisition.

In one of his most famous statements Kraus characterized what they shared:

Adolf Loos and I – he in deeds, I in words – have done nothing but show that there is a difference between an urn and a chamber-pot and that culture consists in just this difference. But the rest . . . can be divided into those who use an urn as a chamber-pot and those who use a chamber-pot as an urn.

Like Loos, Kraus despised the *Wiener Werkstätte* and Josef Hoffmann. As he wrote in *Die Fackel*, attacking both Hoffmann's buildings and clients: 'They have the dirt off the street in their homes, and even that is by Hoffmann.'

Through Loos, Kokoschka quickly came into contact with Kraus who did much to further the artist's career. *Die Fackel* came out on Kokoschka's side soon after Loos took him under his wing. In December 1909 the journal carried an unpaid advertisement asking for someone to publish *The White Animal Slayer*: obviously the *Wiener Werkstätte* had refused to take on the project after making a loss on *The Dreaming Youths*. In March 1910 *Die Fackel* also published an enthusiastic article about Kokoschka (the first entirely devoted to the artist to appear anywhere) by Ludwig Erik Tesar who had written about Kokoschka in his review of the *Kunstschau* the previous year. That article was commissioned by Kraus at the artist's request.

Why both Kraus and Loos became interested in Kokoschka is an intriguing and difficult question. Both were sophisticated, experienced, witty and accomplished. Kokoschka was awkward in company, still immature, often tongue-tied, shy and aware of his lack of a literary education. Kraus, moreover, was not especially interested in the visual arts and his writing reveals that he had little understanding of them. Loos, although obviously a man of acute visual sense, was working in a way which seems diametrically opposed to Kokoschka's. The clean lines of his buildings and the functional emphasis of his designs cannot easily be reconciled with the cultivated awkwardness and marked emotionalism of Kokoschka's paintings.

Loos drew a sharp distinction between art and architecture: the latter, because it was functional, was not art at all. Consequently paintings should be judged by different criteria. No matter how highly Loos regarded Kokoschka's work, however, he and Kraus almost certainly valued the artist himself more for his potential as a disruptive and disquieting force in Viennese life, and Kraus always took 'the wild men to be the better people'.

Kokoschka was now admitted to the select circle around Kraus. He and Loos spent many evenings at a table in the Café Central in Vienna where Kraus was surrounded by friends and those few admirers he was prepared to suffer. It was an exclusive club of which the artist was plainly proud to be a member. He was exhilarated by the wit which he could not match, hungry for the gossip (much of it malicious) and intimidated by the knowledge continuously paraded. If a new issue of *Die Fackel* had just appeared Kraus would expect intelligent criticism and discussion and evidence from everyone that they had read and had understood every word. Kokoschka, afraid of appearing foolish, would pretend that he had not yet seen a copy. He was 'only a painter; and, just as in the East they regard half-wits as sacrosanct,' he 'was granted the privilege of sharing a table with the others, as a mute'. He might have added that in Vienna artists were expected to be stupid: intellectuals were fond of the epithet *Materblüot* (thick as a painter).

Kokoschka did not spend all his spare time with Loos and Kraus listening to their verbal fireworks in the Café Central. They sometimes went to the Yiddish theatre in the Leopoldstadt district together and occasionally visited a brothel where Kokoschka was once horrified by an auction in which the favours of an alleged virgin were sold to the highest bidder. For Kraus, such visits were presumably in the interests of research. Loos, always sexually curious, probably went for the more obvious reason. Both Loos and Kraus were determined to have Kokoschka initiated, worried that he remained sexually inexperienced. But it seems that their efforts were in vain: Kokoschka was not attracted by the opportunities presented.

Loos quickly persuaded Kokoschka to concentrate on portraiture for which, Loos thought, the artist had an obvious gift. Loos would use his contacts to find wealthy people prepared to sit for a young but interesting painter. He would then persuade them to buy their portrait. If they refused, Loos promised Kokoschka that he would purchase the pictures himself. It was an extraordinarily generous offer, especially since Loos was anything but rich at the time.

One of the first of these commissions was a portrait of Kraus whom Kokoschka painted at the writer's home. 'His eyes flashed feverishly into the lamplight. He gave an impression of youthfulness, shut away behind a black curtain, gesticulating animatedly with nervous, fine-boned hands. His voice had a cutting edge.' (Filmclips of Kraus reading in public confirm this impression.)

That portrait, like several others of this period, has been lost, although a later one survives, and there is a photograph of the earlier work which does indeed make Kraus appear more youthful, a fragile figure in a suit several sizes too large for him. Kraus later wrote that 'those who know me will not recognize me in this picture. But those who do not know me will.'

Kraus inspired the implacable hatred of many, the admiration of some and the love of very few. He knew that he possessed one of the finest intellects in Vienna and was not moved by modesty to pretend otherwise. He was incorruptible, accepted no paid advertisements for his paper lest his paymasters restrict his freedom, worked with an intensity that would have ruined the health of most, often slept at his desk and kept his private life secret. No one knew that he, born a Jew, had converted to Catholicism until the day he announced in *Die Fackel* that he had left the Church. From 1911 onwards he wrote every word in his paper himself. As he put it in one of his aphorisms: 'I no longer have any collaborators. I was jealous of them. They put off the readers I want to lose for myself.'

In spite of its wide readership *Die Fackel* did not make Kraus rich. He earned most of his money not from journalism but from public readings of both his own work and that of the few writers living and dead he felt worthy of his attention. These readings were *tours de force* and extremely popular.

In 1924 Elias Canetti, who spent part of his early life in Vienna, attended Kraus's 300th reading which must have been little different from those which Kokoschka heard a decade and more earlier. Canetti remembered more of the electrifying effect the reading had on Kraus's audience than he did of the programme itself. Kraus was met by

the kind of enthusiastic applause which I had never experienced, not even at concerts. He appeared . . . to take little notice of it, he hesitated only a little, standing, the figure slightly bent. When he sat down and began to speak his voice overwhelmed me. It had an unnatural vibration to it like a slow crowing. But this impression quickly fled, for his voice changed immediately and changed and changed again, and very soon one was amazed by the variety of which it was capable. . . . Already the first point – it was actually only an allusion – was anticipated by an explosion of laughter which frightened me . . . it related to something local, to something connected not only with Vienna but which also had become an intimacy between Kraus and his audience.

Die Fackel itself was a mixture of comment, reviews and articles. What Kraus wrote was perceptive, funny and invariably against the mainstream of current opinion. It was written in the most exceptionally precise, although never dry German, has a style which no one could emulate and reads today as vividly as the day it was written.

Here is a selection of Kraus's aphorisms chosen not so much at random as for the ease with which they can be translated. Indeed, most of Kraus's work defies adequate translation.

A snob is unreliable. For the work he praises might actually be good.

If you lack ability, a novel is easier to write than an aphorism.

Emancipated women are like fish come up on to dry land to escape the fishing rod. Even the laziest angler is not interested in rotten fish.

A lightning conductor on a church tower is the clearest imaginable vote of no confidence in God.

I do not trust the printer when I hand over my written words. How can a playwright rely on the mouth of an actor?

Education is what most people receive, many pass on and few possess.

The devil is an optimist if he believes that he can make people worse.

What the painter of pictures shares with the house-painter is that both get their hands dirty. This is precisely the difference between the writer and the journalist.

And, perhaps even with Kokoschka in mind:

In a true portrait one must recognize which painter it represents.

Die Fackel supported Kokoschka at a time when most other Viennese papers did not. However, there was one other Austrian magazine which supported the artist at this time: *Der Brenner* – The Burner – which, published in Innsbruck and edited by Ludwig von Ficker, took up a number of unfashionable literary and intellectual causes before 1914. It encouraged the poet Georg Trakl and the composers Schoenberg and Alban Berg. After 1912 it was secretly subsidized by the philosopher Ludwig Wittgenstein who had decided to divest himself of the large fortune which he had inherited from his father. Wittgenstein also established a foundation which Ficker administered and which once gave money to Kokoschka during the First World War.

In spite of such generosity *Der Brenner* was less important for Kokoschka than Kraus and *Die Fackel*. The former was based in the provinces and had a small, largely sympathetic readership; the latter had as wide a circulation among enemies as among friends.

Kraus was, moreover, instrumental in introducing Kokoschka to a group of interesting writers. One of them was Peter Altenberg, a much older man, whom Kokoschka painted. Another, born in the same year as Kokoschka, was Albert Ehrenstein. They became great friends, maintained a correspondence for years and, in 1911, Kokoschka provided the illustrations to Ehrenstein's novella *Tubutsch*.

Ehrenstein was Kokoschka's only friend of his own age and was to be of crucial importance to the artist at several critical moments of his life. He was born in the poor Viennese district of Ottakring and, like Kokoschka, into a family which had only recently arrived in the capital. His first piece of work appeared in *Die Fackel* in 1910, the year in which he also finished his doctoral dissertation on an aspect of eighteenth-century history. Like Kokoschka he soon moved to Berlin where his work brought him considerably less fame than a long and well-publicized affair with the celebrated actress and beauty Elizabeth Bergner.

46

In Loos Kokoschka found not only a patron and agent but also a second father selflessly concerned for his welfare. He introduced Kokoschka to an entirely new circle of artists, writers and intellectuals whose interests were unlike those of the *Wiener Werkstätte*. He introduced Kokoschka to collectors who, on Loos's advice, began to buy his work. Loos, convinced that clothes make the man, even took the shabbily dressed Kokoschka to Ebenstein, the court tailor who not only fitted him out but also explained anatomy from the tailor's point of view. Ebenstein took no money: payment was to be in the form of a portrait.

Although Kokoschka had produced very few oil paintings thus far (he was, after all, self-taught as a painter; the *Kunstgewerbeschule* had trained him in other techniques), Loos was convinced that he had a gift for portraiture and, as important, that portraiture would enable him to earn his living.

All of Kokoschka's early portraits are of his own or Loos's friends and all of them are half-length. Although for the most part con-ventionally posed, they employ the position of the hands, unnatural relative proportions, other distortions and paint quality to great expressive effect. Almost no information about the character, class or interests of the sitters is provided by their dress or background, and the liberties taken with their features make it clear that physical likeness was less important to the artist than the suggestion of mood.

In technique there are some important differences between one portrait and the next, evidence perhaps of an uncertainty in artistic aim and direction. In that of Frau Hirsch (*c*. 1908) Kokoschka used oil almost like water-colour, establishing the figure essentially in a linear fashion on a thinly washed, transparent background. The portrait of Felix Albrecht Harta (1909) on the other hand exploits contrasts between thick, juicy passages of paint and areas which, although thinner, also reveal the way the brush was manipulated. A third approach produced the portrait of Dr Emma Veronica Sanders (1909). Here the paint looks much drier, gives the impression that it was applied to the rough surface of the canvas with broad hog-hair brushes without any medium and makes the sitter look fragile, her flesh insubstantial and brittle. On the body large areas of white canvas show through. The face has been more carefully worked but its features remain understated. The individual brushmarks create a network of fine, delicate lines making the face look as though it hangs on a web of gossamer.

One still life from this period is known and it is as unconventional as the portraits (illus. 8). Painted in 1909 in the house of the collector Oskar Reichel, whom Kokoschka was teaching to draw, it shows a dead and partially flayed sheep, a tortoise, a brown jug, a white mouse, a tomato, a white axolotl in a small glass tank and a white hyacinth in a pot arranged on a table that is as vaguely suggested and as colourful as the background. The colours, especially the dominant whites, reds, blues and greens contribute to a shimmering, opalescent effect.

The picture was directly inspired by the sight in Reichel's kitchen of a lamb prepared for the *Passach* feast to which Kokoschka had been invited:

I was left alone in the kitchen for a while. The corpse lay on the table. It was Good Friday, and my mind turned to the Son of Man, whose fate was not very different. Every Sunday in the Holy Mass the faithful eat his body, and God be thanked that Christ can no longer feel it, even in sympathy. The lamb's eyes seemed to cloud over and become lifeless as I watched. But the thought that this dead thing was now to be roasted and consumed! When the master of the house lifted it by its stiff legs to give me a better view of it, blood dripped out of its mouth. I had had enough.

Immediately Kokoschka decided to paint the dead lamb and he worked on the picture until the Sunday when the meat was required for the oven.

It is an extraordinary painting and not just because of the juxtaposition of so many unusual objects which have been removed from their expected context. The sheep and the limbless, ghostly white axolotl evoke unpleasant associations which the beauty of their description immediately counteracts. The point of the picture appears to be the contrast between appearances and the feelings they evoke. The various objects even suggest smells visually: the heady scent of the hyacinth, so close to the sickly stench of dead meat; the musty, warm smell of the mouse and sour odour of creatures confined to stagnant water.

In short, it is a painting about physical corruption. As Werner Hofmann has observed:

The colours look as though poisonous essences had been added to them which eat into the canvas. The animals appear to glow from within, the brown jug allows the body of the sheep to show through it. . . . All this morbid charm gives the picture its threatening beauty. It is that residue of animality which Hofmannsthal had discovered as early as 1902 in his *Letter from Lord Chandos*: 'In these moments a worthless creature, a dog, a rat, a beetle, a stunted apple tree, a stone overgrown with moss mean more to me than the most beautiful, submissive mistress in the most happy night ever did.'

This still life and the portraits were unlike the work of almost every other painter working in Vienna at that time. Only Richard Gerstl had already evolved a style completely free from the influence of the Secession and had painted portraits which were more concerned with psychological tension than capturing a faithful likeness. But in 1908 Gerstl had committed suicide at the age of twenty-five after a disastrous affair with Schoenberg's wife and in any case had worked in isolation. Had he lived he might well have competed with Kokoschka for leadership of the younger artists in Vienna. As it was, Kokoschka had no serious rivals by 1909. The future of modern painting in Austria seemed to lie entirely in his hands.

Many writers have sought to explain the importance of these early paintings by Kokoschka and most are content with the observation that they announce the arrival of Expressionism, of a new and unnerving concern for subjectivity, for the primacy of feeling. Some comment less on the style, on the idiosyncratic distortions of form, than on the subject-matter and especially on the type of people portrayed in the portraits.

The same similes and metaphors recur: the sitters are like lost souls, somnambulists; they are haunted by visions, pursued by death. They are emblems of the state of the times.

Certainly they seem to express the fears of subsequent generations and find an echo in much that was spoken and written at the time. 'Decline' was one of Kraus's favourite words.

FIVE

Not long before meeting Kokoschka, Loos had fallen in love with an English girl, Bessie Bruce, who was in Vienna at the Cabaret Tabarin dancing with the Barrison Sisters, one of those all-female English groups specializing in 'The Cake Walk' that were popular in Paris and elsewhere on the continent at the time. Bessie Bruce had also performed at the *Fledermaus* where Loos may first have seen her. Loos, whose sexual tastes were unusual (and eventually brought him a brush with the law) was attracted by her adolescent looks and her lack of regard for conventional social restraints. He never married her but Bessie took his name. She had contracted tuberculosis before they met and Loos almost bankrupted himself by sending her to sanatoria in

Switzerland where half the titled and moneyed consumptives of Europe were desperately hoping that the high altitude, clean air, Alpine sun and relaxation would effect a cure. Some of them, Loos hoped, would pay Kokoschka to paint their portraits, Bessie having made the necessary introductions.

According to all published accounts Loos took Kokoschka to Switzerland in the autumn of 1909 and they went straight to Leysin where Bessie was a patient at the Sanatorium Mont Blanc. The postmarks of letters and postcards tell a different story. The earliest known letter from Switzerland is dated 13 January 1910 when Kokoschka was staying at the Grand Hôtel at Les Avants near Montreux, a village whose relatively low altitude was inappropriate for sufferers from tuberculosis. Kokoschka was not with Bessie at Leysin, a village in the mountains above the other, eastern end of Lake Geneva until 28 January. Before then, from 14 January, Kokoschka was at Yvorne in the Rhône valley.

At least we know what took the artist to Yvorne. Loos had given him a letter of introduction to a famous Swiss scientist, Professor Auguste Forel. Kokoschka arrived at Yvorne on 14 January 1910 and stayed for several days, lodging with a Mme Huguet while working on the portrait at Forel's house. Forel had agreed to sit for his portrait but with bad grace. He announced at the start that he would not necessarily purchase the result.

The portrait of Forel (illus. 9) is remarkable, one of the best of Kokoschka's paintings of this period. We see an old man, his expression both wry and benign, the attitude of his hands immobile, even contorted, frozen into an unnatural gesture. It is on the face and hands that the emphasis of description falls. There is almost nothing to Forel's body at all, as though in his old age his mind had remained alert while his physical powers had begun visibly to fade. This impression is conveyed by an unusual and resourceful use of paint, applied not only with a brush but also with a cloth and even the fingers. According to Forel's wife, Kokoschka painted almost all the picture with his hands and scratched out the hair with his fingernails in the thin paint.

Kokoschka's technique reduces the physicality of his subject to almost nothing, renders it transparent, dissolves it. The paint is very thin in most areas, more like a dye than a layer of material. The drawing is inconsistent, creates a fragile and partially broken network of lines in which the face and hands appear like islands. It is as though the sitter himself had been pressed up against the canvas and left an almost ghostly impression.

Forel's body, like the background, consists of thin washes, apparently random marks left by the fingers and the dabbings of a crumpled cloth, and lines and curious images scratched out with the pointed end of the brush. Some of the lines suggest beams of light falling directly on to the body. Others describe the trees and mountains of a perfunctory landscape to the right of Forel's head. Such scratchings appear on the hands and face, too, although here there is a greater variety in the density and quality of the paint which ranges from thick and juicy passages to dry, chalky marks. The colour is limited; the painting is suffused in a pale pink and green glow.

Kokoschka wrote a graphic account of his work on this portrait. Forel was a zoologist and a Nobel laureate. He was also eccentric and a vegetarian.

Every evening Forel carefully weighed out nuts and apple peel which he solemnly ate. At last he had finished and sat down. 'Can you see all right?' or 'Does it matter if I go to sleep?' was all he ever said to me. And sometimes he did indeed nod off. Then I could really study the way he sat in his chair, and see how the wrinkles on his face increased and deepened. Suddenly he seemed ancient. Myriads of small wrinkles appeared, like the documents of a man's life, and I felt that I must record them all, decipher them like old parchment and hand them on to posterity. His face and especially his hands, fascinated me. His fame meant nothing to me, but the task set by Loos filled my mind.

Kokoschka required many sittings for the portrait. He did not ask Forel to sit still, and moved around him from time to time, gathering information from how he acted. Kokoschka said that he wanted in some way to incorporate the scholar's knowledge in the portrait but he

had never read any of his work and therefore had no idea of what his interests were. His wife . . . and his daughter were often present at the sittings, and they would talk while I painted. Their conversations repelled me. I gradually realized that these people were discussing family affairs before me, a stranger, and were gossiping about relations. 'He has accepted the woman, then?' 'Yes. The family is founded, but there were disagreements, violent quarrels.' . . . Strange problems of marriage and procreation were unrolled before my eyes. It was only at the very end of my stay, when the picture was finished, that I realized that they had been discussing ants. All three were biologists working together on the life of the ant.

This was by no means the only misunderstanding which occurred during Kokoschka's stay with the Forel family. Just before the artist finally left their household he was asked by Forel who 'this man Loos is who so pressingly introduced you.' Forel had entertained and sat for

1. Kokoschka's father,
Gustav

2. The artist's mother,
Romana

3. Kokoschka (*left*), Max Oppenheimer (*seated*) and Ernst Reinhold
at the *Kunstschau* of 1909

4. Karl Kraus in 1909

5. Adolf Loos holding an ear trumpet,
c. 1931

6. Oskar Kokoschka: *Portrait of Adolf Loos*, 1909, oil on canvas, 74 × 93 cm

7. Oskar Kokoschka: *Father Hirsch*, c. 1907, oil on canvas, 68 × 61 cm

8. Oskar Kokoschka: *Still Life*, 1909, oil on canvas, 87 × 114 cm

9. Oskar Kokoschka: *Portrait of Professor Forel*, 1909, oil on canvas, 70 × 58 cm

10. Herwarth Walden
in 1918

11. Else Lasker-Schüler
in 1932

12. Paul Cassirer, c. 1910

13. Alma Mahler

14. The sixth of the seven fans which
Kokoschka painted for Alma Mahler,
1914, gouache and ink on parchment, radius 21.5 cm

15. Oskar Kokoschka: *The Tempest*, 1914, oil on canvas, 181 × 221 cm

16. Oskar Kokoschka: *The Knight Errant*, c. 1915, oil on canvas, 100 × 150 cm

an unknown artist who had simply appeared on his doorstep with a letter from a man Forel had forgotten meeting or perhaps had never even met.

Kokoschka was pleased with the painting; Forel was not. In 1937 Forel published his autobiography, by which time Kokoschka had become famous enough to make Forel think that some mention of the portrait would interest his readers. He remembered that he had made it a condition that

I could work at my table as I pleased while he was painting me. This modern painter, who looked at me especially from behind and from the side, cared nothing for likeness, but only for the expression of moods! As a matter of fact, as the picture turned out, only one eye and the left disabled hand were particularly good and expressive – according to the opinion of experts.

Forel goes on to say that Kokoschka showed him

other paintings, the products of imagination, which ought to have been regarded from the standpoint of the psychiatrist rather than as works of art.

In view of this it is not surprising that Forel refused the picture when Loos offered it to him for 120 francs. But he allowed Kokoschka to store it in his attic from where Loos later retrieved it and offered it to a number of Swiss and German museums. Eventually he sold it to the *Kunsthalle* in Mannheim where it still hangs.

According to Kokoschka, one of Forel's many criticisms of the painting was that it made him look as though he had suffered a stroke. When Loos later heard that the zoologist had indeed had a stroke, although after the picture was finished, he told Kokoschka that he must have 'X-ray eyes'. Others believed the same and that Kokoschka 'knew very well that he was one of the chosen ones. . . . He looked right through people like certain psychiatrists, one glance was enough and he found the most secret weaknesses, the sadness or vices of people.'

Forel's lack of interest in his portrait suggested that Loos's plan for Kokoschka was far too optimistic. It was not enough for Loos or Bessie to effect the introductions and then to trust to luck. Kokoschka's style was too unusual, the liberties he took with the appearance of his sitters too great for him to become an instant success as a portraitist.

On 28 January after the Forel painting was finished Kokoschka moved to Leysin. He was

devoted to [Bessie] from the first. She had the delicate complexion of those

Lancashire girls who work all day at their looms and never see the sun. Even when she was spitting blood into the hated, blue glass bottle that all the inmates of a tuberculosis clinic carry around with them like a holy relic, she had a joyous, childlike laugh. I was supposed to keep an eye on her: but how can you hold back a pleasure-loving young thing like Bessie? When the doctors had gone to bed, she used to climb out of the window and go off dancing with the other patients – those anyway who still had enough life left in them. She was the embodiment of a kind of Englishness that no longer exists.

Any disquiet Kokoschka might have felt at living in such close proximity to a group of terminally ill men and women continuously obliged to register every rattle in the chest and inspect each gobbet of phlegm was eased by the experience of being abroad almost for the first time. (In August 1909 he had spent a few weeks in Munich.) In Les Avants there were fewer dramas. At Leysin Kokoschka painted Bessie

and she introduced me to the Duchess and Count Rohan-Montesquiou. She was a wonderfully thin, tall and pale creature and wore a black velvet costume which made her look thinner still. She was a consumptive and I thought her so wonderfully beautiful that I immediately fell greatly in love with her. Her husband looked very degenerate, a large, effeminate man with a hooked nose and a reddish moustache and a ruched lace collar. His yellow face looked like that of a wax figure. . . . The milieu suited her well, yellowing portraits hung on the walls, the atmosphere was quiet, sad. . . . At the same time I made the portrait of the Count of Verona, a small Italian who was a passionate skater and often spat blood.

This description, like a passage from Thomas Mann's *Magic Mountain*, proclaims Kokoschka's fascination for unusual people in extreme and tragic circumstances. Their appearance revealed not only the severity of their illness but also their mental stress. It was the kind of appearance which Kokoschka found irresistible, which occurred only when defences and the façade of conventional behaviour were down. The pictures are not at all like traditional portraits; they are rather likenesses of emotional types. When Kokoschka showed about twenty-five paintings of this kind in Berlin in 1910, their subjects were not named and they had titles like *A Precious Lady*, *A Brutal Egoist* and *A Man in a Cul-de-Sac*.

After working at Leysin for some days Kokoschka went on to Montreux where Loos had arranged another introduction. In 1904 the architect had been commissioned by a Viennese psychiatrist, Theodor

Beer, to rebuild his house, the Villa Karma, and it was there that Kokoschka was to stay.

He was to paint Beer's mistress, an English aristocrat, as payment for his board and lodging, but that was not the most important reason for his presence there. The psychiatrist was in gaol in Vienna awaiting trial for a serious sexual offence and the English woman was, not surprisingly, undergoing a major emotional crisis. Loos thought that Kokoschka might help to calm her down. His grasp of the situation was insufficient, however. There were hysterical scenes. The portrait was begun but never finished. The lady made advances to Kokoschka which were unwelcome and increasingly difficult to resist without sparking off more scenes. He escaped from the house by climbing out of his bedroom window with the aid of bedsheets tied together.

Kokoschka was not paid for any of the portraits he painted in Switzerland, but he had now developed an appetite for travel and when he returned at the end of April 1910 to Vienna he found the city stifling, marooned in the past. There was clearly little point in continuing to search for portrait commissions, so Loos devised another plan: with Kraus's help Loos arranged for Kokoschka to go to Berlin to work for a magazine.

The magazine was *Der Sturm* which had been founded and was edited by Herwarth Walden. Born Georg Lewin on 18 September 1878 in Berlin and the son of a doctor, Walden had trained as a musician before developing his literary interests and becoming involved with several little magazines none of which survived for long.

Walden was an admirer of Kraus and *Die Fackel* and wanted to establish a German periodical which would complement *Die Fackel* and succeed where all his previous and short-lived attempts at editing magazines had failed. Walden contacted Kraus, and the Austrian, far from regarding Walden's plan as potential competition, advised and encouraged him. He even gave him money and permission to publish articles from *Die Fackel* in the new magazine. Kraus believed that Berlin journalism was even worse than its counterpart in Vienna and, in a spirit of altruism, wanted to encourage anything which might resist the rot.

Walden's first knowledge of Kokoschka came when Walden visited Kraus in Vienna with a view to publishing not a magazine of his own but a Berlin edition of *Die Fackel*. That was probably in late August or early September 1909, for the 16 September issue of *Die Fackel* was the first to give news of its Berlin office, in the Halensee district at 5

Katherinenstrasse. That was Walden's address at the time and it was there that Walden's own magazine was produced.

While Walden was in Vienna he also met Loos who gave him a pile of drawings by Kokoschka and asked him to show them to dealers and collectors in Berlin. Tireless in his support for Kokoschka, Loos then wrote to Walden on 4 October:

The painter Oskar Kokoschka wants to mount an exhibition in Berlin. I guarantee a sensational success. Would Cassirer have room? Is Meier-Graefe coming to Vienna soon so he can see the things? Are you coming to Vienna? Could you spend a few days so that your portrait also joins the collection? Please think about it and about Cassirer (about 15 half-length portraits, among them K[arl] K[raus], Dehmel and me).

This letter not only reveals Loos's habit of playing on the vanity of his contacts by inviting them to be portrayed by a painter who had already made portraits of Kraus and himself, but also his sound knowledge of who mattered in the art world and how, with their help, careers could be made. Cassirer was the most successful dealer in contemporary painting in Berlin and Meier-Graefe, one of his advisers, was the most famous historian of modern art in all the German-speaking countries.

Walden seems to have done little with the Kokoschka drawings which he took back to Berlin. He had other, more important matters on his mind. He had decided by then to found his own magazine which at the suggestion of his wife, the poetess Else Lasker-Schüler, he called Der Sturm – The Tempest. It first appeared in March 1910, cost ten pfennigs and for the next three years ran to eight pages and had an edition of 30,000, an extraordinarily large circulation for a magazine which included poetry, prose and criticism, all of it decidedly avant-garde. Der Sturm concentrated on the work of young Berlin writers such as Rudolf Blümner and the recently arrived Albert Ehrenstein and of authors of an older generation among whom were Peter Altenberg and Kraus himself. It also published essays by Loos.

Herwarth Walden was a strange, inspired and inspiring man. A mane of blond hair parted in the centre and brushed back from a high forehead and spectacles with thick pebble lenses to correct an acute astigmatism gave him the air of a withdrawn and eccentric academic which seemed entirely at variance with the impression created by his thick, sensual mouth and the heavy gold jewelry he habitually wore. He had the kind of appearance which must have made him look middle-aged even when young. A small, frail body made his head appear even larger than it was. Many people thought him ugly; others found his peculiar appearance highly attractive.

Walden, a Jew who considered himself neither Jewish nor German, rather a *déclassé* cosmopolitan, was entirely urban in outlook. He loved Berlin and had no feeling for landscape of any kind. Whenever he was in the country (and he did his best to avoid leaving Berlin) he would react to the scenery in the same way: 'It's all only Thuringia.' This hostility to nature was accompanied by an inability to cope with practical problems. He was maladroit, clumsy and physically weak. He also chain-smoked.

In 1910 he was the total bohemian. Money appeared to interest him little if at all; his life was almost spartan and loans and gifts kept *Der Sturm* afloat. After 1912 when *Der Sturm* had become successful and a new, efficient wife had begun to take charge of his business affairs, Walden began to make money and discovered that he was not averse to the benefits of wealth. But when Kokoschka first knew him he was content with his poverty and appeared to enjoy the disordered life he shared with Lasker-Schüler, as memorable a bohemienne as she was a poet.

By comparison with his wife Walden seemed almost normal. He had married Lasker-Schüler in 1899. She was almost ten years older than he, dressed with extravagant individuality, cultivated a bohemian style in everything, was addicted to morphine and preferred to refer to herself as 'Prince Yussuf' the 'Prince of Thebes' or 'Tino of Baghdad'. They were names which complemented the masculine cut of her clothes.

Walden was Lasker-Schüler's second husband. Her first had been a doctor who probably fathered her son Paul although she proudly claimed that he was the child of a Greek whom she had met by chance in the street one day and never saw again after their single meeting. Paul remained with his mother after her divorce. Unruly and ill-mannered, he went with Walden and Lasker-Schüler almost daily to the Café des Westens, one of the centres of bohemian intellectual life in Berlin. There the three of them sat from noon until late at night surrounded by serious but unrecognized writers and artists, drop-outs and eccentrics, drinking coffee paid for by other customers or even the waiter himself, and eating cakes stolen by Paul from behind the counter when the staff's attention was diverted.

Walden's marriage was unconventional in every sense. He was the first to recognize Lasker-Schüler's genius and, according to some, married her not for love but to protect her from her self-destructive drive. Left to her own devices she would have allowed morphine, sexual promiscuity and alcohol to dominate her life. In public she was outrageous; in private she was excitable, easily angered and always ready for an argument. In public her dress attracted as much attention as her behaviour. The poet Gottfried Benn remembered her dressed 'in a red velvet jacket with gold buttons, with it silk check trousers . . . sandals with little bells sewn to them which tinkled with her every step and with them numerous trinkets on her arms and round her neck. All this crowned by a black jockey's cap.'

Vienna had its fair share of bohemians and eccentrics, but by comparison with Berlin it was a haven of respectability. Vienna was a big city with a cosmopolitan population but it could not compete with Berlin's energy and drive. Vienna was an ancient city, the centre of an empire and proud of its achievements in music and literature. Berlin's population was larger, but the city lacked Vienna's tradition and the self-confidence it provided. It had only been the capital of a united Germany since 1871. Before that it had been the residence of the Hohenzollerns, just one of the more important provincial German towns with a reputation for military training, philosophy, the natural sciences and a lack of culture. Spectacular industrial growth after 1871 transformed Berlin into a great grey and forbidding city which was as active and energetic as Vienna was old-fashioned and comfortable. By 1910 it was well on its way to becoming the true cultural as well as the political capital of Germany.

The affinities between Vienna and Berlin, but above all the enormous differences provided a popular subject for conversation and newspaper articles in both cities. Vienna was old, cultured and beautiful, a temptress who cunningly employed artifice to combat the effects of time. Berlin was young, brash and ugly, a parvenu who sought to compensate with bluster for the absence of an inherited charm. The Viennese had humour and enjoyed life. The Berliner was either cruelly sarcastic or simply crude and was convinced that making money was the same as enjoying life. But at least the Berliner spoke his mind. The Viennese stabbed you in the back while whispering complimentary words in your ear. The Berliner thought Vienna would never change and did not want it to. The Viennese knew the Berliner was right and regretted it. As Kraus wrote: 'Truly I say unto you, Berlin will become accustomed to tradition sooner than Vienna will to the machine.'

Kokoschka had had his fill of Viennese charm and he was tired of old-world attitudes. Berlin with its thrusting optimism, its aggressive, outward-looking stance, would be everything Vienna was not. It would surely recognize and cherish his talent.

Kokoschka arrived in Berlin in May 1910 and the first thing he did was visit a barber. Ever since the 1909 *Kunstschau* he had kept his head shaved and it required regular attention. At the barber's he quickly learned something of Berlin ways for he was easily talked into buying a large number of toiletries for which he had no use, which he could not afford and which he quickly deposited in the nearest doorway once he had succeeded in escaping from the barber's clutches. He had just enough money left to travel from the centre of the city to the west where Walden's offices were located. The Katherinenstrasse was off the far west end of the Kurfürstendamm and it was there that Kokoschka was both to work and live.

From the beginning Kokoschka was impressed and even a little frightened by the energy of Berlin. He was also excited by its modernity. The Potsdamer Platz was already the site of the biggest concentration of traffic in Europe and the entire city seemed

like a network of underground railways, elevated railways, surface railways and tramways, columns of carts, motorcars, motorcycles and pedal cycles, along with rotating advertising signs, flickering giant picture palaces, loud-speakers and café orchestras. . . . And the scraps of newspaper fluttering across the streets!

The conditions of employment enjoyed by Kokoschka while working for *Der Sturm* were anything but ideal. Walden expected him to be a jack-of-all-trades and that was what Kokoschka became. He was the deputy editor, copy boy and delivery man. He read proofs, took material to the printers and cleaned the office. He made drawings for the paper, acted as reporter and critic and even wrote reviews of circus performances. He quickly proved indispensable.

Kokoschka also affected the character of *Der Sturm*. Until his arrival in Berlin it had been exclusively a literary and musical journal. Under his influence it became increasingly concerned with the visual arts, included illustrations and regularly published original graphic work on its front cover. It also made Kokoschka's own work a prominent feature. From May until December 1910 *Der Sturm* printed at least one of his drawings every week. It published a revised text of *Murderer, the Hope of Women* together with a series of illustrations especially produced by Kokoschka for the occasion. It printed a series of portraits of writers and prominent intellectuals in which Kokoschka translated the style of his paintings into pen drawings with a line that was by turns strong and flexible, spidery and scratchy. One of the best of them is of Walden himself; others are of Loos and Kraus; one of the most unusual is of Yvette Guilbert the ageing cabaret performer immortalized by Lautrec who in 1910 appears to have been stranded in Berlin for some time. These portraits were also printed and sold as postcards.

For more than six months Kokoschka devoted almost all his energies to *Der Sturm*. The work was hard and the financial reward negligible, but the experience he gained and the contacts he made were invaluable. He learned to write and draw to a deadline, became familiar with techniques of reproduction and he got to know not only some of the most gifted of the younger writers living in Berlin but also prominent art dealers and museum officials.

Since he was enjoying an extended stay away from home for the first time, it did not matter much that Kokoschka was forced to endure miserable living conditions. The small attic room above the offices in the Katherinenstrasse was primitive, cold, without running water and large enough only for a bed, table and wash-stand. It was badly lit and the only view from its single window was of neighbouring roofs and chimney stacks. Short of money, Kokoschka had to exist mostly on biscuits and tea, stilling his hunger by smoking innumerable strong cigarettes. Sometimes, and especially on Sundays, he would indulge himself by going to Aschinger's near the Zoological Gardens, the cheapest restaurant in west Berlin and famous for its tradition of offering as many free bread rolls as a customer could eat with his main meal. For a few groschen Kokoschka ordered meat balls or a fried sausage and devoured as much bread as he dared.

Walden often went with him and was rarely content with the one portion of hot food and unlimited bread. According to a friend who sometimes joined the party, Walden was always 'the more hungry since Lasker-Schüler was not exactly a good housewife'. After eating 'the bigger half of a dish he succeeded in loudly summoning the manager and bitterly complained that the food was not satisfactory, whereupon another portion was considerately brought for nothing'.

These visits to Aschinger's were not frequent enough however. Kokoschka spent much of his free time in his tiny room thinking about food. The actor, poet and fellow *Sturm* contributor Rudolf Blümner was also living above the magazine's offices and he and Kokoschka would often sit together, comparing and sometimes combining their fantasies in an effort to lessen their longings for food above all, but also for sex and companionship.

One of these fantasies revolved around a girl called Virginia and the two men made up stories about her, weaving them into their own lives. They imagined that they had brought her up from childhood and that she had become extraordinarily beautiful. Fantasy impinging on reality, they began ceaselessly to argue and fight for the right to be her father.

Kokoschka did not confine himself to his attic room. He frequented brothels, more for the warmth and food than for the sexual adventure, and made friends with some of the whores who, attracted by his striking looks and intelligence, were inclined to mother him, give him cigarettes and hot meals. He also became friends with some of the circus and fairground performers whose acts he had reviewed in the magazine. One of them kept his chimpanzees in his flat; another was a girl snake-charmer whose boa constrictors, so lifelike on stage, turned out to be stuffed with sawdust.

Of course Kokoschka also frequented the Café des Westens, that lively meeting-place for the serious avant-garde, those playing at being bohemians and those who were entertained by the spectacle of eccentric dress and behaviour. Something of the flavour of the place, known to Berliners as the 'Café Megalomania' and situated at the Zoo end of the Kurfürstendamm, is captured in a memoir by one of its regulars in 1910, John Hoxter:

In the doorway stands Red Richard presenting arms with a wooden newspaper holder. 'There's a letter for you at the bar.' A nod of welcome from a plaster cast of the Emperor Wilhelm II placed with unintentional symbolism on top of the . . . telephone kiosk. Karl Kraus and Adolf Loos are introducing their latest discovery to the Berliners – Oskar Kokoschka, the painter. Portrait sketches consisting of unusual lines and curly scratches are handed round and Koko enjoys himself making the incomprehensible even more difficult with obscure comments.

It was a bohemian life, but one that was also very full and active. Kokoschka came to know Berlin well, but rarely had the time or the inclination to explore beyond the city centre. He did embark on one trip outside Berlin, however. In August 1910 he went with Walden and Lasker-Schüler on a three-day publicity tour up the Rhine and into the area around the Ruhr putting copies of *Der Sturm* into letter-boxes. As Kokoschka remembered, they

must have presented a fairly strange spectacle, like a circus troupe. Else Lasker-Schüler as the Prince of Thebes in voluminous oriental trousers, turban and long black hair, with a cigarette in a long holder; Walden no less bohemian than his wife, peering round inquisitively through his thick glasses, with his birdlike head, his great hooked nose and his long yellow hair, wearing a worn frock coat, the inevitable stiff upright collar and pointed yellow shoes. I was clad, no doubt with equally comic effect, in a suit made by the imperial court tailor in Vienna. Thus attired we passed through the streets of Bonn, and were of course laughed at and insulted by onlookers, cheered by children and very nearly beaten up by angry students.

By 1910 Berlin had for the first time in its history become a cultural centre of importance. Until unification in 1871 Germany had been a collection of larger and smaller states each of which was jealous of its traditions. Almost all the regional capitals enjoyed grander artistic, literary or musical reputations than Berlin, the capital of Prussia. In painting, sculpture and architecture Berlin had never been able to compete with Munich, Düsseldorf or Dresden.

After 1871 that began to change, and although Munich remained pre-eminent in the visual arts for a time, Berlin was attracting a growing number of painters, the most interesting of whom were, before 1910, exhibiting at the Berlin Secession, an organization which had been founded in 1899 in reaction against the semi-official and conservative association of artists.

Unlike its counterpart in Vienna, the Berlin Secession was interested not so much in architecture and the crafts as in painting and especially in a particular style best exemplified by the work of Max Liebermann, the group's first president. Liebermann was a kind of Impressionist, although his landscapes and figures owe more to Manet than Monet and were also influenced by Dutch *genre* painting.

In 1905 the Berlin Secession appeared to be moving with the times when it showed the work of some of the younger German artists such as Nolde, who was consistently more daring in his use of colour than were Impressionists such as Liebermann. For a few years the Secession's liberal approach ensured that Berlin offered the German avant-garde in all cities an opportunity to exhibit that was denied them elsewhere. Kandinsky and Jawlensky, Russian painters living in Munich, showed at the Secession, as did the *Brücke* – Bridge – group from Dresden.

Then the policy changed, and in 1910 such artists found themselves excluded from the annual exhibition by a jury which suddenly felt threatened by modernism. History repeated itself: under the leadership of Pechstein, a member of the *Brücke* who was now based in Berlin, these painters founded a rival association called the New Secession.

These events, more dramatic then than they appear now, occurred while Kokoschka was in Berlin and they assisted *Der Sturm* in its drive to become the leading avant-garde journal in the city. Walden's magazine championed the New Secession and printed examples of its members' work. It also gave the word Expressionism, coined to describe the style of painting favoured by the New Secession, wide circulation. Walden became for a time Expressionism's loudest (if also its vaguest) spokesman.

These developments, which made Berlin an artistic centre as important as Munich, were especially exciting for Kokoschka. Nothing comparable to the foundation of the New Secession had occurred in Vienna and none of Kokoschka's contemporaries were as radical or original as most of the New Secession's members. What excited Kokoschka most was the realization that painters such as Nolde, Kirchner and Pechstein were working in ways which he understood. Although their styles appeared different (above all in their passion for bright, clashing colours and in their dedication to the landscape), their aim was similar to his. They were all highly subjective in their approach and used their painting as the vehicle for the expression of unbridled emotion.

Kokoschka no longer felt isolated. He now saw that the path he had taken independently in Vienna ran parallel to that being followed by painters in Dresden, Munich and Berlin. It must have been an exhilarating moment.

SIX

While Kokoschka was associated with *Der Sturm*, the magazine gained considerably in authority and interest, not least because of his contributions to it. Walden recognized this fact and was grateful. Lasker-Schüler, who may well have been secretly in love with the young artist, admired his work and often wrote about it.

Kokoschka benefited directly from *Der Sturm*. It made his work, both literary and artistic, far better known in Berlin than it had ever been in Vienna, and brought it to the attention of an influential public. It also stimulated the interest of the brilliant art dealer Paul Cassirer.

Cassirer's family was rich and well-connected. Two of his brothers owned a large cable factory; another was a famous neurologist; his sister married his cousin Bruno, a publisher; another cousin was Ernst Cassirer, a philosopher with an international reputation. When still quite young, Paul and Bruno had founded a publishing house and art gallery but had then divided the business between them. Paul took over sole responsibility for the art gallery.

Paul Cassirer was an outstanding example of the enlightened upper middle class of Jewish descent which played a vital role in the intellectual and cultural life of Berlin. Nowhere else in Europe had the rise of industrial capitalism and Jewish emancipation combined to such positive effect. Both as patrons and practitioners of the arts, the German Jews gave support to whatever was liberal and progressive, and the Cassirer gallery was representative of their activities in general.

Cassirer's gallery quickly became the most successful of its kind in Berlin. It specialized in French art of the recent past and in German Impressionism. It did much to support the Berlin Secession and its leading member, Max Liebermann. Cassirer was so intimately involved with the Secession indeed, that he was eventually elected its president. It was most unusual for a businessman to play such an active role in artistic matters and his election caused some controversy.

Cassirer's gallery made a great deal of money by awakening public interest in what was little known and less understood. By introducing the Berlin public to the work of the French Post-Impressionists, Cassirer ensured that they became popular in Germany before they did in France, and that German museums acquired works by Cézanne, Van Gogh and Gauguin earlier than almost any elsewhere in Europe. Cassirer staged a Cézanne exhibition as early as 1901, for example.

Paul Cassirer was a man of learning, extraordinary charm and outstanding taste. He genuinely loved most of the work he showed at his gallery and frequently bought from his own exhibitions for his own collection. When, in 1909, Cassirer left his first wife and moved in with the celebrated actress Tilla Durieux, he brought with him Barlach's sculpture *The Singing Woman*, several paintings by Manet, Renoir's *Two Children at the Piano*, two works by Van Gogh (one of which was *L'Arlésienne*) and one of Cézanne's landscapes of the Château Noir.

Cassirer was a mixture of businessman, patron and collector. Although his taste was broad, it did not extend to the work of those artists associated with the New Secession. It is therefore rather surprising that he should have taken an interest in the equally, if not more, radical Kokoschka. Before Kokoschka left Vienna for Berlin

Loos had approached Walden, asking him to try to persuade Cassirer to organize a Kokoschka exhibition. It proved difficult, but the dealer eventually yielded and staged the show in June 1910. Although it was not a one-man exhibition (Cassirer hedged his bets by giving over half his gallery to the work of Hans Hofmann, later to become the godfather of American Abstract Expressionism), it was the next best thing and provided Kokoschka with his first opportunity to present a considerable number of his works to the public.

He showed twenty-seven oils of which no fewer than twenty-four were portraits. Seventeen of the paintings were owned by Loos, at least two were loaned by the Viennese collector Oskar Reichel, and the recently completed portrait of Walden belonged to the sitter. A selection of life drawings was included as were eight illustrations for *The White Animal Slayer*.

The exhibition was not a success and apart from an enthusiastic article in *Der Sturm* by Lasker-Schüler and another elsewhere by Kurt Hiller, the press took no notice of it. According to a letter Kokoschka wrote to the Folkwang Museum in November 1910, the lack of success had not surprised Cassirer who felt that Kokoschka was not yet on quite the correct path and had told him that 'unless I follow his moral advice, generously given, I can expect only a prison sentence or a bullet. He is allowing me a period of two years, at the end of which he will take a financial interest in me only on condition that the training methods have worked.'

The nature of Cassirer's advice is made clearer in a letter which the dealer wrote to Walter Serner who, preparing to stage an exhibition of Kokoschka's work in Karlsbad for the summer of 1911, had asked Cassirer for his opinion of the artist.

I believe Herr Kokoschka to be a quite extraordinarily gifted man [Cassirer wrote] who – if he is saved from the misery in which he now finds himself and is supported sufficiently – will surely achieve something great in art. The entire danger for him is that he is split, and because he is forced to earn his living by making quick drawings, he allows himself to be prevented from accomplishing the great things for which his talent is suited. You would be doing something quite extraordinarily good for art if you could . . . give Herr Kokoschka the chance to work quietly for perhaps two years.

The implication of that letter is that the work Kokoschka was producing for *Der Sturm* was preventing him from developing as a painter, especially a painter of portraits. But Cassirer himself did little to give Kokoschka the chance to work quietly, without financial pressure, for two months, let alone two years. At that stage he clearly considered the investment unsound.

He did arrange for one portrait commission, however. He asked Kokoschka to paint his wife Tilla Durieux, one of the most famous actresses of the day, a celebrated beauty and society hostess. She had already been painted by a great many artists, Renoir among them. Kokoschka took little pleasure in the task because he immediately found Durieux unsympathetic. She kept him waiting for sittings, made him the victim of her moods and never let him forget that she was honouring him by allowing him to paint her. Characteristically, Kokoschka thought the project not worth the trouble and never finished the picture. He simply left it, together with all his painting equipment, at the Cassirer house and, without announcing his intention, never returned.

Durieux herself thought little of the portrait which, although unfinished, had reached quite an advanced stage. In her autobiography she mentions Kokoschka only once and in passing, while devoting an entire chapter to Renoir. But the Kokoschka is much better than the Renoir which, with its hot colours and pretty, doll-like face, is one of the least happy examples of his late manner, while the Kokoschka, sketchy though it is, does more than suggest the feline cunning and sexual magnetism of the sitter.

Apart from this portrait and the memorable painting of Walden, half length and in profile, Kokoschka also painted his friend Rudolf Blümner and the writer Peter Scher at this time. This portrait is lost and may well have been not an oil but a drawing or gouache. Scher contributed to *Der Sturm* and because he earned a reasonable living from regular and more conventional journalism, he was expected to subsidize Walden's activities more often than he could afford.

Years later Scher recalled Kokoschka turning up at his home on the outskirts of Berlin to begin work on the portrait.

On a large sheet of ordinary office stationery he began to scrub around and rub with the end of a small pencil. He squeezed paint out of a tube, scratched around in the whole lot with a nail and said that one shouldn't be afraid of using even a hammer and chisel, for what was 'drawing' and 'painting' when the only point was to produce something convincing?

This account testifies to the artist's unusual working methods and also to the power Kokoschka possessed to discern aspects of his sitter's personality and life unperceived by the less gifted eye. Scher thought the picture looked like that of a convict: 'And there, once again, "the

eye of God" revealed itself, for he did not know that some years earlier
. . . I had spent twenty months in prison weaving straw mats.'

There has been much discussion of Kokoschka's 'eye of God', of his
ability to see into the past and future, of his second sight. Several of his
sitters reported the shock they experienced when they first saw his
painting of them because he had revealed aspects of their character
which they had always attempted to hide. Kokoschka also seems to
have been aware, however dimly, of major events in his own future.
Before the First World War he produced several works in which he
appears wounded in the chest, at more or less the spot where he was
eventually wounded during the eastern campaign.

Although the Cassirer exhibition was not successful, it did directly
lead to what was Kokoschka's greatest opportunity thus far. It was
seen by Karl Ernst Osthaus, the wealthy industrialist and the most
generous patron of contemporary art in Germany at the time, who
had founded the Folkwang Museum at Hagen in the Ruhr. Osthaus
was deeply impressed by the show and offered to stage what was
essentially the same exhibition in the following September. This was
not only Kokoschka's first one-man show and his first exposure in a
public museum, it also resulted in the first acquisition of a Kokoschka
painting by a public institution.

Cassirer would later become crucial to the development of
Kokoschka's career; but in 1910 the artist owed more to Walden who
had, after all, persuaded Cassirer to stage the show and who continued
to encourage Kokoschka at a time when Cassirer had not made up his
mind about him. If Walden was important for Kokoschka the reverse
was equally true. It was Kokoschka who persuaded Walden to extend
coverage of the visual arts in *Der Sturm* and who encouraged him to
take an active interest in them himself. While Kokoschka was in Berlin
Walden even began to organize exhibitions of contemporary painting
and sculpture. He staged a show of work by members of the New
Secession and in March 1912, about eighteen months after Kokoschka
had returned to Vienna, Walden founded his own gallery, also called
Der Sturm, which opened with an exhibition of 'Blue Rider' prints and
drawings and work by Kokoschka himself.

Some writers have compared Walden unfavourably to Loos. Loos,
they argue, was selfless, an altruist who supported Kokoschka during
difficult times and for no financial gain. Walden on the other hand is
often seen as a mixture of prophet, huckster and advertising man, as
interested in publicizing himself as any of the artists he represented.
That is too crude a contrast. There was indeed more than a hint of the

charlatan about Walden; he did eventually profit financially from his activities; he certainly lacked many of the qualities which made Loos's personality so attractive; but while he was supporting Kokoschka he was extremely poor and his efforts were largely unrewarded.

In return Kokoschka did not treat Walden well. Like many artists he seems to have regarded dealers chiefly as the source of unlimited supplies of sympathy, understanding and cash. After Kokoschka returned to Vienna he sent many letters to Berlin demanding money and exhibitions and accusing Walden of neglecting him. In April 1912 for example, he accused the dealer: you let 'me quietly starve without lifting a finger'. By 1914 such letters were multiplying and had become mixtures of bitter recrimination and desperate pleas for help: 'Please, you have to help me. I need 500 crowns which I cannot get hold of anywhere . . . send me the money immediately and don't refuse because I have no means and have already used up all my credit.'

In Kokoschka's defence it must be admitted that he had entered into a formal contract with Walden by this time. Precisely when it was signed is not known, but it seems to have been in force by the time he arrived back in Vienna early in 1911. Presumably it was an exclusive contract, but Kokoschka nevertheless occasionally also worked for other Berlin dealers (Gurlitt and Cassirer) and Walden appears to have raised no objections even though Kokoschka was not above playing one off against the other. In 1914 he wrote to Walden, 'I should like to escape from the "Cassirer trust"; where I can I should prefer to send pictures constantly to you, if you provide the marks for them'.

Another letter soon after is more pressing and reveals the exaggerated expectations of Walden which Kokoschka entertained:

My heavy debts and the *personal misery* in which I have been living in Vienna utterly alone, without a friend, forced to be an outsider, forced *to ask for money*. . . . Couldn't you get me a fresco commission in America? I am ready for this, the kind of work most suited to me and I must constantly daub little pictures which can give me no satisfaction.

The contract with Walden lapsed and in September 1916 Kokoschka signed another agreement with him according to which he would provide ten drawings a month and twelve oils a year in exchange for a salary of 2,000 marks a month. Less than six weeks later Kokoschka unilaterally dissolved that contract and made a better one with Cassirer. The result was a legal dispute which was eventually settled without recourse to the courts.

Kokoschka's dealings with Walden do not reflect well on the artist.

Most art dealers can be difficult and Walden was certainly no exception. He did not always pay his artists promptly, sometimes pretended to have lost or mislaid work and was, especially during the early years of the gallery, badly organized. Kokoschka could also be unreliable. Quite apart from reneging on a contract, he often failed to deliver promised paintings and in his letters exaggerated his financial plight and the misery of his circumstances in Vienna. Berlin had transformed the gawky, naïve youth into a self-possessed man with the confidence to make demands of others.

It is difficult to overemphasize Walden's contribution to cultural life in the German capital. *Der Sturm* remained the leading avant-garde magazine in Germany at least until the outbreak of war and although it gradually declined thereafter, it managed to retain some of its influence until 1930. It finally ceased publication in 1932 when Walden left Germany for the Soviet Union.

The *Sturm* gallery was easily the most adventurous of those specializing in contemporary art in Berlin. It put German Expressionism on the map. In 1912 it staged the exhibition of Italian Futurism that had previously been shown in Paris and London and which in Berlin on some days of its run attracted more than a thousand visitors. In 1913 Walden organized a huge show of avant-garde painting and sculpture from all over the world, 'The First German Autumn Salon'. It was the biggest exhibition of its kind ever seen at a private gallery.

Nor was that all. Walden founded an experimental theatre, held weekly soirées at which poetry was read and discussed and music performed, and he published books. The *Sturm* imprint was responsible for some of the most important avant-garde publications of the day, among them Futurist manifestos, Kandinsky's early autobiography and Scheerbart's *Glass Architecture*.

Walden was a born impresario, but until 1912 his energies were dissipated by the constant demands of Lasker-Schüler. In that year he finally recognized that his marriage to the eccentric writer was a lost cause and left her for Nell Roslund, a Swedish journalist who immediately brought some order into his life. She administered the magazine and looked after the finances of all the *Sturm* operations. Walden married Nell Roslund in London at the end of 1912 and when they returned to Berlin they lived in fear of Lasker-Schüler's unpredictable and sometimes violent behaviour. Once she stormed into the *Sturm* offices and, mistaking Walden's secretary for Nell, threatened her with a revolver.

Having left Nell and married for a fourth time, Walden emigrated to the Soviet Union in 1932. At first active in émigré literary circles, he then disappeared. Only in recent years has it been confirmed that he was arrested and died of exhaustion in 1941 while being transported to a labour camp.

In Berlin Kokoschka first smelled real success but his life was not easy. Always poor and able to earn money only by painting portraits which, as he reported to Loos, was an increasingly unpleasant activity, Kokoschka began to long for Vienna again. On Christmas Eve 1910 he wrote to Lotte Franzos, one of his earliest patrons, that his 'entire life is hell'. Perhaps the Viennese, always unappreciative of their native talents, might now be better disposed towards an artist who had established a reputation abroad.

SEVEN

Kokoschka left Berlin for Vienna no later than the beginning of 1911. He was partly prompted by concern for his family, especially his father who was growing old, but he also wanted to see an exhibition at which his work was represented. This was a selection of the work of a number of young Austrian painters presented in the gallery belonging to the *Hagenbund*, a relatively conservative artists' organization that had been founded in 1900. The *Hagenbund* was not responsible for the exhibition; it had simply let its premises. We do not know who organized the event, but it is reasonable to assume that Kokoschka's participation had been arranged by Loos.

Kokoschka did not return to Berlin before the outbreak of war. He was to remain based in Vienna until military service took him abroad again as a soldier. It seems strange that he showed no interest in going back to Germany once the *Hagenbund* exhibition was over. His dealer was there and although his work for *Der Sturm* brought him little money, it had given him the feeling that he was at the centre of things. Fond though he was of his family, he had also come to realize that his mother was possessive and over-protective, and the atmosphere of his home stifling. He nevertheless chose to stay, and although he rented a studio elsewhere, he lived at home, constantly aware of the limitation to his freedom.

With the possible exceptions of Faistauer, Gütersloh and Kolig, all Kokoschka's fellow exhibitors at the *Hagenbund* show are now all but forgotten outside Austria. Kokoschka himself was represented by no fewer than twenty-five paintings, including the portraits of Peter Altenberg, Karl Kraus, Adolf Loos and Bessie Bruce, and a selection of ten life drawings. After the exposure he had received in Germany the previous year Kokoschka probably expected a more enthusiastic reception than he had been given on the last occasion he had shown his work in Vienna.

He was disappointed. The Viennese have always reserved special scorn for local artists, writers and musicians who first made their names abroad and on this occasion relished the opportunity of putting the young Kokoschka in his place. The reviews were worse than in 1909.

One of the Viennese critics hostile to Kokoschka was Arthur Roessler who wrote regularly for the *Arbeiter Zeitung*. Roessler's attitude to Kokoschka was not surprising even though he had a reputation as the most determined champion of the 'new art', for in 1911 Roessler was assiduously cultivating the myth of another Viennese artist, Egon Schiele, and the claims about Schiele's importance which Roessler was making would not easily have coexisted with public tributes to Kokoschka, who presented Schiele with his most serious competition.

Nevertheless Roessler unwittingly put his finger on some of the qualities which, for Kokoschka's admirers, were what gave his work importance.

He brews up his paints from poisonous putrescence, the fermenting juices of disease; they shimmer gall-yellow, fever-green, frost-blue, hectic-red and the substance binding them seems to be penetrating iodide of formyl, carbolic and asafoetida. He smears them on like a salve and allows them to crust scabiously, to form scars. He paints the countenances of people who fade away in the stale air of offices, who are greedy for money, loll about in the expectation of happiness and amuse themselves coarsely. He paints their weevil-like skin, their suppurating flesh steamed in inward heat, softened by dissipation and distressed by disease. Possibly the clumsy portrayal of the disgusting impurity of spongy and porous, leathery and flabby, spotted and speckled, infirm bodies is nothing but the despairing expression of a soul in harrowing disintegration which looks at the world through calcified eyes. Depravity is the attraction of these pictures. They have a certain significance as manifestations of an epoch in decay; judged artistically they are massacres in paint.

Apart from the concluding phrase, this memorable if overblown description might have been written by any of Kokoschka's several admirers. They perceived the force of the portraits precisely in the unnerving clarity with which decline, decay and corruption were mirrored and thus in their uncanny ability to serve as symbols for a decadent society.

Only in *Die Fackel* did Kokoschka receive support. In the issue for 28 February 1911 Franz Grüner wrote that the people represented in the portraits 'look as though they had suffered a grave illness, spent many years in gaol, as though they were suffering from repulsive physical and, naturally therefore, psychological diseases'. Although the language is strikingly similar to Roessler's, Grüner was not criticizing. While admitting that 'the means by which Kokoschka arrives at the effect of his pictures do not lead to a beautification of his models', he pointed out that Kokoschka 'aims at another goal by other means'. Grüner went on to compare Kokoschka with Tintoretto and to assert that the *Hagenbund* show

is the kind of exhibition by a living painter which one sees but very seldom. One will appreciate Kokoschka even more, however, if one remembers that what we are looking at is only intended as a beginning, and how far great painters are accustomed to grow beyond their beginnings.

Interestingly enough, the same issue of *Die Fackel* contains a spirited defence of the apartment house and shop on the corner of the Michaelerplatz which Loos had designed and which had almost been completed. It had already provoked bitter criticism in the Viennese press because of its lack of ornament and relatively anonymous appearance.

Kokoschka could have expected nothing less than intelligent and positive criticism from the paper edited by his friend Kraus, but the extent of the hostility exhibited by other journals and newspapers surprised and hurt him. He was also hurt by a further episode connected with the *Hagenbund* show. He had written another play, *Der brennende Dornbusch* – The Burning Bush – and planned to produce it during the run of the exhibition. The authorities demanded to see a text of the play before the opening night, objected to the play's alleged obscenity and banned the production while the dress rehearsal was under way.

Kokoschka felt humiliated by the response to the *Hagenbund* show and his dislike of the city in which he had grown up grew even stronger and he came to suffer from something close to persecution mania. He was aware that he was the most gifted painter of his generation and concerned that his reputation for intemperance – in his life as well as his art – would damage his career. He also feared that other, less able artists would steal his thunder. Only feelings like these can explain Kokoschka's hostility to several of his contemporaries.

The painter whose progress worried him most was Max Oppenheimer who had been a friend before Kokoschka left for Germany, and whose career seemed to follow Kokoschka's with worrying closeness. Oppenheimer had even been to Germany to stimulate interest in his work. Oppenheimer also specialized in the portrait, had received several commissions (some of them from the same patrons), had exhibited his work widely and had sold work to most of the private collectors of modern art in Vienna. Kokoschka believed that Oppenheimer was imitating his style and was determined to publicize the fact. In letters to Walden written during May and June 1911 Kokoschka asked him to do everything in his power to frustrate Oppenheimer's ambitions. Kokoschka described him as 'a shadow who copies each of my pictures. . . . He has a large exhibition at the Tannhäuser [Gallery] in Munich and has now in addition copied the *Sturm* poster.' Kokoschka, who asked Walden to advise the Tannhäuser of Oppenheimer's plagiarism, was referring to a poster he had designed showing the naked artist pointing dramatically to a wound in his side which does indeed appear to have provided the model for Oppenheimer's own exhibition poster.

In a slightly later letter to Walden, Kokoschka again complained about Oppenheimer and in a way which reveals much of the way Kokoschka now saw himself. A monograph about Oppenheimer had recently been written by Arthur Roessler in which, according to Kokoschka, 'my entire development' had been ascribed to Oppenheimer.

He was discovered at the *Kunstschau*
He has since been the outsider vilified by the critics

He comes close to Grünewald
He is the only modern in Vienna
He sees ghosts, the most secret sufferings of souls
He prefers to wallow in wounds
He will end in madness
All of this is put together from criticism of my work just as the pictures of the
last two years have been assembled from mine.

It was true that Oppenheimer was influenced by Kokoschka, that
his major subject was the portrait, that he was considerably less gifted
and that he prettified some of the more robust aspects of Kokoschka's
style in order to make them more palatable to a conservative audience;
but artists convinced of their greatness, as Kokoschka certainly was,
expect to be imitated. Some even welcome it as proof of their
importance. The bitterness of Kokoschka's complaints about Oppenheimer and the campaign he waged against him reveal a flaw in his
character which had been exposed by frustration and jealousy.

Significantly, it was Oppenheimer's Munich exhibition which
provoked the beginning of Kokoschka's campaign. For he had done
his best to arrange for an exhibition in Munich himself, had toured the
galleries on his way to Berlin but had found them 'booked up, so that
my friend Oppenheimer will be informing the people of Munich
about my art earlier than I can unless Loos comes here and clears the
matter up'.

Kokoschka's appeals to influential friends are also revealing. Did
Kokoschka truly believe that Loos or Walden would be able to
damage Oppenheimer's career? Surprisingly, both of them did their
best. Loos wrote to the Munich painter Franz Marc in the hope that
Marc might be able to use his influence: 'I have also heard from
Sch[oenberg] that you could arrange for a Kokoschka exhibition. It is
necessary especially in Munich where a miserable Kokoschka copyist
and swindler, Herr Oppenheimer, has been able to insinuate himself.'

Schoenberg was later shown the letter by Marc but thought that
Oppenheimer was being unjustly treated. Schoenberg, a painter as
well as a composer (and himself sometimes accused of being
influenced by Kokoschka), confided to his diary:

One doesn't need to call someone who is unoriginal a swindler. Certainly
Oppenheimer is not very nice. His pictures have never misled me about his
lack of genius. He is a 'scamp' but not a swindler. And his pictures have
nothing in common with Kokoschka's. One is being unjust to both men
therefore! For Kokoschka is genuine!

Not all those approached for help were as sensible. Lasker-Schüler was typically impetuous and immoderate. In December 1911 she published a 'Letter to an Imitator' in *Der Sturm* which was so offensive that the unfortunate Oppenheimer might have felt justified in embarking on litigation.

Dear Max O.
Your ostentatious clothes have always given me pleasure. . . . They demonstrated not only courage but also taste. I was doubly pleased to accompany you to your exhibition of pictures in Munich, but the paintings which hung on the walls were not yours – all of them were by Oskar Kokoschka. And you had to take me with you, me who know your model. Did you think me so uncritical, or are you one of those people who adopt the words and gestures of the person with whom they are in love? You are, I take it, in love with Kokoschka and your pictures are gathered flowers and therefore lack roots. The picture of Heinrich Mann was an exception which, as a brilliant copy, pleased me and I saw in its colours and rhythms apart from the writer himself the painter Oskar Kokoschka, not you. Is Max O. present in *Kokoschka*'s pictures? . . . Kokoschka is an old master born late, a terrible wonder.

Neither this nor any of the other hurtful things that were said about Oppenheimer provoked him to take legal action. He remained silent, realizing perhaps that Kokoschka was being hurt by the campaign more than he was. This remained true even when Kraus joined the attack with a witty article in *Die Fackel*. Oppenheimer's career was not affected and Kokoschka's rage can only be imagined when, at the beginning of 1912, Paul Cassirer staged an Oppenheimer exhibition at his Berlin gallery. This prompted another open letter from Lasker-Schüler, this time addressed not to the artist but the dealer.

Sir,
On the day you exhibited Oskar Kokoschka in your salon you moved a hundred years into the future by becoming the first art dealer in Berlin to recognize the eternal value of his creation. I heard with no little astonishment that you wish to stage a second exhibition of Kokoschka on your premises. Copies of his genius. Why during his lifetime? Why water down good wine if visitors with little wit get heart palpitations? I ask you most politely to cancel this exhibition. Oskar Kokoschka is not one of a pair of twins, he hasn't even got a cousin, but he has got an assassin for a friend.

Oppenheimer was not the only Viennese artist to be influenced by Kokoschka. All the younger painters specializing in portraits were deeply affected by his work and none more so than Egon Schiele who, because success proved elusive, did not merit a campaign of vilification. Oppenheimer however, was a threat. He was ruining the market.

While Kokoschka was loudly proclaiming that Oppenheimer was robbing him of the fame that was rightly his, Kokoschka's reputation was actually growing. While Austria remained generally antagonistic to Kokoschka's work, Germany began to hail his genius. In 1912 he not only showed at the *Sturm* gallery but was also represented by six paintings at the huge and prestigious *Sonderbund* exhibition in Cologne. One of them was the *View of the Dents du Midi* which was purchased by the Wallraf-Richartz Museum in Cologne.

Many German critics were now in little doubt about Kokoschka's greatness. P. F. Schmidt wrote in the authoritative *Zeitschrift für bildende Künste* that Kokoschka was 'the first Viennese painter in whom one can say there is genius. He is by no means to everyone's taste for he possesses exceptional individuality. Germany has probably seen nothing so wild and fantastic expressed in colour since the death of Grünewald.'

In 1913 the first monograph on Kokoschka was published. Written by Paul Stefan, it appeared under the imprint of Kurt Wolff of Leipzig, a house which specialized in the kind of unconventional art and literature already generally described as Expressionism and which later bought up the unsold copies of *The Dreaming Youths*. Stefan had earlier written about Gustav Mahler and the composer's widow, in 1913 Kokoschka's mistress, probably persuaded Stefan to turn his attention to the young painter's work. The book not only included reproductions but also the text of three plays. It was unusual for an artist still under thirty years of age to receive this kind of attention and Stefan's book established several of the criteria by which Kokoschka's work continues to be judged.

The artist who starved in Vienna and Berlin [Stefan wrote] had to paint portraits, but he could not see people, only animals and spirits. And for him the human face became a caricature, an instructive peculiarity, a betrayer, the target of his revenge. . . . He thus painted Peter Altenberg for example, not at all as the darling of well-endowed women but as the demonically aroused poet shaken by rage at his world . . . with dreadful eyes, rigid features and maliciously distorted hands which nevertheless cry out for help. Such hands, which appear to grasp bloodily for something beyond the figure are significant for Kokoschka. . . . The pictures of this period reach their object indirectly. Firstly they express the artist Kokoschka, they say what he was suffering then. And they permit an understanding of Kokoschka the visionary. . . . He does not see the individual he is painting, even less what the photographer or 'society' painter would see in the individual, but he sees a human being . . . sees his progeny unto the second and third generation, sees unconscious wishes, aims, repressions.

This concern for the human being, Kokoschka's sense of the humanity of his subjects was what Kraus recognized and cherished in the artist's work. Convinced as he was of the imminent collapse of civilization, Kraus no doubt also responded to the expression in Kokoschka's painting of the mortality of living things, of the corruptibility of matter.

In 1913 Kraus asked Kokoschka to illustrate one of his pamphlets, *Die chinesische Mauer* – The Chinese Wall – which was first published in 1909. Kraus's essay was inspired by a sensational American murder case which filled even the Austrian newspapers at the time. A white woman had been killed by her Chinese lover and Kraus used the incident as a symbol for the decline of western civilization in general, for the decadence of a culture soon to be judged and punished by the yellow races which were immune to occidental customs and weaknesses. What had been a relatively unimportant event in the United States was brilliantly transformed by Kraus into a polemic with universal implications.

Kokoschka's lithographs are not illustrations in any conventional sense. The man he depicts, far from being Chinese, is a self-portrait and his mistress has become Alma Mahler, Kokoschka's own mistress at the time. He also makes use of classical allusions. Only the final lithograph, *The Invaders*, expresses the sense of the text and shows a pack of animals with oriental, human features, their teeth bared, their bodies poised for attack (see illus. at head of this chapter).

The illustrations are concerned more with the battle of the sexes than with Kraus's account of the murder and its consequences and they therefore return to the theme which Kokoschka explored in *Murderer, the Hope of Women*.

In spite of Kraus's support, the exhibitions and Stefan's monograph, Kokoschka still failed to make a satisfactory living from his work. Almost certainly he would have fared better in Germany where he was seen as a pioneer of the new style of Expressionism. But he preferred to remain in Vienna, not least because in 1912 he became deeply involved with a woman – Alma Mahler – for the first time in his life and did not want to leave her.

As the obvious solution to his financial problems Kokoschka now sought a teaching post. Even before he had completed his studies at the

Kunstgewerbeschule Kokoschka let it be known that he wanted to teach there. He had, after all, conducted a life drawing class while still a student. In 1912 he tried again for an appointment and persuaded Alfred Roller, the acting director of the school, to appoint him as a teaching assistant to Professor von Kenner. He taught for ten hours a week and received 150 kronen a month, a by no means negligible salary at a time when a fully trained dressmaker could expect no more than 68 kronen a month for working a six-day week.

His main responsibility was the class for 'general life drawing' which he directed whenever von Kenner was ill or otherwise engaged. One of his students remembered that Kokoschka's classes were a joy:

for Kenner's academic kind of life drawing with charcoal and stump [was replaced] by Kokoschka's free method [employing] nude models in motion, up to six nudes in a Greek dance step which were sketched on large pieces of paper and which he, as an expressive artist, was able convincingly to capture.

Another student recalled Kokoschka's teaching methods, or rather the lack of any, for 'he did not correct our drawings . . . and said nothing of substance about art'.

This lack of correction coupled with a reluctance to talk about art, especially contemporary art, was something which also struck later students when Kokoschka was professor in Dresden. He invariably impressed his students, however. In Vienna he was:

full of good humour and energy; he radiated an atmosphere which inspired us all, 'Work, work, every piece of serious work is worthwhile', he often said, moving among students and easels. They were beautiful words. But he also said by way of instruction, 'Round is old fashioned, angular is modern.' I thought that childish.

That same student also recalled that Roller once summoned her to his office to ask what she thought of Kokoschka's teaching. Apparently the acting director had received a complaint and it was probably one of several. The complaints were taken seriously. Kokoschka had only a year's contract which was not renewed. In May 1913 he wrote to a friend:

I spoke to Roller today, he wants to take the course himself next year. He has learned enough but not understood and wants to take as his assistant that young fellow who is paying court to Frau Roller – after asking me pro forma to suggest my successor. The two will complement each other well since the newspapers have said a few times that the boy copies my drawings.

While Kokoschka was working at the *Kunstgewerbeschule* he was also teaching elsewhere: at the private and progressive school for girls in Vienna founded and run by a friend of Loos, Eugenie Schwarzwald. She was married to a leading administrator at the Ministry of Finance and had the reputation of being a brilliant hostess as well as an inspired teacher. She supported Loos who designed some of the interiors of the school including her study and who occasionally taught art history there. Schoenberg also gave lectures.

Before joining her as a teacher Kokoschka had painted a portrait of her husband and was a regular visitor to her house. Eugenie Schwarzwald had been struck by the artist's acute intelligence and although she found him 'so quiet that those who did not know him might easily have thought him deaf and dumb', she managed to get him to say enough to convince her that he would make a good and imaginative art teacher. In her ideas about education as in everything else, Eugenie Schwarzwald was nothing if not progressive, and the people who sent their daughters to her school (it was for young ladies only) also had advanced ideas.

Kokoschka quickly demonstrated an ability to bring talent out of the least promising pupils by unconventional means. One of his pupils at Schwarzwald's school was Elsie Altmann who married Loos after Bessie Bruce's death. She remembered Kokoschka as

tall, blond, thin, upright, the hair cut short and the unbelievably deep blue of his eyes . . . but no, it was not his eyes that were so blue but his gaze, yes, his gaze was blue. He gave out an inexplicable magic. . . . We were the most feared class in the entire school: wild, cheeky, ill-mannered, uncontrollable . . . and suddenly were a flock of little lambs, quiet and respectful. Who would have dared make trouble for this archangel? We were not very talented; we drew whatever was put in front of us: an apple, a pear, a flower, a woman; and then we coloured it. That was how it was before. But Oskar walked quietly and calmly between the desks, looked into our faces and said, 'Draw whatever you want.'

Such freedom in art lessons was very new at the time and highly contentious. Emphasis on freedom and play was part of the method of one of the teachers at the *Kunstgewerbeschule* however. This was Franz Cizek, one of the first to take children's art seriously and to realize that it cannot be judged by adult standards and ideas. Kokoschka was doubtless influenced by Cizek who had taught him for some of his time at the School of Arts and Crafts. Indeed, a book of collages by pupils of Cizek which was published in Vienna before the First World War contains work remarkably similar to Kokoschka's postcards for the *Wiener Werkstätte* and to the illustrations for *Die träumenden*

Knaben.

But Kokoschka was not quite as liberal as Elsie Altmann remembered him. He did make demands of his pupils even though he managed to create an atmosphere in which they thought they were free and in which their imaginations were excited and stimulated. He often told his class stories and then instructed them to draw whatever came into their heads.

With a magical touch he freed us from all our inhibitions, brought out and developed talents in us of which we had never dreamed. Even I who was not gifted was suddenly in a position to paint lively and brightly-coloured fairy-tale scenes.

That same student also remembered how Kokoschka's teaching career was temporarily halted. One day

and rather unexpectedly the school inspector came to our drawing class. In the past the Viennese school authorities had turned a blind eye to the so-called eccentricities of Frau Dr Schwarzwald, but this time she had gone too far. One simply couldn't tolerate engaging the 'notorious' and 'immoral' Kokoschka to teach drawing to a class of young girls.

Although private, the Schwarzwald school was subject to official inspection and the inspectors made it clear almost as soon as Kokoschka arrived that they did not think him suitable. He had no idea of the importance of the syllabus and no respect for conventional teaching methods. According to one inspector,

he had the girls draw whatever they wanted. . . . Since September of last year only imaginative pictures with figures have been drawn and painted: street scenes, paintings of people, a chaos of childish rubbish, mostly only half finished daubing entirely in the style of the art which he himself, without sense or thought, exhibited at the *Kunstschau*.

The inspector's major criticism was that Kokoschka took no notice of the curriculum which every teacher was obliged to follow. In February 1912 the local education committee withdrew permission for Kokoschka to teach. Eugenie Schwarzwald had to dismiss her art master or have her school closed down.

It is interesting that the inspector referred to the *Kunstschau* in his report. Since he gives Kokoschka's first name as Hubertus throughout, he clearly was not very familiar with the man or his work and had almost certainly not seen the exhibition in question. Nevertheless he was only too aware of the young man's reputation and that reputation, bad enough in official circles in 1909, was made worse by an event which took place between the inspector's visit to the Schwarzwald school and the decision to withdraw Kokoschka's teaching licence.

That was a lecture which the artist gave at the 'Academic Society for Literature and Music in Vienna' on 27 January 1912 and which he called 'On the Consciousness of Visions'. In the final letter from the local education committee this 'lecture about his artistic philosophy' was said to have led to 'noisy demonstrations'.

The full name of the society is misleadingly stuffy. In fact it was an organization devoted to the public performance, exhibition and discussion of the 'new art' and it invited most of the radical Viennese practitioners to air their views. Loos lectured on 'Ornament and Crime' for example and Schoenberg gave a talk on Gustav Mahler. Karl Kraus also gave his first public reading under the auspices of the society in 1910.

Kokoschka, who was probably brought to the society's notice by Adolf Loos, spoke to a full audience, many of whom must have been persuaded to attend by the striking poster he had designed which was a version of the self-portrait, pointing to a wound in his side, first produced as an advertisement for *Der Sturm*.

He spoke for about thirty minutes and what he said precisely is unknown since the notes he used were lost soon after. His delivery was halting and on one occasion he had briefly to leave the podium to collect his thoughts. Much later, in 1921, he did his best to recall what he had said and wrote it down in an essay which he now called 'On the Nature of Visions'. He thought it important enough to publish it on several occasions, once as an appendix to Edith Hoffmann's English biography. We may assume that the substance of this essay is largely that of the 1912 lecture and that it provides insights into his artistic credo which, in spite of major changes of style and subject in his paintings, remained the same throughout his life.

The purpose of art, Kokoschka says, is the revelation of visions which lie beyond normal experience but are conjured up by it in the memory:

One tree left alive in an arid land would carry in its seed the potency from whose roots all the forests of the earth might spring. So with ourselves; when we no longer inhabit our perceptions they do not go out of existence; they continue as though with a power of their own, awaiting the focus of another consciousness. There is no more room for death; for though the vision disintegrates and scatters, it does so only to re-form in another mode. Therefore we must hearken to our inner voice. We must strive through the penumbra of words to the core within.

In such highly poetic language Kokoschka explains that the artist must penetrate the veil of appearances in nature to reveal the essential truths beneath. He can do this only with the aid of the soul, which is 'a reverberation of the universe'.

The essay is extremely difficult to understand and most of those present at the 1912 lecture thought it entirely incomprehensible and little more than a series of unconnected assertions. The press reported a noisy and unruly reception and the evening ended in confusion. Once again Kokoschka had experienced rejection at Viennese hands.

EIGHT

In 1912 Oskar Kokoschka was twenty-six years of age and although in Vienna he had more opponents than friends, in Germany his career looked promising. He was now convinced that he had already secured a place for himself in the history of art. He was one of the first, perhaps even the very first, to have arrived at a new style of painting. Although only his friends recognized the fact, he was the leader of a generation of Viennese painters who had escaped from the influence of Klimt and the Secession and were employing an unmistakably modern language. What Kokoschka had done for painting he had also accomplished in his writing. He knew that in time his plays would be recognized as the forerunners of a new kind of theatre.

In some ways, however, his artistic development had outstripped the growth of his personality. He remained in some important respects immature. He continued to live at home where he was careful to do nothing to offend his parents. He found it difficult to cope with criticism, demanded that the world accept his own estimate of himself and became angry when he found that it did not. He continued to rely for emotional and practical support on those older than himself and chiefly, of course, on Adolf Loos who had long since become a kind of surrogate father. Kokoschka had few friends of his own age. He seemed to seek out older people, to look to them for the maturity he found lacking in himself.

Since his youthful passion for Lilith Lang, Kokoschka appears to have had few girl-friends and there was certainly no one who had engaged his attention for long. When, at the age of twenty-six, he met the woman who was to dominate his life for the next three years and haunt his dreams for years after that, he was obviously ripe for a consuming, passionate affair. And it is significant that the woman who almost drove him mad with love for her was considerably older than he was.

Kokoschka first met Alma Mahler, the widow of the composer, on 14 April 1912 and instantly wanted her. He was not the first to find her powerful sexuality and air of worldly experience irresistible; nor would he be the last. She was one of the most celebrated women in Vienna, desired by many men whose passion was fired by the knowledge that she was by no means unavailable. Had circumstances been different, she might have been a brilliantly successful courtesan.

Alma Mahler found talent erotic. When it was genius accompanied by fame she found it intoxicating. She married Mahler, a man much older than she and no longer in the prime of life, and she basked in his reflected glory, relishing the attentions of the distinguished men with whom, through her husband, she came into contact. She lavished her considerable gifts on her love affairs, vicariously living the life of an artist by shaping the lives of the men in her thrall.

Alma was the daughter of Emil Schindler, one of the best-known painters of late-nineteenth-century Vienna. When Schindler died, Alma's mother married one of his pupils, Carl Moll, a founder of the Secession, a friend of Klimt and one of the most astute and shrewd artists in Austria.

When Moll became her stepfather in 1897 Alma was on the threshold of maturity and although by no means a classic beauty, she was striking enough to attract a great deal of male attention, especially from older men. Her chestnut hair and bright and penetrating blue eyes were her best features, but even without them her bearing and confidence would have made her impressive. She talked well, had wide knowledge, especially of art, music and literature and (this perhaps the most powerful aphrodisiac) she appeared to listen to whatever a man said with rapt attention. This was less because she was genuinely interested than the result of a slight deafness which forced her to concentrate in order to hear.

Klimt, the most fashionable painter in Vienna and a man with an almost insatiable sexual appetite, hotly pursued Alma for a time and may even have been her first lover, although it seems that before her marriage Alma enjoyed the flirtation and the pursuit more than the conquest and probably preserved her virginity. Klimt sharpened her hunger for fame. He was a celebrity and he wanted her.

Alma found herself especially attracted to musicians, partly no doubt because she was musically gifted herself and knew more musicians even than painters. Taught composition by Alexander von Zemlinsky, she was not surprised when he fell in love with her and proposed marriage. She agreed but Zemlinsky could not hope to compete with Gustav Mahler, Vienna's greatest living composer and the director of the State Opera.

Alma met Mahler in November 1901 at a dinner party at which Klimt was also present, as was another of Alma's admirers. The hostess was amused by the combination of guests and no doubt looked forward to some awkward moments. As it happened, the evening was memorable less for the conversation than for Mahler's behaviour. He was transfixed by Alma from the moment he set eyes on her. As soon as the dinner-party ended and he reached home he sent her the first of a stream of letters, each of them more urgent in its demand that she should respond to his entreaties. He was forty-one and she was twenty-two. He was staid and rather dull, but his fame more than compensated for his age and unexciting personality. Alma quickly surrendered, less to Mahler himself than to Vienna's greatest composer. They became engaged just before Christmas 1901 (little more than a month after their first meeting) and were married on 9 March 1902 by which time she was already pregnant.

Alma adored being the wife of a famous man. Already established in Viennese society she now became one of its most ambitious hostesses. The famous and influential longed to be invited to her dinner-parties where she proved an even greater attraction than her husband. Much though Mahler loved her, he did not make her happy. She was always acutely aware of the difference in their ages, frequently angered that his work, which regularly took him away from home, seemed to be as important to him as she was, if not indeed more so. She continued to be interested in other men. She was an outrageous flirt. She had affairs.

One of them was with the young German architect Walter Gropius whom she met at a spa in the Tyrol in June 1910. Their relationship was at first restricted to passionate letters. By September she was wondering: 'When will the time come when you lie naked on my body, when nothing can part us – other than, at most, sleep? . . . I know that I live only for the time when I can become yours utterly and completely.'

That time soon came, when Gustav Mahler took Alma with him to Munich for a concert. She arranged to meet Gropius at the Hotel Regina where they slept together. They were highly resourceful in their arrangements for meetings. Once they contrived to meet on the Orient Express *en route* to Paris where Alma was to meet Gustav for the first stage of a journey to America. It was more than a passing affair. Alma wanted a child by Gropius and even told her mother about the man who was now dominating her thoughts. Mahler also knew about Gropius. Although he believed his wife's protestations that he was just another young man besotted with her and someone she did not take seriously, his worry about a younger rival drove him to seek the advice of Sigmund Freud.

America brought an interruption to Alma's correspondence with Gropius. Mahler then became terminally ill and his wife began to think about Gropius once again. When the composer returned from America to France for treatment, Alma wrote to Gropius urging him to meet her in Neuilly. He did not come, however. Mahler, realizing that further treatment was hopeless, asked to be taken back to Vienna where he died, not quite fifty-one years old, on 18 May 1911.

Alma continued to write to Gropius. He visited the young widow in Vienna and their reunion was passionate, but Alma was genuinely disturbed by Mahler's death and determined to maintain a period of public mourning. Gropius, jealous of Mahler's memory, left her in Vienna and then kept his distance, knowing that he might have to 'wait and hunger for you for years' but assuring her that he would 'always be where and whenever you need me'.

The meetings and correspondence soon began again, however, although they were less frequent. Nor did Alma's public grief dim her interest in other men. She met the controversial biologist Rudolf Kammerer and assisted him with his experiments on toads. Kammerer's wife at least was convinced that the experiments continued in the bedroom although Alma loudly protested otherwise. She also met and had an affair with the composer Franz Schreker.

Alma's stepfather, Carl Moll, introduced her to Kokoschka. Moll had been impressed by the young painter's work at the *Hagenbund* exhibition and had asked him to paint Alma's portrait. The sittings were arranged for Moll's opulent house on the Hohe Warte, one of the most prosperous districts of Vienna. Moll described Kokoschka to his stepdaughter as a 'young genius' and that must have been enough to arouse her interest.

Kokoschka himself claimed that Alma fell in love with him at first sight, but that would have been uncharacteristic. The reverse is more likely and that is how Alma herself remembered it although her memoirs, coloured by sentimentality and self-dramatization, are scarcely reliable. According to Alma Mahler the first sitting for the portrait was eventful:

He had brought some rough paper with him and wanted to draw. After a short time I told him that I couldn't be stared at like that and asked if I might play the piano while he worked. He began to draw, coughing all the time and whenever he hid his handkerchief there were spots of blood on it. His shoes were torn, his suit was ripped. We scarcely spoke and he was nevertheless unable to draw.

He stood up – and he embraced me suddenly and violently. I found this kind of embrace strange . . . I returned it in no way and precisely that appears to have affected him.

He rushed out and in an hour I had the most beautiful letter of love and supplication in my hands.

While Kokoschka often suffered from bronchitis he was never tubercular, so the detail of the blood on the handkerchief must be a romantic touch. So, too, is the description of his clothes. Even at his poorest, Kokoschka was invariably immaculately dressed.

There is no doubt that Kokoschka was affected by Alma Mahler as he had not been by any woman before. He was young, awkward and unsure of himself. She was accomplished, experienced, self-confident and strong. She was also famous and, as Kokoschka knew, desired by many men. She could mould him, give him an identity and facilitate his entry into circles which had always remained closed. Alma was also affected by Kokoschka. Even though he was not yet as famous as her other conquests, she sensed genius in him. She also responded to the raw, undisciplined energy obvious in everything he said and did. He came from a different background; his manners and behaviour lacked polish; he was far too young for her; but her accomplishments, self-confidence and strength would transform him. She would become his muse. She would create Oskar Kokoschka and she would never allow him to dominate her as she would dominate him. When he visited her in her flat they would sleep together but she never allowed him to stay the night. When they were together in her house in the country she insisted that he occupy a bedroom apart from hers. When they travelled abroad he would take another room in the same hotel. She thus protected her independence, either because she was afraid of total involvement or was never interested in having it.

Even seventy years after they were written Kokoschka's letters to Alma are touching and occasionally disturbing to read. They began on the day he met her, quickly became a flood of entreaties, protestations, whimperings and cries of pain. They were most often pages long though sometimes of a few lines only, alternating with telegrams which were even more urgent in their requests and demands and so frequent that Kokoschka had to borrow money to pay for them.

There were a few letters after Alma finally broke with Kokoschka in 1915. Although they became far fewer in number they reveal that he never ceased to think about her, frequently desired her and longed for her recognition of his success. His continuing obsession with her is manifest in other ways. He himself wrote about the affair without ever mentioning her name. As late as 1947 he imposed the condition on his first English biographer and her publisher that Alma Mahler should not be identified.

Kokoschka probably slept with Alma Mahler two days after they first met and his frustration and bewilderment began immediately, for soon after that she left Vienna on an extended trip to Paris. She seems regularly to have left Vienna, her young daughter by Mahler, and her lover to go to Paris, to Scheveningen and elsewhere. He was driven to distraction not only by these frequent absences but also by Alma's determination that their affair should remain secret. She said that it would be improper for them to be seen in public together so soon after her husband's death, but she was probably motivated more by his lack of social graces.

Nevertheless, the affair was common knowledge, at least among Kokoschka's students at the *Kunstgewerbeschule*, one of whom remembered that: 'Every Friday evening after the evening life class Alma Mahler drew up outside the gate of the school in her car, then a rarity, Kokoschka got in and they drove to the Semmering for the weekend.' It was on the Semmering, a beautiful and mountainous spot between

Vienna and Graz, that Alma had her country house.

It was difficult for Kokoschka to keep silent about the passion which consumed him. He told Adolf Loos who strongly disapproved, rightly perceiving the danger which Alma Mahler presented. When Kokoschka told him that he could never contemplate breaking with her and intended to marry her if only she would have him, Loos announced the end of their relationship and left Kokoschka without his staunchest ally. Kokoschka also told his mother about Alma and she disapproved equally strongly. She was worried by the effect the older woman was having on her son who had become short-tempered and withdrawn and in any case always felt threatened by the thought of a permanent relationship.

At the end of April 1912 Kokoschka wrote to Alma in Paris that his

poor family has to suffer a great deal because I scream too loudly and am sharp with them. I cannot change myself quickly into the compliant elder son and brother sympathetic to the hurts of others. My poor mother now suffers greatly from my electricity which needs to be discharged so that I retain clear control of my nerves during the day.

The letters provide the most reliable evidence of the progress of the affair, but the evidence is one-sided. When Alma broke with Kokoschka she asked him to send back her letters to him promising to do the same with his to her. He kept his promise; she broke hers. Her side of the story is known only from her memoirs which are as unreliable as Kokoschka's own.

She says that he was unreasonably, insanely jealous and tried to shut her off from her friends. Although his behaviour was obviously abnormal, he did have grounds for his jealousy. He knew Alma's reputation and he knew about Kammerer. Although he knew nothing of Gropius, Alma did, as we know, continue to write to the architect throughout her affair with Kokoschka.

Alma hurt Kokoschka deeply in many ways. She inflicted the biggest hurt of all when she decided not to have Kokoschka's child, which was aborted. Kokoschka had been ecstatic when he discovered that Alma was pregnant. He had longed for a child, not least because its birth might force Alma to marry him. He never became a father and it was the biggest disappointment of his life.

During the three years of the affair Alma dominated Kokoschka's art as she did his life. According to her, the affair was 'a single, violent lover's quarrel. Never before had I tasted so much cramp, so much hell, so much paradise.' It is difficult not to conclude, however, that

Alma's emotions were considerably less engaged than were Koko-schka's and that she was using him. The affair was not without its happier moments, however. Kokoschka travelled with Alma Mahler to Mürren in 1912 and in 1913 over the Dolomites into Italy and down as far as Naples. These journeys were a source of delight to them both and resulted directly in some of Kokoschka's best work: not only the landscape painted at Tre Croci but also *The Tempest* which was directly inspired by memories recalled at a later moment when the relationship had begun to founder.

Almost everything Kokoschka drew and painted at this time was inspired directly or indirectly by Alma Mahler and the always erratic course of their relationship. He painted her portrait on her own and together with him. He made her the subject of narrative print cycles. He found it difficult to draw any woman from his imagination without giving her Alma's features.

In 1913 he produced lithographic illustrations to his poem *Der gefesselte Kolumbus* – Columbus Bound – which was inspired by the affair with Alma Mahler. Like most of the other similarly inspired work and indeed like the affair itself, these illustrations are a mixture of exultation, misery and self-dramatization. Alma becomes the eternal Eve for whom the man is searching. But she is also the Virgin Mary and the man, Kokoschka himself, thus becomes Christ who must inevitably suffer a horrible death.

The lithographic cycle *Bach Cantata*, which dates from 1914 but was first published two years later, also uses biblical imagery to create an allegory of Kokoschka's personal life. The cycle ends with the sacrificial death of the man. Like *Columbus Bound* therefore, the *Bach Cantata* reveals that throughout his affair with Alma Mahler Kokoschka dwelt on the likely consequences of having committed himself to a woman with the power to ruin him.

By the time Kokoschka was working on the *Bach Cantata* Alma was indeed thinking about ending the relationship. Replying to a letter from Gropius, she wrote to Berlin:

How am I living? – After battles and mistakes – I have regained myself? – I am more mature – more free – above all I know that I have nothing to search for – because I have found so much – everything – in my life. – I halt beside no milestone! – If you want my friendship – you have it. – I greatly desire to talk to you. – Your image is pure and dear to me – and people who have experienced such strange and beautiful things together, may not lose each other. – Come – if you have the time and it makes you happy – come here. – It is *not* resignation which makes me write all this but *clarified, newly cleared* vision.

And she signed it:

Alma Mahler (and no longer anything else in this life).

We do not know whether Gropius responded to this particular invitation, but it is clear that Alma was no longer interested in Kokoschka and was again in hot pursuit of the architect. Significantly, it was in the spring of 1914 that Gropius's reputation had grown enormously. Already known as the designer of one of the first modern industrial buildings in Europe (the Fagus shoe-last factory at Alfeld), he now received glowing tributes from the German and Austrian press for his work on the Cologne *Werkbund* exhibition of 1914. Alma wrote to him in May telling him that she was lonely and suggesting a meeting in July. She wrote repeatedly, even though, unknown to Gropius, she continued to consort with Kokoschka. On New Year's Eve 1915 which she spent with Kokoschka, she wrote to Gropius who had already been mobilized, in terms which make her longing for him clear: 'May *the* time come when I may lead you here – here to me where you with your *steps* have measured the floor for me.'

They met towards the end of February 1915 in Berlin where Gropius was on leave from the front and the reunion was passionate. Kokoschka, now training with the Austrian Imperial Cavalry, had no idea that his mistress was enjoying nights of sexual abandon with an officer of the German Hussars.

Gropius soon had to return to the battlefield after which he and Alma wrote to each other daily. In May or June 1915 she announced that she might be pregnant. This time she had no intention of arranging for an abortion and was determined to marry. Even when she discovered that she was not pregnant she was no less determined:

When you get leave – I shall go – wherever you will see me quickest – I shall bring my papers with me and we shall marry . . . without anyone knowing. . . . I shall remain your wife incognito until you return and can give me your protection.

She signed this letter twice:

Alma M. Gropius; A. Maria Gropius.

Kokoschka had no idea of Alma Mahler's interest in Gropius until after war had been declared and he had joined the cavalry. Even then he had to discover the painful truth for himself. Not that he had ever been free from suspicion: throughout his affair with Alma he was repeatedly driven to despair by her real and imagined infidelities. Jealousy of the dead Mahler was bad enough (the sight of the composer's death mask was enough to make him tremble with rage), but the belief that Alma had lovers still living was even worse.

Kokoschka was convinced that Alma continued to see the biologist Kammerer and he was once confronted by the proof in particularly unappetising fashion. Alma had used some of her not inconsiderable financial resources to commission the building of a villa on the Semmering. She encouraged Kokoschka to believe that it was to be their house and they spent much time there together both while it was being built and after it had been completed.

Kokoschka painted a mural on the wall above the fireplace and it, like almost everything else he produced at that time, was a celebration of their love. The house gave him cause for hope that they would indeed eventually be married; it provided evidence that the emotional security which had so far eluded him was already within his grasp. He dreamed of having a family and of leading an idyllic life in one of the most beautiful places in Europe.

One day he arrived at the house alone to find the living-room full of glass tanks with toads in them. Many of the toads had escaped and were mating. Obscenely coupled, they hopped and slithered across the floor and over the furniture. Kammerer, as Kokoschka well knew, was carrying out research on the midwife toad and he must recently have been at the house conducting his experiments. In a rage, Kokoschka chased the creatures into the garden and smashed all the tanks. When Alma arrived, she once again accused him of unreasonable jealousy.

Despite the mounting evidence of Alma's habitual unfaithfulness, Kokoschka persisted in believing that he occupied a special place in her affections and was unable to contemplate ending the affair. He managed to convince himself, almost as a defence against madness, that she would eventually yield and marry him. He was prepared to do anything, totally to abase himself if necessary in order to keep her. She knew that she could deceive and demean him without driving him away. Once she knew that she was dominant, however, and that Kokoschka was her willing slave, she began to lose interest in him and found the intensity of his behaviour irritating.

At the same time she was afraid of the rages which her inconsistent moods provoked in him and it was probably her fear of violence which prevented her from making a clean break. Before war broke out she had made up her mind and, to judge from some of Kokoschka's letters to her, frequently dropped heavy hints that the affair must end. For whatever reason she repeatedly stopped short of insisting on a final break, however, and Kokoschka continued to visit her both in Vienna and at the house on the Semmering. Perhaps she perceived a solution to her problem in the coming international conflict: once the war had begun she did her best to persuade Kokoschka to volunteer.

Throughout the final stages of his affair with Alma, Kokoschka sought consolation in painting. Again and again he painted his mistress, alone and together with himself, and again and again he captured an expression on her face which is both enigmatic and bewitching, strong yet vulnerable. In these paintings she becomes what he wanted her to be. The greatest of them, now known as *Die Windsbraut* (illus. 15) – The Tempest – suggests both physical and emotional fulfilment. The artist, his hands intertwined, his mistress resting tenderly on his shoulder, lies on a bed which seems to consist of clouds twisting and turning in the turbulent air above a moonlit, mountainous landscape. The picture describes a love too powerful to be earthbound, an intimacy which has elevated the lovers above the mortal and transient and is about to carry them off to paradise.

The picture might also, as Werner Hofmann suggests, allude to Kokoschka's growing sense of alienation from his mistress. The dominant colour, a cold blue-green, supports such an interpretation, especially since there is evidence that *Die Windsbraut* originally contained much more red. The painting is subtle enough to carry several meanings simultaneously. Certainly Kokoschka had Wagner's *Tristan and Isolde* in mind when he conceived it.

The awakening to death makes the expression in the man's eyes frozen and absent. Unity awaits him and his beloved only in the stormy waves of world destruction – thus the private is elevated to the level of the cosmic. It seems that Kokoschka who was led by his mistress to a Tristan-like experience paraphrased Isolde's last words:

> 'To drown,
> sink down
> in the wafting universe
> of the breath of the world-
> conscious –
> greatest desire!'

In a letter written to Alma sometime in April 1913 Kokoschka told her: 'The picture is slowly being finished but always improved', and added a description:

We two with a very strong, peaceful expression, our hands entwined, on the edge, in a semi-circle, a sea illuminated as though by Bengal fire, a water-tower, mountains, lightning and the moon. . . . In the midst of the confusion of nature, to trust one person eternally and through faith to make oneself and the other secure.

The picture is the masterpiece of Kokoschka's early period and perhaps the greatest of all his paintings. Certainly he made nothing else like it, partly no doubt because he never again experienced the feelings Alma inspired in him. It was Kokoschka's friend, the poet Georg Trakl who gave the painting a name: it was *Die Windsbraut* – The Tempest – a word which in German literally means 'bride of the winds'.

Kokoschka's obsession with Alma caused much tension with his family, not least perhaps because his mother was for the first time confronted by a serious rival for her son's affections. Later, too, Romana Kokoschka appears to have panicked whenever she heard that her eldest son and the family's only source of financial support, had become deeply involved with a woman.

But the obsession with Alma did not drive from Kokoschka's mind all thought of his responsibilities. His extraordinary concern for the well-being of his family remained paramount.

In 1914, not long before the outbreak of war, his sister Berta announced that she wanted to marry Emil Patočka, an officer working in the legal department of the Austro-Hungarian Navy in Vienna. The wedding could take place only if the sizeable sum of 10,000 kronen could be raised as security – a military regulation apparently designed to discourage officers from marrying beneath their station.

Kokoschka managed to raise the money, but only after a nerve-racking period in which he wrote to numerous friends, museums, dealers and private collectors asking for assistance. Once the bills for the wedding had been paid Kokoschka was completely without funds. Immediately after the bride and groom had departed on their honeymoon, Kokoschka and his father 'in our top hats and tailcoats . . . stopped outside a wine bar . . . but emptying our trouser pockets we discovered that we had not a penny between us'.

NINE

The war which had threatened for some time and which was finally sparked off in June 1914 by the assassination, by a Bosnian revolutionary, of the heir to the Austro-Hungarian throne, the Archduke Franz Ferdinand, at Sarajevo, began on 28 July. Until then the summer had been remarkable only for its unusually warm weather.

Then came Sarajevo. In the words of Stefan Zweig:

the very last critical days of July and every hour another contradictory piece of news, the telegrams from Kaiser Wilhelm to the Tsar, the telegrams from the Tsar to Kaiser Wilhelm, Austria's declaration of war against Serbia, the murder of Jaurès.

At first the majority of people in Austria were jubilant:

The first fears about the war which no one wanted . . . had suddenly become enthusiasm. Groups of people formed in the streets, flags, bands and music were suddenly everywhere, the young recruits marched . . . in triumph and their faces were bright because they were being cheered, they, the little, everyday people whom no one otherwise respected and fêted.

Austro-Hungary's declaration of war on Serbia was quickly followed by the involvement of Germany, Russia, France, Belgium and Britain. What Kraus later described as 'the last days of mankind' had begun.

Once war had been declared Kokoschka felt that he should enlist but resisted his inclination to do so. What eventually persuaded him was less Alma's advice than a powerful sense of guilt. This emerges from a vividly descriptive letter which he wrote to Alma in July 1914 and in which he recounts events he had observed at a railway station in Vienna.

The woman who went with her husband to the station was blue in the face and smiled. Then she left and jokingly said to him, 'Don't shoot too many Serbians; it's not their fault.' Then she disappeared into the crowd. The man had been drinking to gain courage and had said 'Go now!' and had then staggered off into the concourse. He was then suddenly sober and when he could no longer see his wife he had such a grim expression on his face that I am unable to comprehend why things should be so good for me.

Everyone arrived sleepless at the station, feeling very cold, dressed only in a jacket or a peasant blouse. Those in uniform went hither and thither on account of the 'stormy acclamation of the people' and were then put into the cattle trucks. 48 men in one truck to the border. Again not to sleep but on benches. I am tormented by the worry that my brother might also have to go. In Hungary all those in his category have already been called up. In Vienna this will happen with the second phase of conscription . . . when the war with Russia breaks out everything will be committed.

There are those who see things from above 'objectively' and are enthusiastic for the others and wish them lots of luck . . . but I have a bad conscience, as though I shared responsibility for everything because of my search for enjoyment and frivolity . . . and if nothing but victories come, then that would be the greatest sin of all – but so far there have been so few victories.

This memorable description leaves one in little doubt that Kokoschka was already uncomfortably aware of the suffering the war had caused even at that early stage of the hostilities and of the stark contrast between the plight of ordinary people and the privileged. In letters to Alma he repeatedly refers to his own relative well-being and to the miseries of 'these little, starving and confused boys and men who have known nothing but misery until now, are being driven to their deaths over there or are being crippled, and no one gives a damn about it later'.

Kokoschka's anger and guilt were exaggerated by worry about his brother. Bohuslav, to whom Kokoschka always felt protective, was quickly conscripted into the navy, was serving on a battleship in the Adriatic and might any day be killed. In the autumn of 1914 Kokoschka wrote to the publisher Kurt Wolff that: 'If I were to get some money to keep my relatives' heads above water I should like to volunteer for the army because it will have been an eternal scandal to have sat around at home'. At about the same time he wrote to Albert Ehrenstein, that he was 'now going secretly to war'.

He had still not taken the fateful step by the beginning of 1915, however, and it seems likely that his resolve was strengthened by Alma who noted on the bottom of a letter he wrote to her on 2 January: 'We talked about his artistic future throughout New Year's night. I in part very sharply and like a teacher.' That 'artistic future' must surely have included a consideration of whether Kokoschka would join the fighting.

When Alma wrote that note Kokoschka had just volunteered and she was relieved that he had done so. She had her own reasons to be pleased. Others had theirs and chief among them were Kokoschka's mother and Adolf Loos who realized that the affair with Alma must now be at an end. Loos immediately contacted Kokoschka and asked him if he needed any help.

A letter to Alma dated 3 January 1915 and posted at a military training camp has the heading 'first day of exile'. Kokoschka continued to write almost daily to Alma and the warmth of his letters gives no clue that their relationship was in crisis. Perhaps he believed that some conspicuous act of bravery might be enough to win her back, or that a period of enforced absence might make her realize what she meant to him.

The circumstances of Kokoschka's enlistment suggest that he wanted to make some grand, heroic gesture. For instead of volunteering for some ordinary regiment, he contrived to be accepted as a recruit by a famous cavalry division which was usually open only to the wealthy and high-born. It was one of the most celebrated regiments in the entire Austro-Hungarian army, the one in which members of the imperial family traditionally served.

Kokoschka moreover was determined to become an officer and, as a cadet, had to provide his own horse and uniform. He had recently sold *The Tempest* to a pharmacist in Hamburg and the price was just enough to enable him to buy a mare. The uniform – a light blue tunic with white facings, bright red breeches and glittering brass helmet – was splendid, designed to enable its wearer to cut a dash, impress the ladies and advertise the pride of the regiment. It also ensured that its wearer made an excellent target for the enemy. The cavalry even shaved before every engagement: in action they were expected to be as smart as they were at a court ball.

Before Kokoschka left Vienna for his initial training he gave Alma seven large fans made of swanskin which he had decorated with scenes allegorizing their love affair (illus. 14). They were not all made at the same time: the first was already completed by the end of 1912, the last dates from the end of 1914. It was once thought that there were only six of these fans, but it was then discovered that there had been another in Gropius's possession. At some stage, smarting at Alma's treatment of him, Gropius had burned it.

A great self-portrait *The Knight Errant* (illus. 16) was probably also executed immediately before Kokoschka left Vienna for his military training. It shows the artist clad in the same armour in which he appears on the fans and lying, apparently wounded and on the verge of death, on a rock at the edge of the ocean in a strange and stormy landscape. Written in the lowering sky are the letters E. S., presumably standing for the words spoken by Christ from the cross: *Eli, Eli, lama sabachthani* – 'My God, my God, why hast thou forsaken me?'

The landscape includes two weird figures. One seems to be the angel of death, the other, a strange female creature, half beast, half human, is at a distance from the knight but seems to be shrinking from him. This, inevitably, must be Alma Mahler, the source of all the artist's woes.

There is some dispute about the date of this painting. If it was indeed executed before Kokoschka's departure for the war, it provides evidence for his visionary powers, since within a year he would be lying, gravely wounded and on the point of death in an alien landscape.

While Kokoschka was training and writing daily to Alma (and receiving letters in return) she was growing determined that the affair with Gropius should be revived. The architect had not merely replaced Kokoschka in her affections; he clearly meant more to her than the painter had ever done. She had refused to be the mother of

Kokoschka's child and had always resisted his entreaties that she should marry him. But she very much wished for a child by Gropius and it was she who now suggested that they marry, albeit secretly. Gropius was by now in the German army and the wedding was arranged for the first day he was able to take leave. He married Alma on 18 August 1915 in Berlin. In October 1916 Alma gave birth to a daughter, named Manon after Gropius's mother.

Kokoschka appears to have known nothing of Alma's relationship with Gropius until June 1915 and continued to write letters until the beginning of July, often daily, describing his training, the man-oeuvres, the daily round in camp and, above all, his feelings for her. Since Alma's letters to him no longer exist, we do not know how she reacted. But it is obvious that she often replied.

Kokoschka trained for several months at the cavalry school at Wiener Neustadt and his letters to Alma from there are extraordinarily valuable, not merely because of the insights they provide into the artist's state of mind, but also for the information they give about daily life in the cavalry at that time. Kokoschka's first day consisted of

waiting, waiting in a tight new uniform and helmet until I got a headache and couldn't go on. . . . Everyone uses the [familiar] *Du* form of address because we are comrades, but in spite of their friendliness they are eternally distant from me because they are aristocrats and I don't want to bridge the gap.

He was often hungry because

I don't like to go to a table where officers sit, and to whom I have, stuttering, to introduce myself, because I shall never learn the ranks and the phrases needed to become a proper cog in this stupid machine.

Once his horse had arrived from Vienna he began to learn to ride.

And then exercise on four strange feet on a gigantic field of snow with bushes and edged by mountains. Buglers rushing around and captains scream-ing. . . . Then into a ditch over waves of frozen furrows throwing up dust; many, many horsemen at a canter, blinded by snow so that you get a headache like the very devil afterwards; more and more obstacles, then through the long forests where you snake along so as not to let the snow fall into your collar; and then everything at the trot for you don't know how long . . . and I'm still in the saddle. Suddenly: 'Tarah!' You lurch forward over the horse's ears – a runaway – but you have always to keep in step. Smoking permitted. Dismount alone although your feet hang down frozen on either side like two motionless North Pole explorers. Unsaddle (alone) in the forest clearing, my two friends who always call out, warning me of dangerous places where I might be thrown, show me the place. Then smoke unfurls from everyone's cigarette, the horse is hot, the captain with '48 vintage sideburns and wearing armoured gloves, puts aside his martial virtues, stops screaming and this quietens the ravens which often flew up. And then around 11.30 we galloped back to the stables and into the coffee house. I never thought I could bear it so long with a headache behind my eyes and on a *wooden* saddle.

With such exercises from 7.30 until 1.00 p.m. almost every day and with stable duties at night it was a hard life which Kokoschka bore with fortitude. Given his background and interests, it is surprising that he survived. He did more than survive. He impressed his superiors and received rapid promotion in the ranks. He nevertheless continued to feel out of place and believed that he would never become a model soldier, 'because I am not stupid and still have something between my mouth and seat'. But he wanted to stay in the cavalry because, at least according to him

the infantry is beyond my physical capabilities, the artillery is too sober. . . . At least I have my peace here, for these fellows have known each other since childhood, are on the same level and I shan't bother to do anything more than necessary. Apart from that they take me for something very daft: a 'Cubist' or a 'Secessionist'.

Kokoschka's greatest difficulties in the cavalry were caused by his consciousness of class and social differences. Although he was no doubt pleased to find himself in the presence of the wealthy and high-born, he also felt uncomfortable in the midst of so many aristocrats, with the complicated etiquette he was expected to observe and with the knowledge that, as an artist, he would have been out of place in any regiment. He nevertheless made friends more easily with the aristo-crats than with the sons of *nouveau riche* fathers who had bought their way into the army and who, 'as long as the war keeps their cabbage greasy (in civilian life I had not the slightest notion of their existence) in their vulgarity play the barrack tyrants'.

Kokoschka was quickly appointed corporal and recommended for consideration as an officer. Meanwhile Loos had done an extra-ordinary thing. From a photograph of Kokoschka in uniform he had had a postcard printed and copies of it were now on sale throughout Vienna (illus. 18). Loos no doubt thought that such publicity would benefit Kokoschka's career once the war was over. The wild man and enemy of the bourgeoisie was revealed to be a good-looking soldier, now fighting for his country. Kokoschka was not pleased. He was keen on promotion and worried that the postcards might compromise his chances of preferment.

The First World War was the first mechanized conflict in history, but few of the Austrian generals grasped the fact that the nature of warfare had changed since 1866. Unlike the Russians who 'had learned from the Japanese to camouflage themselves in field-grey uniforms and dig themselves in', the Habsburg commanders retained their faith in the cavalry, and, as Kokoschka says of himself and his comrades: 'We imagined ourselves setting out with trumpets blowing and banners waving and heroically overrunning our enemy – but he was lying low in trenches.'

On the eastern front old-fashioned skirmishes with lances and sabres were common, as was the full-scale cavalry charge with 'ten divisions, drawn up in a semi-circle riding off into the unknown'. Such tactics were entirely unsuited to modern combat. So were the uniforms. The saddles, designed for parade use, were uncomfortable in action for both horse and rider and in hot weather frequently caused the horse's hide to rupture and bleed.

It was not only in the cavalry that old-fashioned and inadequate practices were maintained or that soldiers were unsuitably equipped for modern warfare. Loos, convinced that in this area as in all others Austria was fatally behind the times, was determined to persuade the army to give up the starched wing collar and introduce puttees instead of Prussian-style leather boots. When he too was conscripted, Loos appeared on parade in a comfortable uniform of his own design and promptly found himself put on a charge for insubordination. Only when the war was already lost were Loos's proposals adopted.

Kokoschka was trained, became a non-commissioned officer and went to war. His regiment was commanded by General von Bosch and had the task of protecting the right flank of the infantry and artillery of the combined Austro-Hungarian and German forces on the Russian front. Planning the campaign before the outbreak of war, the Habsburg General Staff had agreed that, in the event of there being an eastern and a western front, the German army should be concentrated in the west while their own forces should be deployed in the east against Russia and Serbia. At first there were successes. Przemysl was taken from the Russians and the advance continued into Grodek, Lemberg (Lvov) (where Kokoschka arrived on 22 July 1915) and Vladimir in Volhynia, the terrain becoming increasingly strange and hostile.

Kokoschka arrived at an unfortunate moment in the campaign. In July there was a sudden reverse when the IVth Army attempted an advance from Lutsk and exposed its left flank. The terrain was swampy and difficult. The Russians hid in the marshes, concealing themselves in tall reeds and emerging from time to time to fall upon the exposed flank between Lutsk and Rovno.

Action was frequent. In August 1915 Kokoschka was in a group which was surprised by Cossacks. Of nine men only five escaped. Kokoschka wrote of such incidents to friends and especially to Ehrenstein, but never to his family which received quite different news: the weather was always warm, the natives were friendly and the war was endlessly fascinating and exciting. Kokoschka knew that his parents were worried about him and Bohuslav and he had no wish to worry them further. He did not ask them for money or for food and clothing because he knew that they could scarcely afford to look after themselves. His friends, however, frequently received requests. Walden was asked for parcels. Kokoschka requested him to send socks, strong cigarettes and, the item vital to officers in the Imperial Cavalry, silk underwear!

On 6 August 1915 Kokoschka wrote to Loos informing him that he had just escaped death at the hands of the Cossacks by a hair's breadth.

In the endless forest and marsh here I fell into an ambush with a patrol. We lost more than half our men. There was hand-to-hand fighting during which everyone thought his last hour had come. By chance two or three escaped. . . . I the last of them, because my horse is weak and at the end went lame!!! Then a life-and-death race, the first of the [enemy] beasts ten paces behind me, with ceaseless shooting and cries of 'Hurrah, hurrah'. I still felt the lance in my liver. With my sabre I urged on my horse to the limit and then managed to reach my people. Now I shall get respect!

As a postscript Kokoschka added that Loos should say nothing of this to his parents: 'I am so happy that I am still alive.'

On 27 October 1915 Herwarth Walden received a brief note from Kokoschka: 'My wounds were more decorative than dangerous. Shot in the head and stabbed in the chest. My engagement broken off, my studio closed, for everything the Big Silver [medal]. I am a pensioner!!!!!'

That laconic announcement conceals more than it reveals. On 29 August, eleven days after Alma Mahler had married Walter Gropius in Berlin, Kokoschka had escaped death by the skin of his teeth at Lutsk. His company found itself on the edge of a vast, marshy forest in which groups of Cossacks were concealed. These would fall upon the Austrians whenever they tried to flush them out. There had been many casualties by the time Kokoschka himself was attacked. As he says, 'I had actually set eyes on the Russian machine-gun before I felt a dull blow on my temple', but in spite of a bullet in his head he was still able to see 'two captains in Russian uniform dancing a ballet, running up and kissing each other on the cheek like two young girls'. The next thing he remembered was an enemy soldier with a bayonet bending over him, a sharp pain in the area of his lung and the distinct impression that he was dead.

Years later, in Prague, Kokoschka recalled the episode in a long, partly autobiographical essay. It remains the best description of the way in which he almost died.

My horse had been killed beneath me and I had been shot in the head through my ear. . . .

I lay for some days on the ground until Russian Cossacks began to kill the badly wounded with their long bayonets (there was no point in moving the wounded; it would only have meant a great deal of work for nothing). I opened my eyes and saw an enemy soldier dispatching several of my comrades, who were screaming loudly, into the other world. Now I knew it was my turn. In my hand, the one that was not paralysed, I felt my revolver which was pointing directly at the man's chest. He could not see the danger because I was in his shadow. He bent over me. I cocked the revolver, my finger squeezed the trigger. The bullet was in the chamber. Then his bayonet entered my jacket and I thought I could not bear the pain but knew that it was only the jacket. There was still time for me to save myself. But I could not shoot the enemy soldier because my mind was not so confused as to permit me to murder the Russian who was only carrying out an order. Now I felt the weapon very slowly penetrating the skin, the fat on my ribs and then going into the ribs. The pain was terrible, truly not to be endured and I nevertheless told myself: 'Just a second more! Just endure!' And then suddenly it ceased as the weapon entered my lung. Then the pain ceased. My head felt light. I was happy as I was never happy again. I floated on air. Blood flowed from my nose, ears and mouth and blinded my eyes. Dying was so simple and easy that I suddenly had to laugh in the soldier's face. But now suddenly his eyes were so shocked, his face was a grimace . . . His hands shook, he let go of the rifle with the bayonet which stayed lodged in my body and then fell over under its own weight. The soldier disappeared from my field of vision.

Left for dead, Kokoschka was subsequently discovered by his own troops. Gravely wounded in the head and lung, he spent some weeks in the field hospital at Vladimir in Volhynia in great pain and visited by hallucinations. Only a miracle had saved him. In spite of his serious wounds he was extraordinarily fortunate. By 22 September 1915 no fewer than 70,000 Austrian prisoners had been taken by the Russian army and there were countless Austrian dead.

Then Kokoschka was taken in an open train back across the steppes, through Poland and to a hospital at Brünn. According to him, it was on that journey that, feverish, unsure whether he was alive or dead, he composed the poem to which, when it was published, he gave the title 'Orpheus and Eurydice'. It was, once again, autobiography transformed into allegory with the aid of a Greek myth.

'Orpheus and Eurydice' is obviously a response to his own escape from the jaws of death, but it was also inspired by the wounding knowledge that he had lost Alma Mahler for ever. The brief note written to Walden in October 1915 acknowledges that the 'engagement' had been 'broken off'. Kokoschka now knew that Alma had married Gropius. He finally realized that he must spend the rest of his life without her.

By 27 October Kokoschka was back in Vienna. By the time he reached the capital the war had begun to affect the civil population. Everything, especially food, was in short supply; there was almost no coal; and the influenza epidemic which by 1918 would be responsible for more deaths than the war itself, had begun to rage.

In the capital Kokoschka was sent for treatment at a hospital. In the Palffy-Spital he was nursed by nuns at night and aristocratic young ladies by day. His lung wound healed quickly, but the effects of the bullet which had passed through his head and out through the back of the neck were more serious. As a result of damage to his inner ear he lost all sense of balance and only regained it partially after a grim fight with himself. Balance remained a problem until the end of his life.

Visitors were shocked by the state of this once robust and vital young man. One of those who visited him was Friederike Beer-Monti who, having already commissioned a portrait from both Klimt and Schiele, now decided that Kokoschka should paint her too. She was so disturbed by the sight of him in the hospital that she could scarcely bring herself to say anything. Kokoschka suggested that she come again later. She could not bring herself to return and the portrait was never painted.

Life in the Palffy-Spital was frustrating. Kokoschka was out of the war for the time being but he was still in the army and in any case too ill to attempt to reconstruct his private life. His parents were proud of him but worried about his health and his continuing obsession with Alma Mahler. What little pleasure Kokoschka enjoyed in hospital was provided by a young countess, Alexandrine Mensdorff-Dietrichstein who, as one of the day nurses, paid him special attention. Before the end of the year he was able to walk on crutches and his progress was due more to the ministrations of the aristocratic nurse than to the military authorities whose treatment of the convalescents left a great deal to be desired. Three times a month a

dashing general still in the prime of life, whose nickname was 'the hyena of the homeland hospitals', would come on a morale-boosting visit. He would play a few rippling arpeggi on the hospital piano and then ask the patients in turn: 'Well . . . are you feeling nearly ready to get back to the front?'

The young countess did something to take Kokoschka's mind off Alma Mahler who, although married to Gropius, was still living in Vienna (indeed, she was never to live permanently with her husband). Worried that talk of her former affair with Kokoschka was damaging her reputation, she did her best to limit the damage. When, soon after Kokoschka was wounded, the Viennese newspapers announced his death, she went into his studio and removed everything associated with her that she could find.

Kokoschka's family, suspecting that Alma's interest in Gropius would not be sustained for long, were concerned that she might decide to begin the affair with Kokoschka again, and knew that he would not be able to resist her. They did everything they could to let Alma know of their hostility. It is said that Kokoschka's mother even paraded up and down outside Alma's house ostentatiously holding a gun in her coat pocket. It was not loaded and we do not know whether Alma was even at home at the time.

The worry was unnecessary. For the time being at least Alma remained faithful to Gropius even though he was at the front and she was hundreds of miles away in Vienna. She was worried lest he think that she was continuing to see Kokoschka. When, in June 1915, a Munich periodical published a poem he had written and illustrated, she was fearful that Gropius would read it and be jealous.

The poem was called '*Allos-Makar*', a Greek phrase which means 'otherwise happy' and is almost an anagram of Alma Oskar. Alma wrote to Gropius saying:

I *never* want to see this person – who has almost destroyed my mind – again. . . . I sense that this is intended to be a kind of message from him – he knows that I am interested in everything new. . . . Look at Allos-Makar carefully – but it does not touch me *at all*! – I sense the artistic value or lack of it – that is all. . . . Isn't it beautiful that you are such a wonderfully strong man that I may tell you *everything*.

Kokoschka convalesced until May 1916. He was considered well enough for duty but not well enough to return to the front so, after ten days as an inspecting officer at two military hospitals at Kloster-neuburg he was transferred to the military press office. He was bored and he was still depressed about Alma Mahler. He attempted to secure an official discharge from the army so that he could paint again. He may even have wanted to die, for, at the end of June 1916, he asked to be sent to the front again. He told his family nothing of this and explained his decision in a letter to Ehrenstein: 'The thing you know about nags at me so much' – presumably a reference to Alma – 'that I must finish with the military one way or another in order to rescue myself at least in work and learn to forget.'

Kokoschka's request was granted, but the military, recognizing that he was still unfit for battle, sent him to the front as a press liaison officer. On this occasion he went not east but south to the Italian front where he was responsible for escorting journalists and war artists and passing them on to army command at Ljubljana.

Operations had only recently begun in Italy, which Austria-Hungary first attacked in the early summer of 1916. Troops had emerged from the mountains to the north-west and aimed to cut off the Italians, particularly on the front formed by the Isonzo river.

On 17 July 1916 Kokoschka reported to his mother that he was accompanying 'the most famous Hungarian painter Rippl-Ronaï who is being handled with kid gloves' and was going to Laibach [Ljubljana] 'where everything is comfortable and in a civilized state', and where he would be working for 'a field-marshal well-known for his liking for art'. Rippl-Ronaï was indeed famous: in Paris he had associated with Vuillard, Bonnard and Maurice Denis, and was a member of the group founded in the 1890s and called the Nabis.

Even as a liaison officer at the Isonzo front Kokoschka's life was frequently in danger. On 30 July 1916 at a place called Selo he was sheltering from an enemy bombardment in a church which took a direct hit from the Italian artillery. He gave the news to Walden in as laconic a fashion as he had told him about his first escape from death: 'Now I've been in the field for quite a long time again. Coughing like an old gentleman and weak as a baby. Here and there the Italians chuck their stuff across at us; recently I was almost buried in a house that got some of it.'

A postcard written to Loos on the day of the bombardment is a little more explicit.

Today I received my second baptism of fire in a village through which the trenches run. Once it was very beautiful but today it is totally destroyed. I had climbed out of the trench and begun to draw the church, had taken from it only a tall votive candle for superstitious reasons although more beautiful things were lying around there, was observed as I was drawing and caught in a cloud of shrapnel which destroyed a house five paces away. Then I had to wait for a second bombardment, then escaped through the ruins.

He concluded by asking Loos to tell the countess who had nursed him of his whereabouts and that he was keeping the candle he had plundered to give to her. The drawing of the church still exists.

The card to Loos does not mention any wounds and there appear to have been none. A later encounter with a grenade in no man's land on 28 August 1916 was more damaging even than his earlier brush with death. He was now seriously shell-shocked and his nerves had gone. Once again he was returned to Vienna and to a military hospital. There he took a significant step. When he had earlier planned to marry Alma Mahler he had formally left the Catholic Church so that he might participate in a civil wedding ceremony. Now he joined the church again.

It would no doubt have consoled him but little if he had known about the progress of Alma's marriage to Gropius in the mean time. Before and immediately after the wedding, Alma's letters to Gropius were loving, beseeching and seductive. By the end of 1916 their tone had changed to one of complaint. She was tired of keeping their marriage secret; she disliked his mother who never hid her disapproval; she hated Berlin and the Berliners and would never be able to live with him in Germany; she failed to understand why he saw her so rarely; he had forgotten her birthday. It never seems to have occurred to her that he was fighting on the western front.

Alma began to see other men. She met the writer Franz Werfel and fell in love with him. By the end of the war they were openly living together.

TEN

The war had almost two years to run, but for Kokoschka it was already over. He had no further desire to solve his emotional problems by flirting with death. He was very ill. His nerves could not be relied upon. He immediately required some further convalescence. He was not discharged from the army but granted extended sick leave. He was released from hospital in Vienna not because his condition had improved but because conventional treatment was incapable of doing anything more for him.

Of the hundreds of artists serving on both sides of the war few emerged from their experiences unscathed. Many (Franz Marc, August Macke, Umberto Boccioni and scores of others) never returned from the trenches. Others, on the German side most notably Max Beckmann and Ernst Ludwig Kirchner, suffered mental break-downs which deeply affected their art. Others still (like George Grosz and John Heartfield) became pacifists, communists or espoused other kinds of radical ideas in the belief that politics were capable of creating the kind of utopian, egalitarian society in which wars were in-conceivable. Walter Gropius, who before the war had specialized in designing buildings for industry and, as a member of the German *Werkbund*, had worked closely with industrialists in making proto-types of useful objects to be mechanically mass-produced, was forced to observe the destructive power of machines in war and came to the conclusion, as did many others both then and later, that the true cause of the conflict was competition between capitalist economies. Once war was over, Gropius became director of a new kind of school of arts and crafts in which the emphasis fell on handicraft, team work and social responsibility: the Bauhaus.

In spite of his frightening experiences and the physical and mental distress he suffered, Kokoschka was not fundamentally changed by the war. He had always been deeply interested in history, politics and economics and read widely. He was thus better informed about the state of the world than most artists who in any case tend to be politically naïve. According to Eugenie Schwarzwald Kokoschka always preferred to talk not about art but the 'world production of petrol and coal, the misery of the people in Whitechapel, the evacuation of children to the country. Then he comes to life. These are the things that touch him.'

When war broke out he was pessimistic not only about the future of the Habsburg empire but of Europe in general. He was angered by the sacrifices demanded of those least equipped to make them and the lack of equality both at home and in the field. By 1916 little had changed to make him more optimistic and the dramatic events which would eventually make him politically more active had not taken place. The Bolshevik revolution was yet to come; Russia fought on, there was no obvious victor on land; Austria–Hungary remained intact and the United States had not entered the conflict.

Released from hospital for a second time, physically weak and mentally scarred as much by Alma Mahler as by the war itself, Kokoschka wanted to leave Vienna. He chose not to retire to a spa or to some rural beauty spot where the pace of life was slow and the food better and more plentiful than in the city, but to Berlin where he would be able to re-establish contact with Herwarth Walden who, in spite of the war, censorship and economic difficulties, continued to publish *Der Sturm* and to run the gallery. By September 1916 Kokoschka had already arrived in the German capital.

Berlin in 1916 was not the dynamic and optimistic city that it had been when Kokoschka first saw it in 1910. Its population was suffering from the effects of the war. Food was scarce, crippled and hideously maimed veterans begged on every street corner, women in mourning were everywhere and there were signs of social unrest. The newspapers were increasingly critical of military policy and in parliament the truce between the major parties had begun to show signs of strain.

Extraordinary though it may seem, however, it was against such a background that Kokoschka came to realize that it would be possible for him to make a new start on his artistic career. That in itself proved a valuable therapy. Walden commissioned him to paint a portrait of his new wife Nell and, in spite of the economic uncertainty, offered him a contract. Walden was not the only Berlin dealer to do so. Cassirer and Fritz Gurlitt also made him offers. At first Kokoschka was inclined to join Gurlitt's gallery but extracted a better offer from Walden, who in September 1916, as we have seen, promised a salary of 2,000 marks a month in exchange for ten drawings and twelve oils a year. The following month Cassirer made an even better offer which Kokoschka also accepted: a minimum of 2,500 marks monthly and without precise obligations. This contract began on 1 January 1917, and when Kokoschka signed it he was breaking the agreement with Walden which he had already made.

At the same time offers of other kinds were multiplying. There was talk of a professorship at the art academy in Dresden; the Insel publishing house proposed a collector's edition of the artist's plays; Max Reinhardt announced that he would direct a play by Kokoschka on the Berlin stage during the following winter. No wonder there was pride in the letter Kokoschka wrote to his father on 23 October 1916: 'At thirty years of age I'm not badly placed, without once ever having made concessions, what?' Soon after he wrote again offering money to his parents and advising them to engage a maid. Finally, although somewhat precipitately, he felt secure enough to tell his father that the anxiety about his choice of career had been unnecessary. Optimistically he told him that he was already better off than he would have been had he chosen a more conventional course.

What Kokoschka meant by concessions were artistic compromises. At the same time he nevertheless appreciated the value of personal contacts and the necessity of exploiting them for all they were worth.

This is revealed by a letter which he wrote to the publisher Kurt Wolff in Leipzig on 21 November 1917. He told Wolff that he 'had, as you know – and this must remain confidential for the time being – a contract with Cassirer for a very high salary. My pictures are therefore very valuable now', and went on to say, ['I am] prepared, in exchange for a professorship at the Academy [in Darmstadt] which would mean a release from a *lack of freedom* in my present circumstances, . . . to express my thanks by donating a valuable picture'. He was offering the painting not to Wolff but to the Darmstadt gallery with which Wolff must have been in contact at the time. Clearly Kokoschka was not too confident that the Dresden professorship would materialize but was determined to acquire a teaching post somewhere.

Some artists are reluctant teachers. They believe that teaching responsibilities diminish their effectiveness as artists and rob them of valuable time. Kokoschka was not one of them. Although for most of his life he was unencumbered by such responsibilities, the few years which he did eventually spend as a full-time teacher were productive and enjoyable both for himself and his students. In any case the duties of teachers, and especially professors, at German art academies then as now can scarcely be described as onerous. Professors were given large studios and a small number of advanced students who were rarely demanding.

It is therefore not surprising that Kokoschka should have been so anxious to secure a professorship somewhere. It would have made him financially even more secure without interfering with his painting. In a country where professors of art are accorded the same respect as successful opera singers and celebrated writers, a professorship would also greatly have enhanced his reputation. A post at Dresden was especially attractive for Dresden was regarded as one of the most important cultural centres in Germany at that time, but a professorship in the much smaller city of Darmstadt, or almost anywhere else, would have been only slightly less valuable.

Kokoschka's efforts to advance his career, and the energy he required to gain friends and influence, suggest that he was rapidly recovering from the injuries inflicted by the war. Yet he was by no means fully recovered, nor, in 1917, could he have been confident of any plans he might make for the future. The war was going badly for Germany and her allies. Who could predict what might occur if the war were finally lost?

Kokoschka remained in Berlin until the end of November 1916. He was still officially an officer in the Austrian cavalry on extended sick leave, always aware that he might be recalled to duty at any time. According to Kokoschka, he was indeed recalled to Vienna and the rail journey from Berlin involved a change at Dresden where, he said, a strange event took place. Waiting at night at the station he was approached by a stranger who claimed to recognize him and introduced himself as Dr Fritz Neuberger. They had a mutual friend, Neuberger said, the poet and *Sturm* contributor Albert Ehrenstein who was concerned about Kokoschka's health and state of mind. He had requested Neuberger to intercept the artist at Dresden and persuade him not to proceed home.

Although Kokoschka did indeed get to know Neuberger in Dresden and relied on his support in many ways, the circumstances of their meeting were different and less dramatic than his own description of them. When Kokoschka left Berlin he already knew that he would be staying in Dresden, as a letter to his mother, written from Berlin on 26 November 1916 reveals. After telling her that he was afraid of being recalled to active service he announced that he wanted 'to go to a sanatorium in Dresden on 1 December where I have friends among the doctors who will protect me there for as long as possible. It is expensive but I can now afford it, thank God, and will only come back when I have to or until I am . . . a professor.'

The promise of a professorship in Dresden was probably more of an attraction than the treatment. For two months Kokoschka had done his best to secure the post and obviously had a greater chance of success if he was actually living there.

The sanatorium, owned by a Dr Teuscher, was in a large and beautiful park called the *Weisser Hirsch* on the edge of the city. The hospital still exists. It seems likely that Kokoschka was given accommodation there, although accounts differ. Most of them claim that Neuberger, whom the artist presumably met only after he arrived in Dresden, found him a room in a guest-house close to the sanatorium.

Fritz Neuberger remains a mystery. He was plainly a sympathetic and fascinating man, widely travelled (he had been in India), with the ear of important people in the military (he was acquainted with General Ludendorff) and in industry. But Neuberger was no reactionary. On the contrary, he seems to have been one of the growing number of Germans who knew that the war was already lost and who hoped that its end would be followed by dramatic social and political changes. Neuberger seems, indeed, to have been deeply involved in plans to bring the war to an end. He may have been one of the group which arranged for Lenin to be taken from Switzerland to Russia through Germany in the famous sealed train, in the well-founded belief that Lenin's return would result in a revolution in Russia and an armistice with Germany.

Such liberal attitudes might explain why Neuberger was attracted to and helped a strange group of actors and bohemian poets which was doing its best in Dresden to forget the war. These actors and poets whom Neuberger had gathered under his wing were living in a guest-house in the same district of Dresden as Kokoschka's sanatorium and the artist was a frequent visitor there.

The group included the playwright Walter Hasenclever, the poet Iwar von Lücken, the actress Käthe Richter, the poet Paul Kornfeld and the actor Ernst Deutsch. Kokoschka took to them instantly and painted two group portraits of his friends which include likenesses of Neuberger and himself. Richter was the one to whom he grew closest. A strikingly attractive, slightly boyish woman with a volatile temperament, she never achieved the fame those who saw her act say she deserved. She fell in love with Kokoschka soon after he arrived and there was a brief but lively affair.

Richter, who was working for the Albert Theatre, treated Kokoschka with great kindness and sympathy. As the artist wrote to Walden on 8 December 1916: 'Katja, thank God, is still here, otherwise I should have died from hypochondria; she protects me from people; the examination is over for today, but at night I got a cardiac spasm from weeping.'

This period of Kokoschka's life is difficult to reconstruct. We know nothing about the treatment he received at the sanatorium and little about the details of his daily activities. That he continued to paint is clear. The two group portraits, done in an extremely free and energetic style, are not the only pictures he produced at this time.

Nor do we know precisely when he arrived in Dresden. Some accounts say that he went there not from Berlin but from Stockholm, but there is evidence enough to demonstrate that what was to be an important trip to Sweden occurred after he had been in Dresden for some time. He left Germany for Stockholm on 3 September 1917.

He went to Sweden to see an exhibition at which he was represented. The exhibition in question, staged in the autumn of 1917 in Liljevalch's Konsthall in Stockholm, consisted of contemporary Austrian art and was organized by the Austrian government as part of a propaganda effort aimed at persuading the neutral Swedes that the Austrians, far from being the murderous savages portrayed in the

Allied press, were highly cultured and civilized. Much emphasis was given to the fact that many of the artists whose work was on show were members of the armed forces.

The exhibition which included about ten of the artist's paintings, did not appeal to Kokoschka. On 24 October he wrote to Ehrenstein saying that he was feeling 'worse than ever', partly because he sensed that the other Austrian artists whose work was also on show represented 'a powerful ring of interests hostile to me'. He added that he was once again having trouble with his lung.

Every week I have to stay in bed for at least two or three days, with a high temperature, my lung simply no longer has its old powers of resistance, devilish pains in the chest, and I certainly feel that my strength and youth have gone, also my health.

Kokoschka's ability to make friends easily ensured that he quickly got to know many people in the Swedish capital, some of them connected with the Stockholm Museum. One of them probably told him about a specialist, working not in Stockholm but Uppsala, who had reputedly developed a new treatment for shell-shock and had already assisted several patients in achieving recovery. His name was Baranyi; he was Viennese, had won the Nobel Prize for medicine in 1915, had been a prisoner of war in Russia in 1915 and 1916 and had become a professor at Uppsala University in 1917 not long before Kokoschka arrived there.

We do not know how long Baranyi treated Kokoschka, but the artist was certainly in hospital in Uppsala for several weeks until he finally left Sweden on 15 November 1917. Baranyi's treatment caused him distress. It involved repeated sessions during which he sat in a chair which was rotated at high speed while he held a heavy weight in each hand. The object was to produce a spasm in the brain. It is difficult to imagine how Kokoschka's condition might have been improved by such torture.

Either Baranyi or Kokoschka decided to end the treatment after little progress had been made. It seems likely that the artist emerged from it worse than he had been when he went to Uppsala, but there was some improvement again after he returned to Stockholm, thanks to the ministrations of a recently widowed Swedish baroness, Karin von Fock-Kantzow, with whom Kokoschka fell in love. With her he enjoyed an idyllic interlude. They would often take boat trips together and he spent most of the salary he continued to receive from the military on daily bouquets of roses which, as the exchange rate

7. Kokoschka (*right*) with his brother Bohuslav, both in uniform, 1915

8. Kokoschka as a volunteer in the uniform of the 15th Imperial Dragoons

19. Kokoschka convalescing in Vienna, 1916

20. Kokoschka with nurses at the convalescent hospital in Vienna, 1916

21. Kokoschka, Berlin, September 1916, photograph dedicated to 'Nell Walden, the artist'

22. Kokoschka c. 1921

23. Kokoschka on the balcony of his studio overlooking the Moldau in Prague

24. Oskar Kokoschka, *The Crab*, 1930–40, oil on canvas, 63 × 76 cm

6. Kokoschka in Scotland, 1942

5. Olda Kokoschka, 1939

27. Kokoschka with some of his pupils at the School of Seeing, Salzburg

28. Kokoschka with Olda

became more disadvantageous, grew almost ruinously expensive. The widow urged Kokoschka to stay in Sweden and marry her, but he refused. Perhaps he saw in her a too-domineering woman who reminded him of Alma Mahler. She certainly dominated the man who became her second husband, a German pilot whose reputation for aerial combat was almost as great as that enjoyed by Baron von Richthofen. His name was Hermann Goering. They met while Goering was making a living as pilot in an air show touring Denmark and Sweden soon after the end of the war.

Having extricated himself from the intense relationship with a woman whose ardour would probably have proved suffocating, Kokoschka returned to Berlin on 15 November 1917 where he again contacted Herwarth Walden but remained only six days. Although he already knew that he had been recalled to active service and had been given permission to remain in Germany only for a further week, he somehow contrived to stay at the sanatorium and postpone indefinitely his return to Vienna, the prospect of which filled him with dread. Something of his feelings for his native city emerges from a letter he wrote from Dresden on 6 January 1918 to Egon Schiele. Schiele, whom Kokoschka considered to be as shameless a plagiarist as Oppenheimer and a pornographer into the bargain, had invited Kokoschka to participate in an exhibition of contemporary Austrian art. Kokoschka replied:

I will not take part in any exhibition in Vienna, a decision by which I have abided for many years. Since there is no sign that the attitude to my work of those circles that concern themselves with art there has improved, I have no desire to feel at home there, even with the least important of my works, ever again.

Kokoschka would do everything he could to remain in Dresden.

ELEVEN

In Dresden, Kokoschka began to feel a little better physically. Mentally, however, he remained confused and vulnerable. The memory of the affair with the Swedish countess and the presence of the always sympathetic Käthe Richter did little to solve his continuing emotional problems. Although he had learned to cope with the loss of Alma Mahler he continued to think about her from time to time and very occasionally to write to her.

The evidence for her continuing influence at this time is entirely bizarre: Kokoschka had a life-sized doll made in Alma's image. Its appearance was as human as expert hands could make it and it was intended to be as perfect a substitute as possible for the person on whom it was based. If Alma remained beyond Kokoschka's reach, her three-dimensional likeness would not be. It would be his to own for ever and it would yield to his every whim.

The preparations for the doll's making and the manner of its manufacture make it clear that what Kokoschka desired was a fetish. He could not make it himself, not only because the necessary skills were beyond him, but because it would not possess the required magic if he were directly involved in its creation. He should not set eyes on the doll until it was complete. It would enter his life in a state of perfection, as seductive as a new mistress.

The first stage in the doll's life was a search for its creator. Kokoschka heard, perhaps from Käthe Richter's family, about a seamstress and doll-maker who lived in Stuttgart and, if some reports are to be believed, was better qualified for the job than anyone else alive: she had once been Alma Mahler's dressmaker. Her name was Hermine Moos, and in September 1918 she exhibited her dolls at the Richter gallery in Dresden.. Not suprisingly she was taken aback by Kokoschka's request that she should make a life-sized doll for him, shocked by the implications of the strange commission and soon came to regret agreeing to undertake the task. For as soon as she did so Kokoschka immediately began to bombard her with letters explaining in both words and pictures how the doll had to look. His letters to her allow us to follow the doll's construction closely and to understand the nature of his obsession.

These letters make it clear that Kokoschka demanded the impossible. He understood that the fetish would never move and breathe but he wanted it to look as lifelike as possible. For example, the wig 'should not be made too quickly for it must be connected organically to the skin of the face and the tiny hairs around.' The hair, like Alma's own, had to be 'chestnut (Titian)'.

A letter of 20 August 1918 is representative of many others.

Yesterday I sent . . . a life-sized drawing of my beloved and I ask you to copy this most carefully and to transform it into reality with the application of all your patience and feeling.

Pay special attention to the dimensions of the head and neck, to the rib-cage, the rump and the limbs. And take to heart the contours of body, e.g., the line of the neck to the back, the curve of the belly. I only drew in the second, bent leg so that you could see its form from the inside, otherwise the entire figure is conceived entirely in profile so that the major line from the head to the instep of the foot enables you precisely to determine the shape of the body. Please permit my sense of touch to take pleasure in those places where layers of fat or muscle suddenly give way to a sinewy covering of skin, e.g., on the shin-bone, the patella, the ends of the shoulder-blades, collar-bone and arm. You can see the . . . layering of the fat and muscles from the position of the white areas of paint which I have applied to show their natural location. The look of the head must be captured exactly and should accurately show that facial expression which I desire but never achieve. The belly and rougher muscle on the leg, back, etc., must be firm and textured! The woman should look about 35 to 40 years of age! Pay attention to the swinging of the arms and legs! The movement of the joints should correspond to the major movements in nature. *The figure must not stand!* For the first layer (inside) please use fine, curly horsehair; you must buy an old sofa or something similar; have the horsehair disinfected. Then, over that, a layer of pouches stuffed with down, cottonwool for the seat and the breasts . . . initially in larger sewn pouches, but then in smaller and smaller layers until the form of the surface imitates nature. When the skeleton is ready perhaps you could bring it here together with the sketch so that we understand each other completely!

The skin will probably be made from the thinnest material available, either roughish silk or the very thinnest canvas and applied in very small areas. I am now trying to learn from a chemist whether it is possible chemically to treat silk so that it sticks to cottonwool without altering the structure or the appearance of the silk. . . . The point of all this for me is an experience which I must be able to embrace!

Instructions like these were not all. Kokoschka also sent the seamstress samples of material and experimented with glues and compared various types of hair for verisimilitude. It must have required enormous powers of imagination and recall, to say nothing of the faith Kokoschka must have had in the skills of the craftswoman. He not only needed to remember the most subtle details of Alma Mahler's naked body, he also had to describe them so clearly to the lady in Stuttgart that she was able to reproduce them from verbal descriptions and sketches alone.

By December 1918 she had progressed far enough for her to have her handiwork photographed. Although the doll remained un-finished, Kokoschka was 'absolutely astounded by the uncanny vitality' the doll possessed, at least in the pictures. But he also had criticisms: 'The hands and feet must be articulated more,' he wrote, 'take, e.g., your own hand as a model. Or think of a sophisticated Russian woman who goes riding. And the foot, e.g., like that of a dancer: Karsavina perhaps.'

He left the craftswoman in little doubt about what he intended to do with the doll when it was ready. He admitted that he wanted to dress and undress it and said that he had already bought some beautiful clothes and underwear during a trip to Vienna. 'Can the mouth be opened?' he asked, 'And are there teeth and a tongue inside? I hope so.'

If it were not for the evidence of these letters and of scores like them, the story of the making of the doll would be scarcely credible. The only explanation for this bizarre episode in Kokoschka's life is that his mind had become temporarily unbalanced.

By January 1919 he was daily expecting

the news from you that my beloved, for whom I am pining away, will soon be mine. Have you succeeded so well in your deception that I shall not be brought down to earth? . . . And does no one know about [the doll] apart from your sister? I would die of jealousy if some man were allowed to touch the artificial woman in her nakedness with his hands or glimpse her with his eyes . . . assure me that you have been able to achieve this glowing skin with the roughness of a peach, with which I have long since covered my desired love in my thoughts, and that the earthly traces of how it was made have either been eradicated thanks to the fortunate inspiration of a creative, erotic mood, or transformed into a new enrichment of the experience of happiness and voluptuousness. Colour may only be applied by means of powder, . . . fruit juice, gold dust, layers of wax, and so discreetly that you can only imagine them . . . When shall I hold all this in my hands?

The doll was completed towards the end of February 1919 and it arrived in Dresden in a large packing case towards the end of March or at the beginning of April. Kokoschka's excitement may only be imagined as he removed the expensive creation and inspected it. But he was dreadfully disappointed. The many letters, the sketches, the tests and experiments, the care with which all the materials had been acquired had proved almost pointless. The doll did not look at all lifelike. The dream was shattered and the motionless dummy, its face rigid in a travesty of a human expression, seemed to mock its owner. Kokoschka wrote to the seamstress in Stuttgart on 6 April, 'I was honestly shocked by your doll which, although I was long prepared for a certain distance from reality, contradicts what I demanded of it and hoped of you in too many ways.'

Photographs of the doll exist and they make plain the reason for Kokoschka's disappointment. The face looks like a mask and the body is covered with what appears to be thick fur which ceases at the soles of the feet. It looks more like some legendary, half-human creature than a real woman.

Kokoschka nevertheless forced himself to make do with the travesty which had so miserably failed to make his fantasy flesh. He made paintings of it (the *Lady in Blue* in the Staatsgalerie Stuttgart is one of them), he made drawings of it (see illus. at the head of this chapter), in most of which it appears in poses suggesting total sexual submission, and he took it for drives in a carriage, carried it into restaurants where he demanded that a place be laid for it, or took it with him to the theatre where it occupied the seat beside his.

These excursions must have amused the sophisticated inhabitants of Dresden and scandalized the conventional majority. The doll can have done nothing for Kokoschka's reputation except in circles where artists were expected to be mad. It must also have alarmed Kokoschka's friends who knew that the doll was the leading actress in private as well as public performances.

Kokoschka's decision to commission the doll is odd enough; his desire to let the world know about it is odder still. For he not only paraded the doll in public, he also allowed some of his letters to its maker to be published in an anthology of artists' writings in 1925.

While the episode of the doll betrays a genuine mental disturbance, a confusion between artifice and reality in a mind distressed by the events of the immediately preceding years, it also reveals Kokoschka's desire to dramatize himself and proclaim the extraordinary nature of his artistic personality to an astonished world. What began as a temporary mental aberration soon became part of a public image as artificial as the doll itself.

Kokoschka took possession of the doll not at Teuscher's sanatorium where he had been living for more than a year, nor at the guest-house to which he had moved sometime in 1918. Called the Felsenburg, this guest-house was run by a Frau Nachtway, was close to the sanatorium and was presumably the place where Kokoschka's friends, Käthe Richter and Iwar von Lücken, were also living.

Kokoschka did not remain at the Felsenburg long, however. When the doll arrived in its packing-case in Dresden, he had found more permanent accommodation. He had been offered rooms in the house of Dr Posse, the director of the Dresden art museum, who lived in some style with his father, a housekeeper and a maid in a Baroque villa situated in the park surrounding the Zwinger. Kokoschka was permitted to share the services of the young and attractive maid. Her name was Hulda and for a time she seems to have been the woman to whom the artist felt closest. In spite of a country upbringing and an inadequate education, she was a person of rare understanding, imagination and wit.

Kokoschka persuaded Hulda to participate in the private charades he designed for himself and his doll. He bought Hulda a cap, apron and black silk stockings which she was expected to wear when giving performances. She would wait on the artist and his mute, motionless mistress, inventing appropriate dialogue and, no doubt, contributing greatly to the creation of a highly charged erotic atmosphere. Kokoschka even gave her a name which he used in private. It was Reserl, a common Austrian abbreviation of Theresa.

What transpired in the privacy of Kokoschka's rooms can only be imagined, but it is clear that Reserl was a willing and resourceful participant in the improvised playlets. It is also clear that Reserl was in love with Kokoschka, that she sensed and sympathized with his confused mental state and did her best to restore his emotional equilibrium. One episode, recounted more than once by the artist himself, provides evidence of Reserl's sensitivity.

Dr Posse's father was a former army general. On the day he died his son asked Kokoschka to make a drawing of him before the undertaker arrived. It proved a difficult and distressing task, for the sight of the corpse lying on a bed in a room upstairs made Kokoschka feel depressed and fearfully alone. After the drawing was finished Kokoschka met Reserl on the stairs as he was returning to his rooms. Noticing his distress, she took him down to the cellar where a large barrel served as a bathtub. It was night by then and the cellar was illuminated only by moonlight. Reserl, 'whom no man had ever seen naked', undressed slowly in front of him and climbed into the barrel, explaining that she was doing so 'because of the dead man upstairs, so that he won't come back in your dreams'.

'What talent', Kokoschka asked, 'enabled this simple country girl to read me like an open book?' Later that night she entered his room while he was asleep and crept into his bed. He remembered her whispering into his ear: 'I am at your service body and soul – dispose of me, sir.'

According to Kokoschka he did not make love to Reserl then or at any other time, but if that is true, she clearly longed for it to be otherwise, occasionally going to extraordinary lengths to protest her love for him. Once she even cut his initials into her breast with a knife. Kokoschka's claim that their relationship never went beyond flirtation is nevertheless credible. Making love to the woman who was not only his maid but also the servant of the doll would have destroyed the fantasy which dominated his imagination, offering in exchange only unsatisfactory reality.

Reserl was obviously a remarkable woman and something of her character emerges from the letters which she wrote to him on the occasions he was absent from Dresden. In one of them, where she refers to Kokoschka, as she habitually did, as 'the Captain', she assured him that

the birds outside your window still sing the same songs, Reserl is still your most obedient servant, but the sun shows itself rarely, probably because it is there with you in Vienna. Or is everything so grey because the Captain is not here?

Today I was in the Pragerstrasse and there were many, many girls who were also young and pretty. Don't you also think, dear Captain, that they were perhaps all looking out for a tall blond man with the blue eyes of a child who hasn't shown himself in the Pragerstrasse for three weeks?

What became of Reserl remains a mystery. She was still in Dr Posse's service in 1924 when Kokoschka finally left Dresden, for the artist wrote to his parents at that time, suggesting that they employ her as a maid. Nothing came of the suggestion. When, some years later, Kokoschka visited the house he saw another servant busying herself outside. Reserl had gone and he was unable to find out anything about her until after the Second World War when he received news that she had died.

There is no mystery about the fate of the doll, however. The games soon lost their magic; the object of Kokoschka's fantasies lay reproachfully in a corner of his room; reality finally dissipated the dream and revealed Miss Moos's creation to be a monstrous aberration. But what was the artist to do with his doll? To dispose of it quietly would have been inappropriate. Its end demanded a ritual as elaborate as any that had previously been acted out in private.

Kokoschka gave a large party, inviting all his friends to meet a new mistress. When they arrived, he explained that she would join them later. The supply of drink seemed endless; the music, provided by the chamber orchestra from the Dresden Opera, was appropriate to the Baroque surroundings and, since the weather was warm, the musicians played outside in the garden which was illuminated by flaming torches and where a fountain played.

According to Kokoschka, one of the guests was a celebrated Venetian courtesan who, as the evening progressed, became impatient to see the person in whose honour the party had been arranged. Finally Reserl appeared carrying the doll, presumably to the consternation of some of those present and the amusement of others. The courtesan was less surprised than curious and demanded to know whether Kokoschka slept with the doll and whether it looked like one of his former mistresses. Most of the guests were drunk by now and the doll was passed from hand to hand. Someone ceremoniously decapitated it and others doused it in red wine. Next morning the police arrived, investigating a report from the postman that there was a headless corpse in Dr Posse's garden. The doll was eventually removed by the dustman.

In his autobiography Kokoschka remembered: 'The dustcart came in the grey light of dawn, and carried away the dream of Eurydice's return. The doll was an image of a spent love that no Pygmalion could bring to life.' This implies that the artist believed the doll had served its purpose: it had assisted him in expunging the unhappy memories of Alma Mahler for ever. Could any psychiatrist have suggested a more radical treatment? What is more, it appears to have been largely successful. Alma Mahler continued to cast a shadow over Kokoschka's mind, but from now on it was considerably lighter and the artist came to terms with his memories. He even recognized that the experience had a positive side: it had made him more resilient; he had learned the danger of allowing himself to be tied too exclusively to one person; and from that moment he was able to regard the frequent and heavy blows of fate as the source of emotional and creative energy.

The critic P. F. Schmidt who, in a review of the 1912 *Sonderbund* exhibition, had written that Kokoschka was 'the first Viennese painter whom one can describe as a genius', visited the artist at this time in Dresden and years later recalled the way in which Kokoschka was living:

Hans Posse, the director of the *Gemäldegalerie*, a fine scholar who lived quietly, had taken over one of the eight lodges which surround the palace in the *Grosser Garten* like planets around the sun and had taken Kokoschka as a lodger. The natural result of living under the same roof was a kind of symbiosis of scholar and artist in the secluded atmosphere of an enchanting Baroque villa in the middle of the green of tall park trees. Kokoschka did not paint there – as a man he loved privacy, as an artist he did not need it. To visit him there meant opening the door to his witty conversation about himself. The guest needed only to stay quiet and allow the expression of a highly vital personality to work on him.

Clearly there was no longer any trace of the hesitant, tongue-tied Kokoschka remembered by Eugenie Schwarzwald, of the self-conscious young painter who scarcely said anything at all. In spite of the grave consequences of his war wounds, Kokoschka appears to have discovered new confidence in Dresden, partly the result no doubt of the attention he was receiving. In 1918 one of the best-known writers about art in Germany, Paul Westheim, published a monograph about Kokoschka, and an equally celebrated art historian, Hans Tietze, wrote an article about his work which appeared in the *Zeitschrift für bildende Kunst*, the leading art-historical journal.

Before that Kokoschka had received renewed attention as a playwright. In June 1917 before he left for Stockholm, Kokoschka attended a performance of three of his plays at the Albert Theatre in Dresden with Käthe Richter in the cast. Earlier still, in April 1917, his *Sphinx and Strawman* was produced in Zurich. Although the production attracted little attention at the time, it is now of considerable art-historical interest: it was staged at the Dada gallery and directed by the founder of the Dada movement, Hugo Ball. Ball also played Herr Firdusi, the leading male role, while Ball's mistress, Emmy Hennings took the part of Firdusi's wife. The production was designed by Marcel Janco. As Ball himself remembered

The play was performed in two adjoining rooms; the actors wore body masks. Mine was so big that I could read my script inside it quite comfortably. The head of the mask was electrically lit: it must have looked strange in the darkened room with the light coming out of the eyes. Emmy was the only one not wearing a mask. She appeared as half sylph, half angel, lilac and light blue. The seats went right up to the actors. Tzara was in the back room, and his job was to take care of the 'thunder and lightning' as well as to say, 'Anima, sweet Anima!' parrot fashion. But he was taking care of the entrances and exits at the same time, thundered and lightninged in the wrong place, and gave the general impression that this was a special effect of the production, an intentional confusion of backgrounds.

Finally, when Mr Firdusi had to fall, everything got tangled up in the tightly stretched wires and lights. For a few minutes there was total darkness and confusion; then the gallery looked just the same as before.

Had Kokoschka been informed of the chaos the production became he might have felt less delight in the fact that this was the first foreign performance of one of his plays. Had he known anything about Ball and his Dada activities he would have been less delighted still. For the Zurich Dadaists were dedicated to the subversion of all traditional artistic values. Kokoschka's attitudes were too conservative to admit such subversive notions to the artistic canon. They would soon become more conservative still.

TWELVE

On 1 March 1918 Kokoschka celebrated his thirty-second birthday. In a letter written to his parents on the following day he said he was shocked to find himself so old and that, if peace were coming, he would have to work doubly hard to make up for everything he had lost during the previous years.

Peace was indeed coming, although another seven months elapsed before the last shot was fired. While Kokoschka was inundating Hermine Moos with instructions for the manufacture of the doll in Alma Mahler's image the war was going badly for the Central Powers. During the days when Kokoschka was impatiently awaiting news of the doll's completion, the collapse finally came.

On 1 November 1918 Austria–Hungary sued for peace and ten days later Germany also capitulated. With the end of the war the old order in Europe passed away. The former Tsar Nicholas II and his family had already been executed by the Bolsheviks in July; now the emperors of Austria–Hungary and Germany were also forced to relinquish power although they were spared the fate of the Russian.

Wilhelm II of Germany abdicated and went into exile in Holland on 9 November; three days later Franz Josef's successor Karl I stepped down from the Austrian throne. In Berlin a republic had already been declared and a revolution had broken out. In Austria–Hungary parts of the empire declared independence even before the victorious Allies met at Versailles to redraw the map of continental Europe.

Defeated, the empire disintegrated and Vienna became the capital of a small republic. A country with a population of fifty million was reduced to a tiny Alpine state with six million inhabitants, more than a third of whom lived in Vienna. According to Kraus, still writing and publishing *Die Fackel*, all that was left of a proud and glorious country was the tourist industry and the operetta.

Kraus, whose mammoth drama *Die letzten Tage der Menschheit* – The Last Days of Mankind – is perhaps the greatest work of literature inspired by the First World War, shed few tears at the end of Habsburg rule. Kokoschka, although always beset by feelings of anger and alienation whenever he was in Vienna, was moved to sadness and nostalgia. For him the empire had been a cosmopolitan miracle, a crucible in which the whole of European culture had fused to form a glittering and unique amalgam. Although happier outside Vienna and Austria, he now felt robbed of a home and was forced to realize that he had become a rootless European.

Kokoschka's sense of loss had already been awakened by the death of Klimt early in 1918. Like so many others, Klimt had fallen victim to the influenza epidemic which had been raging throughout Europe for some time. In a letter to his mother, Kokoschka admitted that he had 'cried for poor Klimt, the only Austrian artist who had talent and character. Now I am the successor.'

In Germany the revolution which accompanied the military collapse was at its most violent in Berlin but affected the entire country. There was street fighting in every major city, atrocities were committed both by the revolutionaries and the government troops called in to restore order. Dresden, too, was the scene of bloodshed and terror. Kokoschka had experienced the revolution at first hand during a brief visit to Berlin:

You needed a pass to get across the street. There was firing from roofs and windows; field guns were stationed at strategic points; impotent oaths of revenge were sworn by the returning soldiers who had been stripped of guns and insignia of rank by the mob. Homosexual sailors, lesbians, whores, black marketeers, and others who disliked the light of day, made life somewhat uncertain even when there was no firing. The street lights were dark because of the coal shortage.

Kokoschka observed the developments with alarm. Everyone, he thought, was as bad, as guilty, as everyone else. As he wrote to an unnamed correspondent on 9 March 1919: 'The revolutionaries employ the same means – hate, slander, a thirst for power – as do the conservative militarists, the vocabulary stays the same, only the heads that fall are different.' At about the same time he produced a lithograph showing a sculpture of a head on whose base is written: 'Liberté, Egalité, Fratricide!'

In Dresden, too, he had sufficient opportunity to observe the effects of the revolution. One night, while crossing the Augustus bridge he saw that:

both banks of the Elbe were crowded with excited onlookers. Some high official had been thrown into the river. The crowd was cheering, and shots rang out. I could see from the bridge how the man, weighed down by his clothes, was trying vainly to reach the far bank. When he got close to it – the river is very wide – he was driven off by gunfire; he turned back and drowned.

In revolution, as in war, normal life goes on, and Kokoschka's life was no exception. He had arrived in Dresden for medical treatment. He liked the city and he liked the circle of people to which he had been introduced by Fritz Neuberger. He decided that he wanted to stay, especially if he could be appointed to a professorship at the art academy.

Dresden was indeed one of the most beautiful cities in Germany, a splendid Baroque jewel on the River Elbe with one of the greatest collections of Old Master paintings in the world. The atmosphere, less hectic than that of Berlin, less hostile to unconventional behaviour than that of Vienna, was congenial and encouraged creativity.

In 1919 the offer of a professorship at the art academy finally materialized and, appropriate to the new spirit of democratic participation which appeared in republican Germany after the revolution, the offer came not from Kokoschka's future colleagues, nor from the Ministry of Education, but from elected student representatives. His appointment ran from 1 October 1919.

There is no mystery about the reasons for Kokoschka's eager acceptance of the offer. He had been anxious to secure a position at an academy for some time, both for financial reasons and for the status it bestowed. The professorship assured him of a salary which, together with the money regularly remitted by Cassirer, meant that he could support his family more generously and enjoy a better standard of living himself. It also provided him with a spacious studio in the academy from whose windows he could enjoy a splendid panoramic view of the river and the buildings along its banks.

According to one of his biographers, J. P. Hodin, Kokoschka enjoyed the freedom to concentrate on his own work but took little pleasure in teaching which he was entitled to arrange as he wished. It seems, however, that Kokoschka took his teaching responsibilities seriously. Unlike most of his colleagues and indeed most professors at all other academies throughout Germany, he taught almost every day, kept regular hours and cultivated a close relationship with his students.

One of those students, Hans Meyboden, wrote about his former teacher almost thirty years later, by which time he was naturally able to remember few specific details of life at the academy. He recalled Kokoschka's generosity: he once gave three students part of his salary to enable them to undertake a long foreign trip which, he explained, was necessary for the further development of their work. And Meyboden remembered that Kokoschka taught less by issuing directives than by creating an atmosphere in which creativity and originality might flourish.

What initially surprised us [Meyboden wrote], was that in all those years nothing was ever said about 'modern painting' and no criticism was ever made of what others did. We only heard, 'You must do it better.' With Kokoschka [in the museum] we only stopped in front of paintings by the great painters of the past. Kokoschka talked about a twig in a winter painting by C. D. Friedrich with such eloquence and passion, presenting it as an instructive model, that the modesty of the picture, its call to truth emerged naturally, of themselves. And in that lies the entire mission of his teaching: he became a teacher, as he said himself, in order to discover whether what he had found out for himself also had something to say to others.

Especially telling here are the references to the lack of discussion of modern painting as such and to the use of the German Romantic artist Caspar David Friedrich as a model. They reveal an innate conservatism which, although perhaps strengthened by the experience of the war and the political and social chaos which came in its wake, was no recent acquisition.

Even as a young man in Vienna when producing his most original and unconventional work and widely attacked for his radical attitudes, Kokoschka had little time for the work of his contemporaries, either Austrian or foreign. The artists he most admired were already part of art history: painters such as Anton Maulpertsch and other seventeenth- and early eighteenth-century Austrian illusionists strongly rooted in Venetian traditions. What is particularly striking about Kokoschka's formative years is the lack of specific influences by those artists who were the heroes of his contemporaries. Egon Schiele's style is unthinkable without the example of Klimt. Although Kokoschka admired Klimt, was grateful to him for his support and even dedicated *The Dreaming Youths* to him, there is almost no evidence of Klimt's influence in Kokoschka's work. The French Post-Impressionists and Fauves who crucially affected the styles of Kokoschka's German contemporaries (Kandinsky and Kirchner, for example) were of no interest to him. Nor were the Cubists and Futurists whose influence can be traced at one time or another in the work of the vast majority of avant-garde artists of Kokoschka's generation throughout Europe and beyond.

Kokoschka had never been especially interested in contemporary art, and always preferred to visit museums rather than galleries specializing in the work of living artists and, if pressed, would express scorn for Picasso, Kandinsky and virtually every other practitioner of modernism (Boccioni, Gris, Braque and Metzinger were among the few exceptions). That explains why in Dresden the Old Master collection formed an important part of his teaching.

Although most of his students admired him, relations with his colleagues were never easy. Many of them envied his success and resented the influence he exerted on his students. While his teaching methods were liberal, never prescriptive, most of his colleagues taught in the old-fashioned, unimaginative way on which art academies had relied for a century and more.

Each week the evening life class was conducted by a different professor. A student remembered that 'the week with Kokoschka was like a fresh breeze, full of turbulence and one surprise after another', but the professor who followed him taught

crabbed methods of industrious copying. In order clearly to demonstrate his reliable ability, he had taken up a seat in the front row, visible to all, and like a virtuoso conjured up – with his left hand, just imagine! – his astonishing copies of reality that were totally lacking in spirit.

Not for Kokoschka were such theatrical performances. He preferred to emphasize the importance of vitality in drawing and created an atmosphere in which it might be achieved.

Nevertheless some of Kokoschka's methods appear to have been old-fashioned even then. He had his students repeatedly draw simple objects – matchboxes, for example, stressing the spatial relationships between them: 'All romanticizing painting, all "German soul in the attic room" was banned . . . sober, rigorous investigation, nothing else.' Then drawings and paintings were made from life-sized lay figures and, following that, Kokoschka, reviving the practice that he had introduced when himself a student, had children pose as models. They were given brightly-coloured cloth to wrap round themselves and were encouraged to move, thus forcing the students drawing them to grasp quickly the essentials of each pose.

How did the master act when he came across a bored naked model [standing] in front of the students' tired eyes [one of those students asked], eyes that could not see the wood for the trees? . . . A solemn silence descended as the girl, commanded by Kokoschka began very slowly to bend her knees. This command was significantly preceded by sympathetic enquiries about the [girl's] living conditions which spoke to the respectable human being in the paid model. The girl moved up and down, up and down, Kokoschka stood beside her and, speaking carefully, pointed to the miracles that were revealed on the knee: taut stretching and quiet relaxing, the shine and shadow of the skin, the coming and going of movement, the entire spot full of miracles, the entire person full of miracles! The misery of posing for 1.50 marks an hour had fled; it was a scandal, as Kokoschka said, if you didn't know how to make something splendid out of it!

Outside the academy Kokoschka was occasionally attacked for his conservative attitudes, and there is an obvious irony in the fact that the man who had once been repeatedly denounced for his wildness was now the target of critics who found his ideas staid and irrelevant.

The most vituperative criticism came from the extreme left of the political spectrum whose voice grew more strident during the early 1920s and for whom all art not directly concerned with social questions was a dangerous anachronism.

On 15 March 1920 a group of armed political demonstrators gathered outside the Zwinger in Dresden where the Old Master paintings are housed. Speeches were made: a rifle went off by mistake; a bullet passed through the window of the gallery hitting a painting by Rubens and causing serious damage.

This event moved Kokoschka to action. He wrote an open letter to the inhabitants of Dresden which was published in more than forty newspapers throughout Germany. He also had the letter printed as a poster and put up on walls and hoardings throughout Dresden. The letter was a plea for the universal acceptance of the importance of art. Art was immortal while the issues which inspired the demonstration, no matter how grave they then appeared, would quickly seem negligible. A great work of art on the other hand must at all costs be preserved for future generations.

I direct the most urgent plea [Kokoschka wrote], to all those who in future intend to argue with the gun about their political future – whether radically left, right or centre – no longer to hold their planned war exercises in front of the Zwinger gallery but somewhere like the shooting ranges out on the heath where human culture is not in danger. . . . The German people will later see more point to and take more pleasure at the sight of . . . paintings than in the spectacle of all the protesting Germans of today. I do not dare hope for the success of my counter-proposal: that in the German Republic as in classical times, *disputes will in future be settled by duels between the political leaders*, to take place, perhaps, at the *circus*.

This pronouncement from the professorial *cathedra* provoked a speedy, bitter and brilliant response from the left. Two of the leading Communist artists in Berlin, John Heartfield and George Grosz, who had been attacking the establishment in words and pictures even before the revolution, published a long article in answer to Kokoschka's letter which they called *Der Kunstlump* – The Artistic Guttersnipe.

Works by Rubens, Rembrandt or any other Old Master are irrelevant to today's society, they argued. The revolution is more important than any painting. For Heartfield and Grosz, Kokoschka was a 'cultural phrase-maker' and an 'art whore'. 'We urge everyone,' they wrote, 'to take a stand against the masochistic reverence for historic values, against culture and art!'

This essay, which employs to exhilarating effect intemperate language, satirical dialogue in Viennese dialect and allusions to the size of Kokoschka's bank account inspired further, less impressive attacks on Kokoschka which worried him sufficiently for him to take precautions when walking alone at night in case local revolutionaries had taken the left's calls for action too literally.

The *Kunstlump* controversy eventually involved the official German Communist Party newspaper *Die rote Fahne* – The Red Flag – which typically sat on the fence and lashed out not only at Kokoschka but also at Heartfield and Grosz. The controversy is now of little more than historical significance. Who, contemplating Ruben's *David and Bathsheba* in the Dresden Zwinger today, can doubt that Kokoschka was right to describe political events as transient and great works of art as of enduring importance? Who can today remember what precisely sparked off the demonstration of 15 March 1920? (It was the Kapp *putsch*.) Yet the controversy shows that by the time Kokoschka began to teach in Dresden he was no longer a member of the avant-garde. Since his début in Vienna the artistic ground had shifted beneath his feet causing a rift which separated him from a younger generation of artists who shared almost none of his aims or beliefs. If they were not, like Grosz or Heartfield, politically committed and convinced that the pre-eminent purpose of art was social and pedagogical, they were like many of the artists at the Bauhaus, abstractionists, determined to expunge all traces of the real world from their work, and to demonstrate that painting, like music, was an autonomous, pure art form.

As time went on Kokoschka seemed to many to be more isolated still: an artist belonging to no group or school and working in an anachronistic style. To others, however, he had already achieved the status of modern master and the very distance between his work and that of his more experimental contemporaries was proof of his achievement.

That Kokoschka's work was now relatively less adventurous than before the war is beyond doubt. He had succeeded in revolutionizing portraiture, a genre to which he had devoted the greatest effort. Now he turned his attentions increasingly to cityscapes which, for all their accomplished use of colour, dramatic shifts of viewpoint and perspective and atmospheric brushwork, were not intended to disturb. Critics have argued that his best period was past and they point to his increasing popularity to prove it.

Kokoschka was indeed highly popular now, at least in Germany and among those wealthy enough to collect pictures. He was understandably anxious to inform his parents of his success and his letters home are full of news of major and minor triumphs. In 1921 he wrote about the celebrations in Berlin to mark Cassirer's fiftieth birthday to which he had been invited. It was an outstanding event in the social calendar and Kokoschka was flattered to be there.

I thought it was to be an intimate occasion [he wrote to his parents], and I went with my brightest tie and in my light-coloured suit, and what did I find? 150 gentlemen in evening dress and ladies in *décolletage* at a banquet. I got to know the old Liebermann and wrote beneath one of his drawings printed on the menu 'Crown Prince OK' because some pretty Berlin girls had asked me for my autograph. At first he was angry about it, but then told people for days that I had paid him a witty compliment. For that made him H.M. The only thing he couldn't forgive was the fact that I seemed to be very lucky with women. That was what this almost 80-year-old man said. He's a real rascal and it does me good that today I can do more than he can.

The pride is unmistakable and understandable. Liebermann was the best-known painter in Germany, the star of Cassirer's gallery and a social lion as highly regarded for his wit and lively conversation as for his art. If he was the artistic king of Berlin, Kokoschka was the heir apparent who, at least in letters home, was cheeky enough to treat him as an equal.

Cassirer must by then have been delighted by his investment in Kokoschka, for he was now one of his most profitable artists. Given the inflation which had already begun to ruin the German economy and which eventually reached its peak in 1923, Kokoschka's success did not make him wealthy, however. Only painters who, like Klee and Kandinsky, already sold work abroad could rely on a regular source of hard currency.

Kokoschka would have been more secure had he not been so generous, not only to his students but also and especially to his parents and to his brother Bohuslav who, returned from the navy and the destroyer in which he served during the war, was again living with them. Kokoschka was frequently assailed by feelings of guilt: he should perhaps have been living with them, too, especially since his father was now old and infirm and Bohuslav's devotion was preventing him from leading a life of his own. Kokoschka knew that his brother wanted to be a writer and believed him to have talent. For the rest of his life he believed that Bohuslav had not been able to do justice to that talent because of his responsibilities at home.

Kokoschka also knew, however, that unbearable tensions would have resulted had he decided to return home permanently, that it was better both for him and his family if he lived alone and earned enough to support them. In any case, he visited them as often as he could. On one of these visits Kokoschka learned that his father's doctor had advised the family to move from their small flat to a larger property in the country. Bohuslav had already found the right kind of house with its own garden in a pleasant suburb of Vienna but, inevitably, there was not enough money to pay for it. Back in Dresden, Kokoschka wrote a cheque for much more than he could afford and posted it before writing to Cassirer with a request that the dealer cover it. It was a foolhardy act, for in Germany it is a criminal offence to issue cheques without having sufficient funds to cover them.

For some time Cassirer sent no word and Kokoschka grew increasingly worried. Perhaps he would not only be arrested but also lose his dealer, angered by being taken for granted. Eventually Cassirer appeared at Kokoschka's home in Dresden and agreed to guarantee the cheque. He also settled a number of outstanding debts. That was not the end of Kokoschka's financial problems, however, merely the beginning of a series of new worries which lasted for years. For the house still had not been purchased outright. It was mortgaged and Kokoschka was expected to make the monthly repayments.

In the letter to his parents about Cassirer's birthday party, Kokoschka boasted about Liebermann's envy of his success with women and in the correspondence with his parents Kokoschka rarely missed the opportunity to tell them about his romances, some of them probably fictitious and made up to tease his mother who frequently told him that it was time he married and settled down. One letter reports that he had 'fallen in love approximately 19 times and with nothing but serious Queens of Hearts in Frankfurt, Berlin and here'. Another hopes that 'mother will forgive me and not be inconsolable, but I admit here loud and clear that I have got engaged again, but simultaneously to *three* ladies'.

The bantering tone of such letters was no doubt in part intended to reassure his parents that Alma Mahler presented no further danger to his emotional stability and that, no longer morbidly obsessed by one unattainable and dangerous woman, he was enjoying a rich and varied life full of exciting romantic encounters. Indeed, this was to some extent the case. He was involved with several women at this time who were by all accounts attractive and charming. Each of them knew about the others and none appears to have complained, sensing perhaps that Kokoschka was not prepared to be tied down. Nevertheless the artist's friendship with them was real and enduring: he remained in touch with them until the end of his life.

In spite of the happiness these women brought him, Kokoschka did occasionally think about Alma Mahler. In May 1921, by which time she had left Gropius and was living in Vienna with the writer Franz Werfel, she received a letter from Kokoschka:

I am sitting in front of the picture which I once made of us both on which we look as though we are suffering and you are giving me the ring. It came into my hands by chance because there will be an exhibition here of my most important works, a kind of survey of my life until now . . . I have given everything away, your ring, your red necklace, your coat, even my memory.

That picture is almost certainly the double portrait of about 1913 which shows the couple, staring out of the canvas with melancholy gaze. (It is now in the Folkwang Museum, Essen.) With the exception of *The Tempest* it is probably the best of all the pictures inspired by the affair with Alma Mahler. It is not surprising that Kokoschka was moved to contact Alma again when he saw it.

It was about this time that Kokoschka met two women with whom he fell in love. One of them, and for a time the more important, was a Russian called Anna Kallin. Born in Moscow in 1896, she was twenty-five when she met Kokoschka in Dresden in 1919.

Anna Kallin, musically gifted, extraordinarily intelligent and well-educated, left Russia for Germany with her father in 1912 and apart from a period of internment after the outbreak of the war, had studied at Leipzig University until 1919. Then she moved to Dresden in the hope that she would become a musician. Since Käthe Richter was by now working in Berlin, Anna Kallin quickly became Kokoschka's closest friend and his letters to her reveal the depth of their relationship.

They were quite different in tone from the tortured, reproachful and sometimes self-pitying letters to Alma Mahler, and they provide evidence of the extent to which Kokoschka had matured and gained in self-confidence since the end of the war. They are playful and light-hearted and occasionally delightfully funny.

In 1921 Anna Kallin left Dresden and followed her father to London; but the relationship with Kokoschka continued. He travelled to England to see her, she visited him in Dresden and they met elsewhere on the continent from time to time. He refused to meet her in Paris, however, since, as he explained in a letter, he had 'been engaged in a kind of fight with the French since before the war. Therefore I have never been tempted to travel there.' In a passage which reveals much of his attitude to himself as an artist, he continued by saying: 'You must not overlook the fact that I invented and am now the leader of an intellectual movement called Expressionism . . . as long ago as 1907!!!' He had no use for Paris. He was as important as any of the artists there.

The exhibition to which Kokoschka referred in his letter to Alma Mahler of May 1921, the 'kind of survey of my life until now' took place in Dresden during that summer. It was large and important and it was well received. It was nothing like as significant as a show staged the following year, however. This was at the Venice Biennale where Kokoschka was one of the artists who represented not Austria but Germany.

The Venice Biennale was more important then than it is now, and any artist chosen to exhibit in one of the national pavilions had every right to assume that it marked a significant stage in his career.

The exhibition is very striking [Kokoschka wrote to his parents in May 1922]. I really have got the main room, painted black, the main wall completely full with the new pictures in burning colours which beat everything done by the French, the English, etc. For that reason I am also very visible and have been angrily attacked as the Lenin of painting. That is very good as a beginning . . . and I hope that the foreigners, especially the Americans, etc. . . . will discover me.

The Americans were vital since they could pay for work with hard currency. Kokoschka was in financial difficulties at the time, not least because of the inflation. In the same letter to his parents he complained about his financial position.

In one month while I was away *everything three times* more expensive. And tax simply shameful. A month ago I had to pay 20,000 marks for 1920 and I now again have to hand over at least as much for '21 and in a few weeks for 1922. I really hope that the exhibition will mean some kind of path to freedom for me, since one can't develop sufficiently under such conditions and I want *to be everything* or nothing at all.

Significantly, the letter does not mention that Kokoschka had met Alma Mahler in Venice. He came across her, apparently by chance, in the Café Florian in St Mark's Square. Venice was an appropriate place for a reunion which provoked, although only in Kokoschka, bitter-sweet feelings of nostalgia for an inaccessible past. Mrs Mahler was uncharitable. She noticed that his face was becoming more and more like that of a child, that 'he has something of Dorian Gray about him. His vices must be leaving their traces somewhere else.'

She failed to congratulate him on his triumph at the Biennale. She was cool. Bitterness and recrimination erupted quickly. He point-lessly recalled the past, referred to his experiences in the army and accused her of persuading the officers in his barracks to assault him, only instantly to admit that he had also treated her cruelly and regretted it.

This at least is Alma Mahler's version of the event; but Kokoschka recalled it differently. When he chanced upon her in Venice she had lost her figure and he no longer found her beautiful. He was confronted by the evidence of the difference in their ages which had never disturbed him before. She no doubt sensed this and took her revenge in her autobiography. Even in retrospect she did her best to keep the upper hand.

It was not Alma Mahler who cast a shadow over Kokoschka's success at Venice but a review in a German newspaper. The *Berliner Tageblatt*, expressing the views of many German nationalists, regretted the decision to allow a 'foreigner from Austria' publicly to represent German culture abroad. It would not be the last Kokoschka heard of German culture, nor of his unsuitability to represent it.

In 1922 and 1923 the inflation grew to ruinous proportions. This was the period when the only healthy businesses were the black market and the printing of banknotes, when workers, Kokoschka among them, collected their wages in suitcases and immediately went to the nearest shop to buy whatever they could before the money became worthless.

At the same time the political atmosphere, fraught since before the end of the war, worsened. The victorious Allies had forced Germany to surrender unconditionally and had then imposed extortionate reparations which, had it ever been possible to pay them, would have trapped Germany in a state of bankruptcy for several generations. Foreign troops occupied the industrial heartland, valuable German patents passed into the hands of foreign companies, Germany was ruined, its populace demoralized, its politicians confused and impotent.

Unimaginable austerity, pessimism and bitterness contributed to the political turmoil. The Social Democratic government which had been forced to accept the poisoned chalice from the Allies was attacked from both left and right. The left accused it of perpetuating the old order and, as the revolution showed, was prepared to use violence in order to introduce a system of government inspired by the Soviet Union. The right accused the government of weakness and refused to accept that the German army had been defeated in the field. The right also believed that violence provided the only key to success. In 1920 it staged a *putsch* and briefly unseated the government which was restored by the concerted action of the trade unions and a general strike.

Although the greatest violence was seen in the capital where the effects of the economic collapse were at their most visible, the apparently intractable problems were obvious throughout Germany. In Dresden, Kokoschka's pessimism grew. He thought that Germany had been completely written off by the rest of the world, that there was no hope for it. He also realized with something of a shock that he was approaching middle age and, like many a man faced with the fact that half his life is already over, he took stock of his achievements so far, found them wanting and decided that radical action was required.

He decided to leave Dresden and Germany. He decided to travel. The immediate cause of this decision was the news that it was his turn to become Rector of the Academy in 1924. He could not refuse, but he knew that administrative responsibility would frustrate, worry and exhaust him. He did not announce his departure. He did not give notice of his resignation. Having packed his bags he left a letter explaining his decision with the porter at the academy and continued to the railway station. It was the reckless act of a man who had decided to embark on a new stage of his life.

THIRTEEN

Kokoschka left Dresden in August 1923 and immediately travelled to Switzerland with Anna Kallin. It was as though he wanted to recapture the youthful excitement he had experienced on his first visit to Switzerland fifteen years before. He again went to the same part of the country, to the mountains above Lake Geneva where, in the village of Blonay, he lived and painted for some months. He might have gone to a canton where German and not French is spoken and where other lakes and mountains would have provided him with motifs as spectacular as those of the Suisse Romande, but he was drawn back to the area he already knew and where three decades later he would make his final home.

He remained with Anna Kallin at Blonay until October 1923 when he received news that his father was seriously ill. Anna Kallin left for London where her parents were living and Kokoschka immediately rushed to Vienna.

As soon as he arrived Kokoschka took charge, doing his best to ease the emotional stress of his mother and brother:

I . . . found doctors, kept my mother and younger brother out of the way in another part of the house so that they should not witness [my father's] death agony, organized everything for the funeral, rode to the crematorium on a stormy night, sitting beside the coachman on the box, and saw my father consumed in flames. I had come away from Dresden without the slightest idea of how much a death in the family can cost, and I had to run in despair to a rich lady in town, a friend of Alma Mahler's, to ask her for a loan.

Kokoschka took responsibility for everything. It was a typical reaction, based on the belief which never left him, that he was the only member of his family strong and resourceful enough to cope with a crisis. It did not occur to him that his own strength was sapping that of his brother whom he prevented, especially at moments of stress, from achieving true maturity.

Bohuslav was now thirty-two years old but his older brother continued to regard him as a boy and thought it natural that he should continue to live at home and look after their mother rather than strike out and make his own way.

Kokoschka himself had long since gained his independence and although always aware of his responsibilities clearly recognized that too close a contact with his family would drain his emotional resources and sap his artistic strength. Nevertheless he remained living at home in Vienna for an entire year believing no doubt that he owed it to his mother and brother to play the role of family head until they had come to terms with the absence of Gustav. Only in October 1924 did he once again turn his back on Austria and Vienna.

The next ten years were probably the best of Kokoschka's life. He had recovered from his war wounds almost completely, was fit and in the prime of life. Freed from the responsibilities of teaching, he was able to devote all his energies to painting and, supported by the Cassirer gallery whose fortunes greatly improved after the stabilization of the German economy in 1924, he could sell almost everything he produced. For a decade Kokoschka travelled ceaselessly, at first in Europe and then to more exotic places. His destination immediately after leaving Vienna in October 1924 was Paris, the city which he had previously never wished to visit.

Perhaps the reason for the new attitude towards Paris, then the unchallenged capital of the world of art, was a growing confidence in the quality of his work, a new belief that he, as a Central European painter, was now able directly to compete with the internationally celebrated figures concentrated in the French capital. A more obvious reason, however, was the fact that Adolf Loos had already decided to do some work in Paris and Kokoschka no doubt felt that if he accompanied him, their old friendship, damaged by the affair with Alma Mahler, would be strengthened. The two of them went to France with another Viennese painter whom both had known for years, Sebastian Isepp.

Loos and Kokoschka seem to have been determined to rediscover their lost youth, to live like bohemians again before advancing age prevented them. At first they moved into an attic on the Ile Saint-Louis with almost no furniture and already occupied by a motley group of unsuccessful artists and rootless anarchists and intellectuals from every part of Europe. All of them slept on the floor. After a few weeks that proved too much for them, and Kokoschka, Loos and Isepp moved to the Hôtel Foyot which was only a shade grander.

Loos had business to attend to. Unlike Kokoschka, he already had a reputation in Paris, thanks largely to an exhibition of his designs held at the Salon d'Automne in 1923. After the war Loos had been appointed chief architect of the Vienna housing association, an official municipal body concerned with providing accommodation for working families and at the same time aspiring to the highest possible architectural and aesthetic standards. The new, socialist city government had realized the importance of Loos's ideas and for the first time in his life the architect had found himself appreciated by the authorities. But disillusionment with the housing authorities quickly set in. Loos resigned and decided to work from then on in the French capital.

Kokoschka was to regard Paris as his base for the next few years but never remained in the city for long. Loos, on the other hand, stayed until 1928, designing offices, hotels and two private houses. One of them was for the Dada poet and artist Tristan Tzara and the other (which was never built) was for the black dancer and entertainer Josephine Baker whose act, both humorous and erotic had been popular throughout Europe for years. Loos also designed the Paris branch of Kniže, the gentleman's tailor and outfitter whose main shop in Vienna he had created in 1912. Loos always owed Kniže money and it was presumably in settlement of one such debt that Kniže acquired

Loos's unique collection of Kokoschka portraits sometime in the 1920s.

In spite of his increasing reputation Loos was physically and mentally in decline. He had contracted syphilis years before (probably at about the time he first met Kokoschka) and the disease was now taking its toll. It was in Paris, probably in 1932, that Kokoschka last saw the man to whom his early career owed so much and whom he regarded almost as a surrogate father. According to J. P. Hodin, Loos

wanted Kokoschka to have dinner with him in the Restaurant de Paris, where lobster in red sauce was on the menu, but Kokoschka declined. Several days afterwards he visited Loos and found him in bed. He stared at Kokoschka for a long time and then said: 'Today we will eat together.' Putting his hand under the horribly dirty sheet he drew out a huge lobster in tomato sauce. He sat up and swung it in the air. Kokoschka saw the fever in his eyes, and his body through the torn, disarrayed pyjamas. . . . The carpenter whom Loos had trained for many years, and who now worked for him if he ever had a commission, came to Paris to fetch him and put him in a clinic in Vienna. He died there, never regaining his clarity of mind.

In Paris with Loos in 1924 Kokoschka did little work. He enjoyed living like a student again without responsibilities. He relished the long hours of leisure, drinking and talking in bars and cafés until far into the night and looked forward to his daily visit to the Louvre.

But Kokoschka avoided the circles in which the city's most famous artists moved. He did not go to the Café du Dome or the Deux Magots; he was not interested in meeting Picasso, Matisse, Brancusi, Léger, Max Ernst or any of the other artists then at the height of their careers; he did not court the attention of Gertrude Stein or any of the other wealthy American collectors based in Paris and with an enthusiasm for anything that seemed most advanced in art.

Apart from the writer Céline, the people whom Kokoschka got to know in Paris were lesser figures like Jules Pascin and the Englishman Augustus John. It was as though Kokoschka shunned the Paris celebrated in the art journals and society columns either because he was scornful of the publicity machine and the big business aspect of the art market or because he was apprehensive about the reception he might receive.

Kokoschka was regarded in Central Europe as one of the leading painters of the age, but the Parisian art world was blinkered and arrogant, notorious for its haughty attitudes to any artist not connected with the school of Paris. It was better to avoid any risk of such treatment and to get to know the French capital without allowing himself to become too committed.

That explains why in December 1924 after only two months in Paris Kokoschka decided to return to Berlin where he stayed until February 1925. While Kokoschka was there Cassirer suggested that he travel around Europe, painting as he went. Landscapes of famous places would find a ready market and the dealer was prepared to finance a lengthy trip. Cassirer not only provided him with money but also with one of his business associates as a travelling companion. This was Jakob Goldschmidt who was not only responsible for all the travelling arrangements and for making sure that all the work produced on the trip reached Berlin safely, but also for ensuring that Kokoschka worked as hard as he could.

In February 1925 Kokoschka and Goldschmidt began their travels. They visited Genoa, Monte Carlo, Nice, Marseilles, Avignon, Aigues Mortes, Vernet les Bains, Toulouse, Bordeaux, Biarritz and then continued on into Portugal and Spain. So much work was produced, most of it landscapes, that Cassirer was able to stage a highly successful exhibition of the artist's travel paintings by the summer of that year.

From May until the end of June 1925 Kokoschka was again in Paris and then set off on his travels once more. He first went to Scheveningen and The Hague, journeyed on to London for ten days in July, returned to Holland from where he went to Switzerland. From October 1925 until January 1926 he was at his mother's house in Vienna, no doubt recovering from the strain of almost a year of ceaseless wandering.

Kokoschka's contract with the Cassirer gallery was extraordinarily generous. It guaranteed an annual salary of 30,000 marks and when Kokoschka heard the terms he was 'half unbelieving, half ironical'. His reaction is easy to understand: the contract meant that he was now secure, even rich. Although his mother and brother remained a heavy financial responsibility, he could now travel to his heart's content and in some style.

When he was not driving a hired car he was travelling by train and first class. In Goldschmidt he had an unofficial secretary. His clothes were tailored and of the finest quality. He ate and drank well and lived in the best hotels. When, after a short visit to Amsterdam, he went to London to paint in 1926, he rented a house in Park Lane before moving to the Savoy. At Park Lane he engaged the services of a butler and a maid. As ever, he kept his mother informed of his progress, proudly referring to his luxurious circumstances. From the Savoy he wrote to her: 'We in Vienna are like negroes or savages by comparison with the real world of the English.'

The luxury which the Cassirer contract made possible did not become a permanent feature of Kokoschka's life. The contract was not generous enough to permit the artist regularly to afford suites at hotels as exclusive as the Savoy. If he lived extraordinarily well from time to time it was because he spent what money he had profligately, preferring to enjoy himself when he could between recurring periods of impecunity.

Kokoschka now relied especially heavily on Cassirer to whose business acumen his success was for the most part due. But if Cassirer's touch had not deserted him in financial matters, his private life had become troubled and tragic. Tilla Durieux had left him for a wealthy banker and divorce proceedings were begun. She it is who describes the final meeting with the lawyer at which both parties were present:

We were all sitting round the table about to sign when Paul suddenly got up, mumbled his excuses and left the room. Immediately a shot rang out in the next room . . . I rushed in . . . and found Paul lying on the floor. He cried out: 'Now you shall stay with me!' The bullet, aimed at a relatively harmless spot, had been deflected along a rib-bone and had entered the spine.

Within hours Cassirer was dead.

Cassirer shot himself on 7 January 1926 and Kokoschka heard the news in Vienna where he was briefly visiting his mother. He must have been both saddened and alarmed, for the death of his dealer meant that his financial security was once again in jeopardy. Fortunately, Cassirer's partners, Walter Feilchenfeldt and Greta Ring, decided to keep the gallery open and they were as enthusiastic about Kokoschka's work as Cassirer himself had been. In some ways they were even more energetic in their efforts to bring it to the attention of an international public.

When Kokoschka heard the news of Cassirer's suicide he rushed to Berlin and stayed in Germany until March. Then he moved to London by way of Amsterdam. He stayed in London until October 1926, evidence of his growing affection for the city. Then he travelled yet again to Berlin where, apart from a visit to Vienna for Christmas, he remained for part of 1927. In the summer of that year he went back to Vienna to supervise repairs to the family house. Once they were completed he departed for Venice.

This bland rehearsal of Kokoschka's constantly changing whereabouts does not do justice to a programme of travels which would have exhausted a man ten years younger. Kokoschka was already forty years of age, at a stage in life when most men relish the comforts of home. Yet Kokoschka obviously wanted to avoid putting down roots anywhere, was wary of acquiring ties or possessions of any kind and was hungry for the kind of experiences which only constant travel could provide.

Although one of the best-known painters in Germany, Kokoschka still lacked a large following abroad. In an attempt to enhance his international reputation the Cassirer gallery arranged a large exhibition at the Kunsthaus in Zurich in 1927 which was hugely successful. Another show at the Leicester Galleries in London the following year proved disappointing, however. The British public, still guided by French standards in artistic matters, remained unreceptive to Central European painting of all kinds and especially to Expressionism. It was also no doubt deterred by the high prices asked. The Cassirer gallery was not the first to believe that an artist's reputation can be enhanced by high prices since most collectors are persuaded that there is a connection between artistic quality and monetary value. Thus, in London, £1,350 was asked for each of several of Kokoschka's landscapes. In those days it was an enormous sum, on a par with the price of work by the best-known painters from Paris.

Meanwhile Kokoschka continued to travel and he now went further and further afield. In 1927 he even planned to visit the United States for the first time. W. R. Valentiner, a German art historian then working at the County Museum in Los Angeles, arranged for Kokoschka to be given an entry permit and even sent him tickets, only to discover on the day the artist was due to arrive in New York that he had stayed on the other side of the Atlantic. About six months later a card arrived from the Middle East making excuses.

Valentiner did not hide his annoyance and this rare instance of unreliability on Kokoschka's part proved to be of enormous consequence. When, some nine years later, Kokoschka was living in exile in Prague and increasingly desperate to reach a safer haven, he tried to secure permission to go to the United States but failed. According to Valentiner, 'it was not so easy to arrange permission for him to come' after Kokoschka's earlier decision not to take up the invitation.

In June and July 1928 Kokoschka was painting in Ireland and in February 1929 he went to Cairo, Jerusalem, Beirut, Athens and Constantinople. At the end of July he was in Venice and from the middle of August until the end of September 1929 he worked in

Scotland. He then returned to Paris and in March 1930 struck out for North Africa where he painted at Algiers, Tunis and Djerba. After spending the summer in Rome and Anticoli he went again to Paris which he appears still to have regarded as his base. On most of these travels the director of the Amsterdam branch of the Cassirer gallery, J. H. F. Lütjens, went with him to make the necessary arrangements and look after his well-being, but in 1929 he was accompanied by his old friend Ehrenstein.

This was the period when Kokoschka was dubbed the *Mitropamaler* – the Cook's Tour painter – and it is easy to see why. It is also easy to understand why he was sufficiently wounded by the taunt to remember it and refer to it years later in his autobiography.

Travel, it has been said, is a substitute for real experience and it is tempting to see Kokoschka's *Wanderlust* as an avoidance of all difficult artistic problems. Moving from city to city painting the landmarks as he went, he was presented with a constant stream of picturesque motifs which, to someone with a fluent and assured style, posed few technical or imaginative difficulties.

The landscapes which Kokoschka produced on his travels are not to everyone's taste. In their loose handling and high-key colours they recall Impressionism and at their worst they can appear slack and even meretricious. At their best, however, they exhibit a confident and unusual grasp of space and light, and combine a wealth of complex detail and a sense of atmosphere to give coherence to buildings and nature on a grandly panoramic scale.

The best of these landscapes (for example, the views of the River Thames) employ unconventional compositional methods. The view-point is often very high and seems to shift continuously. Strong foreground motifs are frequently eliminated so that everything seems to exist in the middle distance. In most of them there is no single dominant focal point: the eye glides from one part of the composition to the next as it might in nature, enjoying an exhilarating sense of distance and atmosphere. Such paintings are much more than mere exercises in topography.

Although portraiture concerned Kokoschka far less during this period than before, he did paint several people on his travels, not only friends but also the rich and famous. In Paris in 1924 he painted Nancy Cunard, and two years later in London he painted Fred Astaire's sister Adèle (who had also changed her name from Austerlitz), an equally wonderful dancer permanently living in England since her recent marriage to Lord Charles Cavendish. Although the best-known of the portraits of this period, neither has the force, the power to disturb, of Kokoschka's earlier work. Adèle Astaire, sitting with her legs drawn up on a couch with a piano to one side of her and her dog on the other, has the staring eyes and rigid expression of a puppet. Only a shade more life animates the likeness of Nancy Cunard.

Kokoschka's three pictures of animals, all of them made in Regent's Park Zoo in London in 1926, are much more impressive, however. His 'portrait' of a mandrill is especially fine. 'As I painted him,' Kokoschka wrote, 'I saw: this is a wild, isolated fellow, almost a mirror image of myself who wants to be alone.'

It was clearly also the wildness and strangeness of the tigon which inspired him to paint this rare animal, a cross between a tiger and a lion, in its cage. It looks like some mythological beast, menacing yet at the same time playful, qualities which Kokoschka no doubt also recognized in himself.

In London Kokoschka had been introduced to Julian Huxley, then president of the Royal Zoological Society, who gave him permission to paint at the zoo outside opening hours. Often however, the work continued after the first visitors began to arrive in the morning. One day when Kokoschka was standing at his easel in front of the tigon's cage he was recognized by one of those visitors. As the painter banged on the floor to bring the beast back from the other end of the cage he 'was startled by something touching my shoulder. There stood my old friend Ernst Reinhold, the "Trance Player".'

The *Trance Player* was a portrait, one of Kokoschka's earliest, of a Viennese friend who had directed and acted in some of the artist's plays. They had not seen each other since before the war. Reinhold had abandoned his acting career, had become a Buddhist and had recently been in Ceylon studying in a monastery.

The chance meeting led to one of those extraordinary experiences which regularly punctuated Kokoschka's life and led him to believe that he possessed second sight and other abnormal powers. Kokoschka and Reinhold visited the botanical gardens at Kew together and they were almost the only people there.

On a bench [Kokoschka wrote], I saw a governess, of that English type with powerful teeth and cold eyes which would have been more than a match for any Victorian child, however obstreperous. In her charge was a half-grown girl with the reddish-blond hair I love so much in Van Dyck's portraits, blue eyes, and a red and white striped dress, bell-shaped, like the gramophone horns of those days. Her little feet, in their short white socks and black patent-leather shoes, danced enchantingly in the red sand on the floor of the palm house, enticing one to approach under the tall palm fronds and between the hanging orchids. My interest was aroused by a low, long Chinese table in the centre, on which was a miniature landscape with rocks and ancient dwarf pine trees. The little girl seemed rather bored, so I lifted her up to show her this landscape. I could feel her heart pounding violently against her ribs, like a landed fish in a basket. I showed her the grotto, and behind it, all in miniature, a waterfall, meadows and hill-pastures, stretching away into the distance. Suddenly the little girl that I thought I was holding in my arms was dancing away into the depths of the landscape like an elf. The child had disappeared. I looked for her, ran round the table, and finally asked Reinhold if he had seen the child or at least the governess. No, he had seen no one. . . . He maintained that the place had been empty ever since our arrival.

This supernatural experience, the more convincing because of the vivid details, was as strange as the one which took place when Kokoschka was a child and playing with the little girls in the park near his home.

FOVRTEEN

By October 1930 Kokoschka had grown tired of travelling, and although the Cassirer gallery urged him to undertake another journey, he returned to Paris where he stayed until September 1931. When Pascin, the French painter whom Kokoschka knew best, committed suicide Kokoschka rented his house, No 3 Villas des Camélias, from his widow. He moved there in June 1931. In September Kokoschka returned to Vienna where he stayed until February 1932. He moved into the modest home he had bought for his family in Liebhartstal on the outskirts of the city where he continued to paint although the rate of his production now slowed. One of the visitors to his studio late in 1931 was one of the most respected historians of modern art,

Julius Meier-Graefe, who published an account of his visit in the *Frankfurter Zeitung*:

Kokoschka's studio is a small room . . . he has more success than he needs. All writers on art with the exception of the Viennese maintain that he is the greatest, the finest, the most inventive of painters. Even in Paris they have written such things and he did not pay them. A whole pack of critics, *le grand peinture . . . le peintre plus fin* [sic] *. . . l'artiste le plus riche . . .* The English, too, the finest artist . . . But not in Vienna.

Oskar Kokoschka is happy in his Viennese seclusion. He is well. He has become fuller, in his painting, too.

Although Meier-Graefe exaggerated the attention given to Kokoschka's work in France and Britain, he was right about the continuing lack of interest of the Viennese. Kokoschka's reputation continued to be greatest in Germany, and in 1931 it was enhanced still further by a large retrospective exhibition at the Mannheim Kunsthalle, one of the most important provincial museums in Germany which for some years had owned several paintings by the artist, among them the portrait of Professor Forel.

One review of the exhibition provides chilling evidence of the change that was occurring in public attitudes in Germany, not merely to Kokoschka's work but to contemporary art in general. The review appeared in the Mannheim Nazi newspaper, the *Hakenkreuzbanner* – Swastika Banner – and it employs a vocabulary which, although familiar then only to readers of such journals, was to become common during the next few years. 'Seen through alien spectacles, the works may perhaps appear excellent; considered in a properly German way, they are the bubbles of the fermentation process of the Bolshevikization of German art.'

In 1931, however, opinions such as this carried little weight in museum and gallery circles. Not until Hitler became Chancellor two years later did the oppression of such artists as Kokoschka begin. But the writing was on the wall and only a few optimists and fools failed to see it there. Kokoschka was neither an optimist nor a fool.

In spite of the Mannheim exhibition, 1931 was not a good year for Kokoschka. The Cassirer gallery failed to renew his contract, pleading poverty as a result of the economic crisis which had been sparked off by the Wall Street crash of 1929. The business was indeed in dire financial straits but Kokoschka, now faced again by the prospect of no regular income, believed that there was some other reason. He had made Cassirer and his successors a great deal of money since the war; now they were abandoning him. He had, he considered, every right to be bitter. The result was a lengthy and rancorous dispute carried on not in private but in the correspondence columns of the *Frankfurter Zeitung*. Kokoschka remained in Vienna until the end of February 1932, then he returned yet again to Paris where he remained until May 1933. From then until September 1933 he worked at Rapallo, from where he returned to see his mother.

Kokoschka was based in Vienna until 1934. It was a relatively uneventful period in the artist's personal life but one of alarming change outside it.

Like Germany, Austria had become a republic in 1918 and both countries were plagued by a number of common and intractable problems. Economic difficulties exacerbated by ruinous inflation were accompanied by political extremism and instability. Some problems were unique to Austria, however. It had lost more territory than had Germany and experienced a more severe crisis of identity. It was also deprived of almost all its former sources of raw materials, and this fact, together with the consciousness that a great empire had been lost, made many Austrians feel that their new and tiny country was neither politically nor economically viable. In addition, there was a precarious imbalance between the capital and the rest of the country. Vienna not only contained more than thirty per cent of Austria's entire population, it was now also badly located: no longer at the centre of an empire and at the fulcrum between east and west, north and south, but in the eastern corner of a small country, and with almost no hinterland on two sides.

The imbalance between Vienna and the rest of the country was both demographic and political. Only the capital – 'Red Vienna' – was solidly socialist; elsewhere, where the economy was overwhelmingly agrarian, more conservative parties were in the majority.

In parliament the two dominant factions were the Social Democrats and the clerical Christian Socialists. In 1918 they agreed on only one thing: union with Germany. But this aim, even had it been acceptable to the Germans, was quickly frustrated by the victorious Allies. Throughout the 1920s the polarization of left and right increased and the antagonism between the major parties was scarcely greater than that between the extremists and moderates within the parties themselves.

Paramilitary organizations sprang up on both sides, their ranks swollen by the growing army of unemployed. In 1927 one of the frequent skirmishes between sections of the socialist *Schutzbund* and the conservative *Frontkämpfer* resulted in fatalities. At the subsequent trial the *Frontkämpfer* were acquitted and on 15 July 1927 the workers of Vienna rose up in their anger. The populace had their first taste of civil war, during which the various paramilitary forces fought each other and the police. The Palace of Justice was burned down and many people were killed.

This marked the beginning of the end of parliamentary democracy in Austria. The end itself came in March 1933 when the Christian Socialist Engelbert Dollfuss, Chancellor for less than a year, dismissed parliament as unworkable and established a dictatorship. Although he banned all parties of the left, the move was directed as much against the extreme right, now supported by Adolf Hitler. In July 1934 there was an attempted *putsch* in Vienna. Hitler's agents planned to kill the entire cabinet but succeeded only in murdering Dollfuss, who was immediately followed as Chancellor by another Christian Socialist, Kurt von Schuschnigg.

In 1931, however, parliament still functioned and Vienna continued to be governed by moderate socialists who pursued an enlightened social and cultural policy. In 1931 Kokoschka was commissioned by the Vienna city council to paint a view of the Austrian capital. He chose an area close to his home, the Wilhelminenberg and painted a multitude of children playing on a sunny day in a park in front of a panorama of the city. The picture had just been finished when Meier-Graefe visited the studio.

It was commissioned by the city [he wrote] in spite of the fierce opposition of the Viennese. To the left, the corner of the façade of a former archducal palace in the Liebhartstal, now a children's home. The palace faces a broad flat area which could be anywhere and one assumes anywhere but Vienna. On the flat area countless dancing and playing children run about. Oskar Kokoschka has made it both easy and difficult for himself in this, the most recent of his many pictures of cities: easy, because he took the best landscape that was close to his house; difficult, because he could scarcely have chosen a more thankless motif from this city that is too rich in its attractions. . . . The flat area, enlivened by the many groups of dancing children does honour to this inventive artist. The picture itself laughs, dances and sings. The spirit of this city could scarcely have been better personified.

According to Kokoschka this was his 'first picture with a political meaning', although that meaning is not immediately clear. The children were orphans living in the former palace of an archduke which the city authorities had confiscated and were using as an orphanage and the picture of the children (based indirectly on a Brueghel) playing games with great excitement 'was meant as a demonstration against the reactionary state of affairs'.

Until then Kokoschka had been scarcely interested in conventional politics. What concerned him were the larger issues: the passing of the old order in Europe, the increasing influence of science and technology and the effects of the monopoly ownership of raw materials, especially oil. Now, and at a moment of crisis in Austria and Germany, how could he fail to take a stand? He was alarmed by the growth of the authoritarian state, by the increasing suppression of individual rights and by the threat posed by the Nazis who, committed to union between Germany and Austria, were daily becoming more powerful in Vienna and elsewhere.

By the end of 1933 the banned parties of the left were gathering their strength for an assault on the Dollfuss dictatorship. On 12 February 1934 a detachment of police searching for weapons at a working-men's club in Linz was fired upon and the police then stormed the building. A general strike was declared and the extreme right seized the opportunity for a show-down. In Vienna, the army, the police and the paramilitary forces moved into the working-class districts of the city and bombarded apartment blocks with heavy artillery.

The *Schutzbund*, the illegal army of the left, resisted. This was civil war, and although the fighting continued for little more than a night and a day, hundreds died and several public buildings were razed. After the speedy victory of the government forces martial law was declared. For days afterwards violence flared up from time to time and for several nights the flames from burning buildings lit up the sky for miles around.

When the battle began Kokoschka was on a visit to Budapest. When he heard the news on the radio he immediately returned to Vienna where he found his mother, bemused and afraid, looking at the flames in the sky from an upstairs window.

Karl Kraus, who continued to write and publish *Die Fackel* single-handed, took no immediate public stand on these events. Like the appointment of Hitler as German Chancellor in January 1933 which provoked Kraus to remark 'zu Hitler fällt mir nichts ein' ('On the subject of Hitler nothing occurs to me'), developments in Austria were grave and alarming enough to reduce even him to silence. Kraus, together with so many intellectuals in Germany and Austria, was unable to see the situation clearly. He believed that Dollfuss was the only man capable of saving the country from Nazism and that the tactics of the left were calculated to make matters worse. When, a month after the brief civil war, Dollfuss was assassinated, Kraus was reduced to tears, but continued unrealistically to hope that Schu-schnigg, the new Chancellor, would continue Dollfuss's policies and prevent the union with Germany which the Nazis desired.

Kokoschka was less confused and less optimistic than Karl Kraus. He had no doubt that Nazism would come to Austria and that, as in Germany, it would be welcomed by the majority of the population. Unlike Kraus, moreover, Kokoschka was suspected of being a socialist sympathizer. Why else would he have been commissioned to paint a picture by the socialist city authorities in 1931? The events of 1934 made it plain that he was in danger, even if the Nazis failed in their attempt to gain control and achieve the union with Germany they so wanted.

Kokoschka knew very well what a Nazi Austria would mean in personal terms. In Germany, the vilification of all artists, writers and musicians opposed to the new, official art policy began almost as soon as Hitler became Chancellor in January 1933. Max Liebermann, a Jew who on the night of Hitler's accession is reported to have said, 'I can't eat as much as I should like to throw up', was one of the first to resign from the Prussian Academy of Arts of which he had been president for twelve years. As he explained to the press:

Throughout my long life I have attempted with all my strength to serve German art. I am convinced that art has nothing to do either with politics or [racial] origins. Since my point of view is no longer of any value within the Prussian Academy . . . I can no longer belong to it.

Within days Kokoschka wrote to the *Frankfurter Zeitung* about Liebermann's resignation pleading for reconciliation:

My life is only half over, my work not yet completed and what I have achieved is problematic, misunderstood, persecuted and neglected – my life has been thus since my eighteenth year. It is a thorny path like that of almost all artists. Therefore, I may be allowed to speak for all my German colleagues on behalf of Max Liebermann whose work is done. I know that it requires no courage to stand up for Max Liebermann and say: if his decision is already irrevocable, then the parting should occur in friendship, so that there will be no tragic misunderstanding between teacher and pupils which would only damage the creation of the new art in Germany.

No one was misled by the conciliatory tone, least of all the Nazi cultural authorities who immediately increased their scrutiny of the *Frankfurter Zeitung* and let their displeasure be known.

The Nazis were delighted by Liebermann's resignation and would have been pleased had Kokoschka, himself a member of the Prussian

Academy of Arts for some time, followed Liebermann's example. But Kokoschka was not prepared to play the German government's game. They would have to find grounds for his expulsion. As early as July 1933 the committee of the academy requested the Ministry of the Interior to investigate Kokoschka's racial origins in the hope that some trace of Jewish blood would be found. They were disappointed and Kokoschka remained a member of the academy until 1 July 1938 when he was expelled.

A Jewish background was, of course, not the only reason why an artist could be persecuted by the Nazis. As Kandinsky, Klee, Grosz and countless others discovered, an allegiance to modernism was enough. Even Nolde, a member of the Nazi Party since the 1920s, was not immune from vilification.

Modernism was international. It was therefore un-German and had to be eradicated from German art. It was also élitist and allegedly inaccessible to the common man. A speech made in 1934 by Hans Hinkel, a leading Nazi cultural mandarin, makes this abundantly clear. Hinkel had visited an exhibition of

paintings representative of Impressionism and other isms. Here were Kokoschka and others from the Berlin Kurfürstendamm. If one had taken down one of these paintings . . . and handed it to a worker, he would not have known which was the top or bottom. . . . If a prominent expert had then explained that what Kokoschka had made was the art of the future, the well-meaning worker would have believed it and thought: I am too stupid to judge for myself; I am not an expert. If I speak today of a new German art I am thoroughly convinced that it will be . . . an art of the people or nothing. An art only for experts was never art. . . . We are convinced that a new German art should give something to the people of our own blood and kind. In their hearts they should be moved by the work to joy or sadness . . . if art does not provide that, then it is not art and has never had anything to do with it.

Kokoschka sensed that he would have to leave Austria before it was too late. The death of his mother in 1934 loosened his last strong ties with Vienna and sped him on his way. Kokoschka's mother died soon after the civil war in Vienna. For four nights she had stood at her window observing the fires burning several miles away in the city centre. On the fourth night she had a stroke. Kokoschka was convinced that worry had caused her death.

She was buried not in Vienna but in Hollenstein where she was born and brought up. Oskar and Bohuslav accompanied the body there to a plot on the top of a hill with a view of the mountains and fields she had known as a girl. On the grave they placed a model of the house in Liebhartstal.

After the funeral Kokoschka left Vienna for Prague. He would never live in his homeland again.

FIFTEEN

There were several reasons why Kokoschka went to Prague. It was the native city of his father; his sister Berta lived there with her husband; the artist had friends there. Because of his family background Kokoschka also had a claim to Czech nationality which he eventually took. The political atmosphere was also considerably easier than that of Austria. Indeed Czechoslovakia had been the great success story among those nations which had gained their independence in 1919 after the break-up of the Habsburg empire. Its industries boomed (heavy engineering and armaments made it one of the most powerful economies in the world between the wars) and it succeeded where Austria, Germany and Hungary all failed, in establishing a stable democratic government. For liberal Austrians living under the Dollfuss regime it was a kind of paradise.

It was no wonder, then, that Czechoslovakia attracted so many refugees from both Germany and Austria, especially as they required no visa, no work permit and the borders were not well guarded. As Heinrich Mann, one of the countless Germans who sough Czech exile, wrote:

During the fateful years when Hitler's Germany was allowed to grow up . . . the state of Masaryk, the President-Liberator, opened its arms to us. We – the whole of persecuted Germany, the intellectual, the freedom-seeking Germany – were not only not treated with indifference . . .: Prague received us as relatives.

Kokoschka already knew an art dealer in Prague who was anxious to work on his behalf. His name was Hugo Feigl and he first met Kokoschka in Paris. Feigl heard that the artist was 'not getting on very well . . . and seems to be irritated by the Paris art world'. In less than an hour Feigl was

in Kokoschka's studio. . . . It was an unusually roomy studio with bleak walls, entirely without furniture, and with a large picture leaning against one wall. . . . At the back of the room Kokoschka was sitting to an English sculptress for a head and shoulders. He jumped up to greet me. When I suggested that he should come to Prague and paint some landscapes for me he nearly kissed me. 'That has long been one of my dreams. My sister is there too and I would like to see her again.' After the first meeting six or seven months passed and I began to feel that Kokoschka had forgotten the suggestion which seemed so fascinating to him in Paris. But one clear sunny autumn day he appeared . . . in my shop in Prague, saying: 'Here I am. I am going to make Prague my home for the next few years.' The next day he had settled down to paint.

Prague was then and still remains perhaps the most beautiful city in northern Europe with its mixture of Gothic and Baroque buildings, its narrow, winding streets and picturesque squares. Although much smaller than Vienna (it had about a million inhabitants) it enjoyed a rich and varied cultural life. German, moreover, was one of the languages most widely spoken in the city which, in Habsburg days, was regarded as second only to Vienna for the quality of its university, music and galleries.

Hugo Feigl proved an important ally. He had contacts within government circles and managed to arrange for the President, Masaryk, to sit for his portrait. Kokoschka was invited to be

Masaryk's guest at his summer residence for the duration of the work but preferred to remain in Prague from where he 'was collected every morning by his official car with the registration number 1, at the sight of which the sentries at his gate sprang to attention'.

Kokoschka had never met a head of state before and was never to meet one who impressed him so much. Masaryk was an intellectual (he had been a professor before entering politics) and a democrat. Kokoschka discovered that they shared many interests and enthusiasms, not least for the educational ideals of the Czech philosopher Comenius whose picture book for children, *Orbis Pictus*, had delighted Kokoschka even before he could read and which had remained a source of inspiration ever since.

Comenius appears in Kokoschka's portrait of Masaryk, holding a chart illustrating the five senses. To the right is a view of Prague. It was not commissioned by Masaryk or the Czechoslovak government. It was bought by Feigl who took it with him when he fled to the United States just before the German army marched into the Sudetenland. It now hangs in the Carnegie Institute in Pittsburgh.

Masaryk was ill when Kokoschka was painting him. In December 1935 he resigned as President and was succeeded by his Foreign Minister Beneš. Beneš was opposed by those who wanted Czechoslovakia to pursue a foreign policy sympathetic to Germany in the hope that Germany would leave its small neighbour in peace. Beneš did realize, though, that his government would have to tread warily and take seriously the warnings that were almost daily being issued in Berlin. Life became more difficult for the German refugees living in Prague.

The international situation had become dangerous. While Germany made increasingly threatening noises to its neighbours, the Nazi terror at home began in earnest. The concentration camps were filling and not only with Jews. The fortunate managed to get away: to France, Britain, the United States but also to Czechoslovakia which continued to let them in. Refugees, some of them artists, seemed to arrive in Prague with every main-line train.

In spite of the difficulties facing the Czech government the refugees from Germany were allowed great freedom. They continued to work, publish and make anti-Nazi propaganda. In the summer of 1937 émigré artists formed themselves into the 'Oskar Kokoschka Association'. They took their lead from a number of similar, older organizations, the 'Bert Brecht Club' among them, already founded by writers and theatre people. By using Kokoschka's name they acknowledged his status as the most celebrated painter in Czech exile. One of the members was John Heartfield who with his savage photomontages was carrying on a brilliant campaign against the Nazis. Perhaps he enjoyed the irony of being a member of a group named after the man whom in 1920 he had attacked as a *Kunstlump*. The Kokoschka Association existed until 1938 by which time most of its members had left Prague to find exile elsewhere, above all in Britain where the Association was absorbed by the 'Free German League of Culture'.

In Germany in 1937 the Nazi campaign against modernism in the visual arts reached its climax with 'The Degenerate Art Exhibition' in Munich. The exhibition consisted of outstanding examples of the kind of contemporary painting and sculpture held to be un-German and therefore degenerate. All the works in the exhibition had been confiscated from public collections in Germany.

Kokoschka was represented (by nine paintings) as was everyone else whose work was 'modern'. The organizers were not content simply to hang these models of degeneracy on the walls and allow visitors to make up their minds for themselves. Strident texts on the gallery walls and in the catalogue compared the works on view to African and other primitive art and to photographs of and drawings by the physically deformed and deranged.

On page 31 of the catalogue three drawings were reproduced. As the caption explained, two were by Kokoschka and the third was the work of an inmate of a lunatic asylum. The reader was invited to guess which was which. On the facing page was a quotation from a speech given by Hitler at the party congress in 1933: 'To distinguish oneself by conscious lunacy in order to gain attention betrays not only an artistic failure but also a moral defect.'

It is often forgotten that the Degenerate Art Exhibition proved remarkably popular. Two million people had seen it even before it left Munich on an extended tour of the Reich and it is fair to assume that most of the visitors, whether party members or not, agreed with the purpose of the exhibition: to unmask all 'modern' art as an elaborate confidence trick and as the product of disturbed minds.

The exhibition was merely the most visible aspect of the government's policy for the visual arts. For some time the authorities had been confiscating examples of 'degenerate' painting and sculpture from the public museums. They also banned the exhibition of the work of 'degenerate' artists and in some cases forbade such artists to work even in private. Some of the confiscated work was burned by the Berlin fire brigade; most of it was sent to the Theodor Fischer gallery in Lucerne, Switzerland, where it was auctioned on 30 June 1939 and passed, mostly at low prices, into the hands of Swiss and American museums or private collectors.

It must be said that not all German museums were punctilious in their observance of the law. Most curators had become Nazis or had been replaced by those who were already party members, but the directors of a few galleries resorted to deception in order to preserve something of their collections. Although the director of the Mannheim Kunsthalle, G. F. Hartlaub, was dismissed in 1933 to make way for someone more sympathetic to the official policy, and although no fewer than fourteen prints and drawings by Kokoschka were confiscated from the museum in August 1937, none of the artist's paintings was lost. Somehow the portrait of Professor Forel which Mannheim had acquired in 1913 was kept out of sight and out of harm's way until the Nazi nightmare was over.

In general though, museum officials did their duty, and for the most part enthusiastically. In Dresden Kokoschka's old friend and landlord Dr Posse at first attempted to frustrate the official policy, fell foul of the agents sent from Berlin to supervise the butchery of the collection and was sent on leave. Convinced that resistance was hopeless, however, Posse then promised to co-operate and returned to his post. Eventually he was given responsibility for acquiring works, most of them plundered from foreign collections, for the new museum in Linz which Hitler envisaged as the world's greatest repository of masterpieces.

To this day Dresden has lacked even a single example of the work of a man who for more than five years had intimate connections with the city. Only one painting by Kokoschka now hangs in the Dresden gallery and that is on loan from the Hungarian state collection.

Between 1933 and 1937 scores of Kokoschka's paintings and hundreds of his prints and drawings were removed from museums throughout Germany. Many passed into safe hands, either through Lucerne or along more clandestine routes; but some were lost, apparently for ever.

There is an obvious sense in which an artist's work remains his personal possession even after it has been acquired by others. Kokoschka was therefore not unique in experiencing a deep sense of personal loss at the disappearance and probable destruction of so many of his paintings. Occasionally after the war one would reappear, often under unusual circumstances, and this would give Kokoschka hope that others still existed and would yet be found. Once, in Venice, he was approached in the street by a stranger who introduced himself and then proudly announced that he was the owner of several important works which he had acquired from a prominent Nazi.

Kokoschka was surprised neither by the degenerate art campaign nor by its virulence. When, not long before the annexation of Austria, a large Kokoschka exhibition was organized in Vienna, the artist wrote to Schuschnigg, the Chancellor, urging him not to return any of the pictures on loan from German collections since they would be safer if they remained in Austria. The authorities were powerless to act even had they wished to and the works were sent back as soon as the exhibition closed. Some of them returned in 'The Degenerate Art Exhibition' which included Vienna on its tour after the *Anschluss*.

The exhibition which provoked the letter to Schuschnigg was organized to mark Kokoschka's fifty-first birthday in 1937. It was the first large showing of his work in his native city. It was held, appropriately enough, at the Museum of Art and Industry, an institution with close connections with the School of Arts and Crafts where Kokoschka had studied and taught, and it was staged at the instigation of Carl Moll, Alma Mahler's stepfather, who had admired Kokoschka's work ever since he had seen it at the first *Kunstschau*.

Moll's introduction to the exhibition catalogue makes it clear that for him at least Kokoschka's loss to Austria was a tragedy. 'You have been lost to your homeland,' he wrote. 'It reproaches you with avoiding it, you reproach it for looking the other way.' Moll was speaking for many but by no means for everybody. One writer commenting on the exhibition recalled Eugenie Schwarzwald's support of Kokoschka before the war and was of the opinion that 'had [she] not, obviously in an attack of madness, appointed this perverse portraitist as a drawing master in her girls' school, yes indeed, girls' school, then this . . . exhibition . . . could not have taken place now, for he would probably have starved long since'.

Although his work was in danger in Germany, Kokoschka himself was, for the time being at least, safe in Prague. He was not especially happy, however, for concern for his future and that of his family distressed and depressed him. His financial circumstances were also very bad: few collectors are interested in buying paintings at moments of political and economic instability and although Hugo Feigl did his best, he could not provide Kokoschka with a reasonable income.

What little pleasure Kokoschka had was derived from the city itself and its associations with his family. He must often have walked past the house in the Stàlenà Ulice in the city centre which had once belonged to his father's family and thought about the dramatic changes in the world since the time the Kokoschkas had carried out commissions for members of the imperial court.

At least the city itself had changed but little since then and was as beautiful as ever. In the summer of 1935 Kokoschka rented a studio in the attic of a Neo-Renaissance building on a picturesque stretch of the River Moldau not far from the Charles Bridge. From its windows Kokoschka could look down on the river and across at the twisting alleyways and lanes on the slope which was crowned by St Vitus's Cathedral. He painted several views of the Moldau from that window and several other landscapes from other vantage-points in the city. In spite of his recurring depression they are some of the best paintings of a city he ever executed.

Hugo Feigl was not Kokoschka's only friend in Prague. Soon after Kokoschka's arrival he contacted a lawyer and collector whom he had first met in Berlin at the opening of one of his exhibitions at the Cassirer gallery. His name was Palkovsky and he quickly invited Kokoschka to his house for a meal. There Kokoschka met Palkovsky's daughter Olda, then studying law but with a greater interest in art and art history.

It was an unlikely match. She was much younger than he, taller, more taciturn and of a more practical turn of mind. He could not speak Czech and her German did not extend beyond what little she had learned at school. Nevertheless they seem to have taken to each other instantly and in Olda Palkovska Kokoschka at last found the kind of woman who had previously eluded him. She was mature beyond her years, courageous, reliable and well-organized. Astute, imaginative and gifted, she was completely unselfish and provided the ideal foil to his excitable, quixotic temperament. It is entirely possible that but for her level-headed refusal to panic, her determination and ability to organize, Kokoschka would not have survived the next few years.

With her black hair, dark eyes, strong, open face and elegant figure, Olda Palkovska was also extremely attractive. Her parents must have planned an entirely different future for their charming, well-educated daughter and were no doubt alarmed by her obvious interest in a middle-aged painter who, although famous, was virtually penniless. For his part, Kokoschka was suspicious of the lawyer and his wife and an easy relationship never existed between them even during the period when they were all living in London.

Kokoschka relied increasingly on Olda both emotionally and practically, but he did not marry her even though she made it plain that she was not averse to the idea. The marked difference in their ages was one reason, but far more important was the uncertain future. At a time in which the world threatened daily to collapse, to embark on a marriage would have been foolhardy.

Early in 1938 the international situation became grave. On 12 March 1938 Germany annexed Austria, to the delight, so it seemed, of the majority of Austrians who, when the *Wehrmacht* marched in triumph through the streets of Vienna, turned out in force to cheer the soldiers to the echo.

Hitler was a member of Kokoschka's generation. Born at Braunau in 1889, he was also Austrian and also considered himself a painter. Indeed, in 1906, while Kokoschka was studying at the *Kunstgewerbeschule*, Hitler applied for admission to the academy in Vienna. It is tempting to speculate that his rejection was the source of much of the frustration which drove him into politics.

The annexation of Austria occurred at the end of winter and it was already clear that worse would come before the summer was out. Germany was now demanding self-determination for the German-speakers in Czechoslovakia who were concentrated in the area inaccurately described as the Sudetenland. Britain and France, desperate to placate Hitler and avoid another European war, were prepared to sacrifice not merely part, but all of Czechoslovakia in order to preserve the peace.

In August 1938 German forces were mobilized and in September Chamberlain, the British Prime Minister, visited Hitler. The fate of Czechoslovakia was sealed, when, at the Munich conference of 29 September, the Sudetenland was transferred to Germany. On 5 October Beneš resigned as President of Czechoslovakia. Within five months the dismemberment of the country was complete.

In Prague, these events were observed with mounting horror. For Kokoschka they merely confirmed his worst fears. He had to move on before it was too late. He did not find it easy to take the final step, however. As a letter to Ehrenstein written in the winter of 1937–8 reveals, he did not want to leave Prague 'as long as there is the direct danger of war. . . . The people here are so thoroughly decent and so brave that one could only be ashamed. Unfortunately all my patrons have bolted. I must now stop writing since we cannot have any light because of the black-out.'

The more direct the danger of a German invasion, the more urgent Kokoschka's need to leave Czechoslovakia. No matter how he felt about abandoning the country which had given him refuge, it was clear that it would have been madness to remain. But where could he go? France was a possibility; but he had never liked or, more important, trusted the French. With great foresight he recognized that Paris was not a city in which safety could be assured at a time of crisis. America was another and better possibility and Kokoschka had begun to make overtures to people he knew there as early as 1936.

One of them was W. R. Valentiner to whom he wrote on 25 March:

I was stupid not to have come to the States with you, for by now I would have been world-famous over there, whereas here in Europe the houses of cards collapse as soon as you build them. I recently painted Masaryk; it is an important composition (I studied him for a long time in person). I have done a couple of landscapes for local museums and now I am free again. Could one paint the President of the United States? I was invited by the Russians to go there, but I have heavy debts and a brother in Vienna and have to keep on sending money which is not allowed from Russia . . . so, my friend, if you come to fetch me in an aeroplane, this time, I shall certainly be there.

After Kokoschka's earlier failure to appear in the United States at the appointed time, Valentiner was presumably reluctant to make fresh arrangements, especially since it was by now not as easy to secure permission from the authorities for long-term visitors from Europe. But Valentiner or someone else did nevertheless arrange for an invitation for Kokoschka to teach at Mills College in America and it arrived in 1937. Why Kokoschka decided not to accept it is both unclear and surprising. Perhaps the reason was concern for his family and the belief that communications from America would be unreliable. Bohuslav remained in Vienna and as the brother of a notorious, 'degenerate' artist was already receiving the unwelcome attentions of the authorities. His sister would also remain in Prague with her husband. A more likely explanation is that Kokoschka believed that he would not be able to secure permission for Olda to accompany him and was not prepared to abandon her to an uncertain fate in Prague. Significantly he did not tell her about the approach from Mills College until some years later when all danger had past. In any case Kokoschka was too much of a European to contemplate transplantation to a foreign culture with equanimity. England remained the best if not the only choice.

It would be an exaggeration to say that Kokoschka was entirely unknown in England. He had once exhibited at the Leicester Galleries and in the summer of 1938 was represented in an exhibition which attracted a great deal of attention even though it was a critical failure.

This was the 'German Art Exhibition' at the Burlington Galleries which was organized by Herbert Read, Roland Penrose and others as an answer to 'The Degenerate Art Exhibition', still touring Germany. It was accompanied by a book, *Modern German Art*, published by Allen Lane as a Pelican Special and written by Oto Bihalji-Merian under the pseudonym Peter Thoene.

Staged more as a propaganda exercise than to provide the British public with a belated opportunity to see something of contemporary German art (about which it was in almost total ignorance), it met with an almost complete lack of comprehension on the part of the London critics for whom most German painters were either too wild or too sentimental. As an anonymous critic in *Apollo* wrote:

German art suffers, it would seem, most from 'bad form'. Like the German language itself, it lacks clarity; it is incontinent, both in its furor, the *furor teutonicus*, and in its sentiment – its *Schwärmerei*. It has therefore never produced a really great *painter*, for their really great men of old – Matthias Grünewald, Dürer, Holbein – were, as painters, only half great.

One of the many people who assisted with the exhibition was Fred Uhlman, himself a painter and a refugee from Germany. One of the critics told him, 'I paid 2s 6d for seeing the exhibition, I would willingly pay 5s for not having seen it.' Another admitted hating the Nazis but added, 'One can't deny that Hitler was right calling them degenerate.'

The exhibition was staged in July 1938 when Kokoschka was still in Prague and a letter from London informed him that he was to be represented in it. Since there was very little modern German art in private or public hands in Britain at the time and since there was no opportunity to secure loans from Germany or Austria, the selectors were very restricted in their choice of work to put on show.

Kokoschka believed that he was represented mostly by poor examples of his work and attempted to withdraw from the exhibition. He also believed with, as we have seen, good reason that the very idea of the exhibition was a mistake since it would confirm the general public in their suspicion of much contemporary art and thus unwittingly make propaganda for and not against Nazi Germany.

Kokoschka was also angered by the catalogue in which it was stated that he 'at first worked in the Art Nouveau style, then allied himself to Expressionism and now painted in the style of the French Impressionists'.

Any suggestion that he had ever worked in styles originated by others was bound to make him angry.

In *Modern German Art*, the book published to accompany the exhibition, Thoene presented a picture of Kokoschka much more in keeping with the artist's image of himself as an isolated visionary. Kokoschka, he wrote,

left the realm of naturalistic truth, which seemed to have been conquered by modern technical developments, in order to track down the submerged, causative phenomena which underlie visible things. He kept the traditional contour of life, even though he filled it with baroque ecstasies and broke it up. Confining himself to the range of apparently traditional forms, he delves down by dream-routes to explore hidden strata of existence, which he portrays with vaporous, suppurating, flashing colours.

Kokoschka has little in common with the masters of late French Impressionism, which explains his solitary position. The essence of things is of greater moment to him than their appearance. But in the pure technique of painting he is bound even less to the German Expressionist school, for next to truth it is beauty in art which he loves above all.

Although Kokoschka was unhappy about his inclusion in the London exhibition, it at least established contact with Herbert Read. Read was an important and influential man in English artistic and literary circles, able, if anyone was, to recommend foreign painters for residence permits. In a letter of 17 May 1938 the artist told Read:

You would put me very much in your debt if you could make it possible for me to paint your Mayor, Sir Hoare Belisha. I have also written about this to [our] friend Augustus John. I have to start at the beginning again and therefore need powerful protection and if possible permission to work in England. Otherwise I am lost – since your Lords have generously handed over my homeland Austria to the Nazis as a present.

If Read replied, his letter has not been preserved. If he tried to arrange for Kokoschka to come to England he was unsuccessful.

As the situation grew worse during the spring and early summer of 1938 Kokoschka's desperation grew. He was at a low ebb. His miserable circumstances, the awareness of imminent catastrophe and above all his fear of being trapped soured his relations even with Olda and her parents. Desperation and confusion prevented Kokoschka from facing important decisions and had it not been for Olda he would probably have been mesmerized by fear, immobile in Prague until it was too late, but Olda was prepared to make decisions for him. By the summer of 1938 it was difficult to leave the country even with a Czech passport, but Olda announced that she would accompany Kokoschka to Britain and for days stood queuing in order to get visas and buy tickets. Since Czechoslovakia was virtually surrounded by hostile countries, the only sure means of escape was by aeroplane.

Even though it was possible to pay for the air tickets in Czechoslovak currency they were difficult enough to get since all flights to countries not under German control were fully booked weeks in advance. Even with a visa, which Kokoschka and Olda did not require since they both had Czech passports, entry to Britain could not be guaranteed, for the immigration authorities could still refuse permission and had begun to turn back large numbers of people.

On Friday 16 October Olda announced that she had managed to book two seats for a flight which left for London the next morning. She was determined that they would both be on it even though there was no guarantee that they would be admitted into the country.

On the Friday evening before the flight, Kokoschka and Olda went to a café frequented by foreign journalists where by chance they met a Canadian correspondent whom Kokoschka knew. When he heard of the pair's predicament the Canadian told them that he was also travelling next day to London although by an even earlier flight and that he would take up their case immediately with a diplomat he knew. This was Lord Robert Cecil who had been associated with the League of Nations, had won the Nobel Peace Prize in 1937 and, being a Cecil, was a man of influence.

Armed with this vague promise, Kokoschka and Olda left Prague for London on 17 October 1938 by the KLM flight which departed at 8.30 a.m. On its way to London it landed in Rotterdam to refuel.

Even if Kokoschka and Olda were allowed entry into Britain the future was bleak. All the foreign currency they were allowed to take with them amounted to no more than £10. Apart from a few clothes hastily packed the night before, Kokoschka took a small painting which he hoped to be able to sell and some of his painting equipment.

The sense of guarded relief as the small aeroplane took off from Prague airport can be imagined. Olda remembered both the relief and apprehension, especially when a stewardess gave her some fashion magazines to read.

When the aeroplane landed at Croydon, then London's international airport, the last few minutes standing in the queue in front of the immigration desk must have been scarcely bearable. We do not know whether the Canadian journalist kept his promise, whether Lord Robert Cecil used his influence to ensure that Kokoschka and Olda were allowed into Britain, but they were admitted. When they presented their passports they were nodded through without a murmur.

SIXTEEN

A letter from Kokoschka to his friend Adolf Arndt, dated 20 October 1938, briefly relates the events of the first few days in London. Kokoschka wrote that he and Olda 'were allowed to take only £5' with them 'and a small picture' which was

in store awaiting payment of £4/7/– together with my painting equipment. The bags stayed in Prague and will perhaps arrive here at Christmas. I was at my most afraid at passport control, but Lord Cecil had recommended me so that I immediately (as an exception!) was allowed in for 3 months; yesterday Sir Kenneth Clark, director of the National Gallery, advised me to stay here and he will arrange everything for me. Today I am invited to tea by the director of the Tate Gallery, Rothenstein, who is working very hard on behalf of my art; tomorrow to the Courtauld Institute.

This letter, brimful of the optimism of someone who has escaped disaster by the skin of his teeth, also demonstrates Kokoschka's ability to seek out the most influential people in the shortest possible time. He was better informed than most other refugee artists in England and less reserved in soliciting introductions and asking for help.

The letter to Arndt continues:

If I wanted, I would probably be able to secure the right kind of position here . . . but I should prefer to be able to work soon, free from all external honours and invitations and above all to have someone here to whom I could leave the problem of existence without embarrassment for the next few days.

Kokoschka quickly introduced himself to the most important museum officials in London, but it took him some time to understand the English way of doing things: that vague promises of help were usually no more than the expression of a desire not to offend and were rarely, if ever, kept. Talk of positions, of honours, of gallery directors working energetically on his behalf was unrealistic. More reliable promises and real help came not from the British establishment but from refugee friends already in London and especially Emil Korner, the economist, who had been financial director of the Witkowitz steel works near Ostraua and had fled from Czechoslovakia. Korner lent Kokoschka £100, a sizeable sum in those days and enough for a frugal life for several months.

The loan, given in the form of a single, large white Bank of England note, was very necessary since Kokoschka's energy in cultivating museum directors and dealers was not enough to assure him of the work he so desperately needed. All he secured from Rothenstein, for example, was an invitation to donate a painting to the Tate Gallery.

This was not surprising. Like all the other artists now living in England who were household names in Central Europe, Kokoschka was scarcely known in Britain where, as the reception of the 'German Art Exhibition' showed, French standards reigned supreme and it was widely believed that there could be, almost by definition, no such thing as a great German artist.

In England in any case all modern art, including that made in France, was highly suspect. Advanced styles – Surrealism, for example – tended to reach London at least ten years late and even then failed to be widely understood and appreciated. During the early years of the emigration London, and especially Hampstead, was the home of an extraordinary number of great artists, architects, writers, composers and intellectuals, almost all of whom failed to make their way in England and most of whom eventually travelled on to the United States where a warm welcome was assured.

At different times during the years 1936 to 1941 Piet Mondrian, Lazlo Moholy-Nagy, Marcel Breuer, Walter Gropius and Erich Mendelsohn, left London. Others, among them John Heartfield and Ludwig Meidner, stayed until the war was over. Freud, the only celebrity whose fame had preceded him, also remained in London until he died.

Kokoschka gravitated to Hampstead, that part of north London whose physical height was matched by the intellectual elevation of many of its inhabitants. At first he and Olda lived in a boarding house at 11a Belsize Avenue. Then, on 31 October 1938 they moved into a furnished flat at 45a King Henry's Road.

Although nothing came of Kokoschka's grander hopes, he did have more success than most of his fellow artists then struggling to survive. Fred Uhlman, who had assisted in the organization of the 'German Art Exhibition' had married an English aristocrat, Diana Croft, whose brother Michael was an art collector. In 1938 he commissioned Kokoschka first to paint a portrait of himself and then, some months later, of another sister, Posy. He also introduced the artist to wealthy friends in the hope that they too would sit for him. Another important patron during these early years in London was Edward Beddington-Behrens, who arranged for commissions from a wide circle of friends.

In Prague Kokoschka had not been politically active. Even his contacts with the association of émigré artists named after him were minimal. Apart from a poster and a drawing of 'La Passionaria' which expressed support for the anti-Fascist cause in Spain, Kokoschka produced no political art in Prague. In London the situation was different and almost from the moment he arrived Kokoschka took a keen interest in refugee organizations and in assisting the propaganda effort.

The most important of these organizations was the *Freier Deutscher Kulturbund*, the Free German League of Culture. It was founded in December 1938 in Fred Uhlman's Hampstead house where, among those present at that first meeting, were the distinguished writer and critic from Berlin Alfred Kerr, the film producer Berthold Viertel, Stefan Zweig, one of the most famous Austrian novelists, and Kokoschka himself. They were all elected presidents of the new association. Only Kokoschka remained in office until the end of the war, however: Viertel and Zweig soon left England for America and

Kerr resigned in 1941 by which time the association was dominated by communists.

The circumstances in which the *Kulturbund* came about are interesting and representative of the efforts of many English people to assist artists from the continent not merely to gain admission to Britain but to find employment and accommodation when they arrived there.

In the summer of 1938 the collector and Surrealist painter Roland Penrose (one of the organizers of the 'German Art Exhibition') received a letter from the brother of the Czech playwright Karel Čapek which requested English artists to help the *Kokoschkabund*. The result was an 'Artists' Refugee Committee' whose headquarters were in Fred Uhlman's house. As Diana Uhlman remembered: 'Somehow we raised enough money and support to bring the whole group of about 22 people over to England. We also helped a great many other refugee artists in different ways.'

The committee persuaded various well-known people to act as guarantors (necessary for the granting of visas) and also to apply for work permits on behalf of the mistresses of artists who did not wish to leave them behind. These work permits were for domestic workers and the fact that work permits for foreign nationals wishing to become cleaners, housemaids and cooks were freely available, speaks volumes about English society at the time.

As the refugees arrived, one group of friends in Hampstead 'arranged to give square meals to two or three of them at a time on a rota basis. Others arranged English classes. . . . Incidentally, I had to spend a small portion of our fund on marriage licences.' The artists had to marry their mistresses to make them acceptable to the 'landladies or hostesses of 35 years ago' who could not contemplate having their houses cleaned by any domestic living in sin.

The Refugee Committee was highly successful and the Free German League of Culture grew naturally out of it. It quickly became the most important organization of its kind in Britain. It published a magazine and regularly staged plays and reviews. By May 1940 it had branches in many cities outside London, counted 1,226 Germans and 102 Britons among its members. Its honorary presidents included distinguished Germans such as Einstein and Thomas Mann (both of whom were living in the USA) and Britons such as Vaughan Williams, Julian Huxley, J. B. Priestley and Gilbert Murray. Kokoschka was not only involved in activities organized by German refugees. He occasionally wrote for newspapers such as *Der Zeitspiegel*, Mirror of the Times, published by exiled Austrians and he participated in some of their activities.

Kokoschka and Olda had been living in England for almost a year when the war which had been threatening for so long finally broke out. When, on 3 September 1939, France and Britain declared war on Germany after the *Wehrmacht* had marched into Poland, Olda and Kokoschka were no longer in London. They had moved to Polperro on the southern coast of Cornwall where it was much cheaper to live than in the capital.

Their feelings on the outbreak of war must have been confused. They must have been relieved that the uncertainty was over but even more apprehensive than ever about the future. Germany was not only strong, it had also signed a non-aggression pact with the Soviet Union which secured its eastern frontier and allowed it to concentrate on the battle in the west where Britain and France were ill-prepared and morale was low. Not that the effects of the war were felt in Britain during the autumn of 1939; it was a period in which most people waited anxiously for something dramatic to happen.

Kokoschka and Olda had arrived in Polperro on 9 August 1939 and moved into a cottage on the cliffs above the picturesque fishing village which, like Newlyn and St Ives, had attracted many artists to live and work there since the late nineteenth century. Kokoschka and Olda remained in Cornwall for nine months.

In Polperro Kokoschka began to work with coloured pencils, a medium which allowed him to combine linear effects with the transparency of water-colours. He also produced four oil paintings in Polperro. The most important is *The Crab*, now in the Tate gallery, London, which shows the giant creature of the title against the background of Polperro harbour in a storm. The crab appears to be about to pounce on a tiny man desperately swimming for the safety of the shore. According to J. P. Hodin who later discussed the painting with Kokoschka:

The theme was hospitality. . . . The destiny of the hunted man becomes a parable of the times. How could the artist forget the suicides committed in the first confusion in the airports and harbours of England by the men who thought they had reached safety, but who were turned away?

According to Edward Beddington-Behrens, however, the artist's friend and patron who eventually bought the painting, Kokoschka told him that the small figure in the sea represented both himself and Czechoslovakia. The Crab stands for Chamberlain who would need only to stretch out a claw to effect a rescue but simply sits there watching.

In addition to two landscapes of Polperro Kokoschka also painted another political picture in the Cornish fishing village. This was *Private Property* which appears to be lost and is known only from photographs. It denounced the greed implicit in the capitalist system as one of the major causes of the war.

Kokoschka and Olda had to move away from Polperro because foreigners were not permitted to live on the coast after the fall of France in June 1940. Presumably it was thought that some of them might wish to signal to enemy ships and submarines. Germans and Austrians, moreover, were declared enemy aliens and interned, many of them on the Isle of Man. At least Kokoschka was saved from that humiliating fate. Protected by his Czech passport, he was a citizen of an occupied allied country with a government in exile in London. Kokoschka was not sorry that he had to leave Cornwall, however. The climate there was not good for him and he had felt very tired and ill for most of the time he was in Polperro.

In common with all other refugees and many Britons, Kokoschka believed the internment laws to be counter-productive. It might well be that some of those who had sought refuge were Nazi spies and saboteurs; but the vast majority were staunch anti-fascists of whom great use could have been made had they been free to contribute to the war effort instead of languishing behind barbed wire. At least on the Isle of Man in summer the female internees did something to test the patience and sense of propriety of their guards by insisting on sunbathing in the nude on the beaches.

Back in London, Kokoschka and Olda at first sought lodgings in the Strand Palace Hotel and then, in July, moved to a house in Boundary Road, Hampstead. The bombing raids and the damp (which badly affected Kokoschka's worsening bronchitis) forced them to move yet again, this time to a block of modern flats in the Finchley Road which, although no less likely a target for the German bombs, was equipped with central heating.

Conditions in London at that time were bleak. The bombing raids had begun in earnest and living conditions were grey and dispiriting. Food and clothes were rationed; travel was difficult; the fear that Britain would soon be invaded and fall to the German army was ever-present. Many of Kokoschka's friends managed to get away to America and, for a time, the artist was again in a state of near panic. By June 1940 he was searching for a way to get Olda to the United States even if he were unable to accompany her. His state of mind emerges clearly from a letter he sent to W. R. Valentiner in April 1941:

I must admit that I find it difficult to understand the bureaucratic methods of some American officials, for they are often the cause of martyrdom and even of the death of those who are subject to the sadistic-religious mania which has spread from Germany and is unconsciously supported in neutral countries by officialdom. I understand the reasons for immigration control, but the small difficulties, caused perhaps to neighbouring countries, would be as nothing compared with what the refugees could expect at home. . . . I was only a persecuted artist, an unwanted immigrant, even though the University of Chicago had invited me to come and teach . . . not only as the greatest artist of the time, but also as a man who wanted to initiate American youth into the mystery of true art. If I die during the war it will be thanks to the red handkerchief of Mr.

But even though, as it seems, Kokoschka received at least one invitation to work in the United States, the necessary visa was not forthcoming. He and Olda were obliged to stay in London and cope with the bombing and the other worsening problems of daily life. It would be wrong to pretend that Kokoschka and Olda were miserable in London, however, or that they repeatedly thought of leaving Britain. There may have been a moment of panic when France fell, but they soon realized that it was possible to survive in England. Olda Kokoschka remembers these years with pleasure and is thankful that she and her husband remained in London rather than move to the United States, where it would have been even more difficult to live without financial security.

On 15 May 1941 Kokoschka finally married Olda, whose quiet determination, refusal to panic and magisterial bearing helped him emotionally to survive what, he now realized, had been the most difficult years of his life. The wedding took place in an air-raid shelter, the temporary location of the Hampstead registry office, and Kokoschka's best man was another refugee artist, the sculptor Uli Nimptsch, only recently released from internment. Olda's parents, who had managed to escape from Prague and had been living close to the Kokoschkas in Finchley Road since September 1940, were not present at the ceremony because they had not been told about the wedding. There were no celebrations. Olda thinks they all went to the cinema afterwards.

Friends of the Kokoschkas, the economist Korner and his wife, had assisted the couple ever since their arrival in England. Korner had bought a large house near Port William in the south west of Scotland and he urged Kokoschka to take a holiday there and benefit from the peace and quiet it provided. It was the House of Elrig later made famous by Gavin Maxwell. The Kokoschkas stayed there from the beginning of September until the end of October 1941. It was the first of almost annual visits to Scotland, the last of which occurred in 1946.

Between 1939 and 1943 Kokoschka painted a series of political pictures. With the exception of the scarcely polemical painting of the children playing outside their orphanage on the outskirts of Vienna, the graphics later inspired by the Spanish civil war, and the self-portrait executed in Prague in 1937 which the artist called *Self-portrait as a degenerate artist*, these are the first political works in Kokoschka's *œuvre* and were to be his last. The two executed in Polperro have already been discussed but they were not the earliest. Kokoschka had already begun another before he moved to Cornwall, which was not completed until 1941. This is *The Red Egg*, an allegory in which a roast chicken representing Czechoslovakia flies away from a plate on which it has laid a red egg. Prague burns in the background. Hitler and Mussolini appear near the table; under the table sits a cat wearing a French Republican bonnet and in the middle distance the British lion, its tail curled into the sterling sign, sits on a pedestal bearing the legend IN PACE MUNICH.

Alice in Wonderland, a comment on the *Anschluss*, followed in 1942, the year in which Kokoschka also painted *The Loreley*, in which the consequences of British prevarication and loss of naval supremacy are satirized. *Marianne-Maquis*, also of 1942, hints at French cowardice.

The last of these political allegories dates from 1943. It is called *What We are Fighting for* and, according to Kokoschka, 'was the one I meant most seriously'. His own description of the painting cannot be improved upon.

A bishop is blessing the troops, and with his free hand is dropping a penny into the Red Cross collecting-box; an endless procession of prisoners file along with hands raised; in a rickshaw pulled by Gandhi sit the Governor of the Bank of England, Montague Norman, the President of the Reichsbank, Hjalmar Schacht, and a Marshal of France; in the foreground lies a starving mother holding an emaciated child who is playing with a rat. The prospering American munitions industry appears as a globe-like monster with two levers for arms, one pulling out a blue rabbit, signifying peace, as an emblem of hope for the future, while the other crams human bones into the armaments machine which turns them into cartridges. In the right foreground stands a bust of Voltaire with the inscription CANDIDE, i.e., 'the best of all possible worlds'.

Few of the great modern painters have been moved to make

paintings which directly comment on political events. This is not because of their lack of interest in the issues but rather because they considered that art was no longer capable of moving minds, that the language of advanced art, although in itself radical, was either inappropriate or inadequate to the task.

There are exceptions, but they are very few. They are to be found in the German art of the 1920s, especially in the work of George Grosz and Otto Dix. There is also Picasso's *Guernica*. But neither he nor the Germans resorted to the ossified allegorical language which for so long had served academic painters wishing to make statements of this kind. Yet Kokoschka did use such language, and in spite of all the modern trappings of style, it inevitably let him down. The nature of the message is also entirely unexceptional. For all their obvious sincerity these works fail.

Perhaps one of the reasons for the failure of these political paintings is that they were inspired less by anger than by despair. Throughout the war Kokoschka was depressed and confused. Unlike most of the refugees and many of the British people, he knew he could not see the struggle in terms of absolute good and absolute evil, and he feared that whichever side was defeated it would be all Europe that would lose. He also perceived distressing parallels between the Habsburg and the British empires. He had experienced the destruction of the former, now he was a witness to the decline of the latter.

The effects on Kokoschka's state of mind of the hardships he was experiencing can be clearly judged from photographs of the artist. In 1939 he was fifty-three years old but appears younger. His hair is dark, his face relatively unlined. By 1942 he seems to have aged by more than a decade.

One other painting, a portrait, belongs to this group of political pictures. In June 1941 Germany invaded the Soviet Union which now became Britain's ally. In March 1942 Kokoschka received a commission, arranged by his patron Beddington-Behrens, to paint the Soviet ambassador to London, Ivan Maisky. The fee was extraordinarily generous – £1,000 – and even though the Kokoschkas were in dire financial straits, the artist donated the money to the Soviet government on condition that it be used to help the wounded – German as well as Russian – who had fought in the battle of Stalingrad. The painting was later donated to the Tate Gallery.

In 1941 Kokoschka was approached by another refugee who wanted to write his biography. This was Edith Hoffmann, an art historian who devoted the major part of her energies to the task for the next two years. The book which was eventually published in 1947 (with a foreword by Herbert Read and a lengthy appendix by Kokoschka himself) is an astonishing achievement, written as it was without access to any documents and to none of the major paintings produced before the war.

Hoffmann had to rely heavily on Kokoschka's memory for details of his life and work and this was not her only problem. Kokoschka had a clear idea of how the book should be written and what was to be included and what left out. Hoffmann was expressly forbidden to name Alma Mahler or Anna Kallin, for example, was obliged to allow two of Kokoschka's essays to be printed after the conclusion of the biography and had to agree to the closest scrutiny of her manuscript. Faber and Faber, who published the book, became accustomed to letters from the artist's solicitor insisting on additions and deletions. It is extraordinary that the biography proved to be at all reliable; yet it remains the best book about Kokoschka in English.

When Hoffmann began to work on her biography, the Kokoschkas were living in a flat in Park Lane in Mayfair (to which they had moved in December 1943) and the artist worked in a studio in another building in the same street. Edward Beddington-Behrens had arranged the accommodation. In peacetime one of the most exclusive and expensive districts of London, Mayfair had been deserted by most of its inhabitants during the war and it was therefore possible to live there for little money as long as the nerves were strong enough to withstand the constant fear of being hit by a bomb.

The flat was at 55, the studio at 99a Park Lane and according to J. P. Hodin, who saw the studio for the first time in 1944, it was

a big quiet room with a skylight. . . . Hanging from the ceiling was a ring with a celluloid parrot and a multi-coloured electric light bulb.

On the chimney-piece to the right I saw some crinkled silver and gold paper, a few dried-up flowers, a porcelain partridge, a piece of rock crystal and some pink shells.

That arrangement of objects served as the artist's landscape 'to help him forget that he was in a city' and was, apart from the painting equipment and a large, throne-like chair used for portraits, the only personal touch in a room left unchanged since the previous tenant had departed.

Although the war was coming to an end, the dangers from the bombing to those living in London were as great as ever. By then the Germans had resorted to the 'doodle-bug', the pilotless rocket-bomb called the V1 which, although often erratic in its course, frequently fell to earth with devastating effect. While Kokoschka was working in his Park Lane studio on a portrait of Kathleen, Countess of Drogheda, one of these rockets exploded in Hyde Park on the other side of the road. Kokoschka and his sitter were lucky to escape with their lives. As it was, all the windows in the house were shattered by the blast except for those in the studio. In view of this dramatic event (which entirely failed to disturb the composure of the Countess) it is surprising that the completed painting was at all successful. In fact it is one of the best of Kokoschka's later portraits.

By no means all of Kokoschka's experiences in Park Lane were as unpleasant or dangerous. One day there was a knock on the door and a prosperous-looking man smoking a cigar stood outside. Kokoschka recognized him instantly, even though he had not seen him since his visit to London in 1926. His name was Ben Tobert and he was the taxi driver assigned to look after Kokoschka when the artist was painting the tigon and other animals at the Regent's Park Zoo eighteen years before.

Tobert had heard that Kokoschka was living in London and had discovered his address. Thanks to Kokoschka, he explained, he had become a wealthy man. He had watched fascinated as Kokoschka had inspected the windows of antique shops on their trips through London together and had listened carefully to the comments the artist made on this piece and that. After the war had begun Tobert had bought a large quantity of silver very cheaply and had made his fortune by selling it to America. In gratitude he now wanted to present the painter with a racehorse. A more inappropriate gift to an artist living in reduced circumstances in a flat in the middle of London can scarcely be imagined.

SEVENTEEN

The end of the war in May 1945 did little to restore Kokoschka's spirits. Europe lay in ruins. The past, already partially obliterated in 1918, was now gone for ever. Most of the old Habsburg empire was occupied by the Russians; the western parts of Austria and Germany were occupied by their Allies; the cities of Berlin and Vienna had been divided between the Allies into microcosms of the countries of which they were the capitals. At best political expediency, at worst crass stupidity ruled.

Kokoschka made his feelings plain enough in a letter written to Alfred Neumayer in 1945:

the world to which I should like to return, the world in which I travelled as a happy wanderer, naturally no longer exists. Great cities have disappeared from the face of the earth, great countries have become deserts. Not even murder has ceased: it is being continued coldly and systematically. No less inhuman than the murder with weapons and machines. Power politics has extended the blockade of starvation beyond the 'cease-fire'. The destruction of cultural monuments (only the sad remains of my native city Vienna tell of her former glory) is connected with the eradication of humanist values in a way which makes the unfeeling attitude to human life which we despised in fascism seem almost normal. 10,000 children in various liberated countries are being subjected to death by starvation, cold and spiritual despair, only because they belong to undesirable minorities. Their only crime is that they belong to a language group which is not that of their rulers. Hitler's seed is growing. His diseased brain dreamed up the idea of collective guilt and the post-war world unhappily remains faithful to the crazy notion of a madman by conducting trials according to such concepts. I cannot live in such a world! I feel personally responsible for the crimes of the society of which I am a member.

Uppermost in Kokoschka's mind was the fate of the German-speakers in Czechoslovakia and the war crimes tribunal at Nuremburg. He felt impotent and isolated in Britain. It would be fair to say that Kokoschka had never been particularly fond of Britain. Although he was grateful for the refuge he had been given, enjoyed the common respect for privacy and admired the tolerance of individual opinions however extreme or eccentric, he, like so many other foreigners, found the complexities of the class system incomprehensible, the insularity frustrating and the belief in the superiority of everything British (in spite of all evidence to the contrary) astonishing. He was also demoralized by the pervading lack of interest in the visual arts.

He considered moving to America or returning to Austria where, as letters from the great and the good continually announced, he was assured of a warm welcome. In 1946 the Mayor of Vienna sent him a ten-page telegram urging him to come home and accept the honours that would be showered upon him.

Not only anger at what he took to be either cynical or naïve prevented him; the state of Vienna itself was a sufficient deterrent. As he wrote (in English) to a friend in October 1946:

In Vienna there are only 4 or five posh restaurants for the 'liberators', where the 'natives' are not allowed. Not even soup-kitchens, these 4 robber-armies have organised, and although it is over a year that they have installed themselves in ruined Vienna at the place where the Nazi oppressed the people before. Exactly in November the Unra stops supplying the 300–400 calories distributed to the populace. Of course younger woman get sometimes a few cigarettes free for becoming whores, the bordells are the only Planwirtschaft [planned economy] on which all 4 Big Power agree whole hearted in Vienna . . . such is the fate of the first invaded country which had been left without help from outside . . . all the food comes to England where they fear starvation as during the victorian days when they ruled the whole world and had the biggest and dirtiest slums.

Kokoschka's pessimism about the future of the world emerges even more clearly in a long essay which he wrote in December 1945 (A Petition from a Foreign Artist to the Righteous People of Great Britain for a Secure and Present Peace) and which sets out his fears and criticisms of international power politics, of the effects of an overriding faith in science, technology and progress, of the lessening of respect for the individual in the modern, bureaucratic state, and the deleterious effects on the education of children of standardized theories imposed from above. Kokoschka felt this essay so important that he insisted (in the face of some opposition from his biographer and her publishers) on having it included as an appendix to the English biography which appeared in 1947.

The essay is rambling and difficulties in translation blunted the urgency of its message in places; but forty years later many phrases strike a clearly contemporary chord:

In spite of their better knowledge of the fatal results the scientists will continue their researches.

Political economists are as intolerant as clergymen in their inability to admit that ideologies diametrically opposed to each other may be equally inaccurate.

The weakening sense of individual responsibility strengthens the superstitious belief that salvation can be found in a kind of super-state.

Once the biologist has fixed heredity on utility lines, 'the greatest happiness of the greatest number' is only a question of time necessary to produce by black magic the mind which bears no 'dangerous thought'.

Such clear-sighted fears, strengthened by the new Soviet hegemony in Central and Eastern Europe and by the western Allies' willingness to see the world divided into essentially two spheres of influence, were in part, of course, inspired by personal considerations. The only countries where Kokoschka had a considerable reputation were those which were no longer able to offer him a secure or comfortable life. He was grateful to Britain – 'the only country to admit me' – in his hour of need and the country in which he felt able freely to speak his mind; but he could not see much prospect of a secure future in a country which continued to be unimpressed by his achievements and which was now increasingly turned in upon itself. At a moment of austerity almost as great as that suffered by the defeated countries, Britain was experiencing a crisis of identity uncannily familiar to anyone in touch with the mood in Austria after 1918.

There were other reasons for the strength of Kokoschka's emotions. Throughout the war he had been unable to communicate with his sister in Prague or with his brother in Vienna. In 1945 he quickly learned that Berta had been very ill and that Bohuslav, meanwhile married and with a two-year-old son, was virtually starving. At first Kokoschka felt that there was little he could do apart from sending money and sacrificing valuable ration coupons on food parcels, but in 1946 when Berta's husband died he went to Prague for the funeral. Not until 1947 did he visit Vienna, however.

The old resentment at the way Kokoschka had been treated by his native city welled up at regular intervals. Former Nazis, denying their past or glibly explaining it away, were insinuating themselves into the new social fabric, and the only people manifestly free from taint, the communists, were working hard to establish a new kind of dictatorship. Above all, however, Kokoschka continued to be bitter about what he felt was Vienna's neglect of his achievement and its enthusiasm for the work of some of his contemporaries who had not been obliged to leave their native land. He was already over sixty and, with most of his life behind him, was anxious to shape the judgement of posterity while he could. He felt that he should already have been universally celebrated as the grand old man of modern painting but had been prevented from receiving his due by the war.

Others had meanwhile flourished and Kokoschka reserved special scorn for the artist of whom he had always been suspicious and with whom he had always seen himself as in competition: Picasso.

In 1946 Picasso was, according to Kokoschka, 'causing great excitement' in London

as the persecuted 'degenerate' artist. A little late. We were there earlier and have not in the mean time become the owners of a series of profitable houses in the Rue de Rivoli. I find it daft to become a property speculator for my old age. Am merely curious whether he leaves it to the Communist Party in his will or to the millionaires who will go bankrupt in the next Wall Street crash.

Although British law entitles any resident who has been in the country for more than five years to apply for nationality, the law was suspended in the case of refugees from Europe, and only after the war was over were the usual regulations reintroduced. In 1947 Kokoschka applied for a British passport and received it. He might have exercised his right to become an Austrian again but he did not and remained British until the end of his life. Repeated attempts by the Austrian government to persuade him to change his mind came to nothing until 1975 and then under extraordinary circumstances.

It must have been galling for the Austrian authorities. Anxious to revive the cultural life that had been suffocated after the *Anschluss*, desperate for cultural heroes untainted by Nazi associations, it was denied its claim to the greatest and most internationally famous Austrian painter. It resorted to subterfuge. When offers of a professorship, of sinecures and of a generous pension were rejected, the government resorted to a legal change. Previously citizenship could only be bestowed on someone who personally applied for it. Now it became possible to grant citizenship by proxy. In 1975 the Chancellor, Bruno Kreisky, himself applied on Kokoschka's behalf without, it seems, the artist's knowledge. The new law is called the *Erlass Kokoschka* and remains in force although it has not been used since.

A British passport made it considerably easier for Kokoschka to travel and his first trip to the Continent after the war was to Prague where he visited his sister and then to Vienna where he wanted to search for his brother Bohuslav. The house in Liebhartstal had been requisitioned during the war, was in use as a store and in a sad state of disrepair. Bohuslav had been in hiding for a time and then found work as a labourer. He, his wife and son, unable to move back into the house, were now living in a shed in the garden.

The return to Austria was exciting and dangerous. Kokoschka travelled by train which passed through the Russian zone of occupation. Then

during a blizzard at night, in a wilderness somewhere beyond Linz, Russian soldiers stopped the train, and with fixed bayonets directed all the passengers holding British passports to get out. Carrying a heavy package of medicines, food and so on, I was forced to scramble up a steep slope, and fast, or risk ending up with a bayonet in my back. Resistance would simply have led to my arrest. I stood in the freezing cold, trying to decipher official forms printed in English, which the soldier in charge could not have read even if they had been in Russian. I was shivering and helpless. And then the engine driver recognized my name. . . . He hid me for the time being in his coal tender. The other passengers were made to wait for a train that did not touch the Russian zone; my train went on.

Vienna was in a sorry state. Spared the kind of bombing that had reduced Berlin to a wasteland, the city had nevertheless sustained severe damage. In the centre, the cathedral had lost its roof and was half destroyed.

Kokoschka did everything he could for the welfare of his brother's family. He met the Mayor of Vienna, contacted everyone of influence he could and took steps to ensure that the house would be restored to Bohuslav and then returned by air to London. He remained worried about his family for some time and especially about his sister, obliged to live out her last years in a country now hostile to all German-speakers. The most obvious remedy would have been for Berta to leave Prague and join Bohuslav and his family in the house in Liebhartstal; but Berta had never got on well with her brother and Kokoschka knew that the solution was unworkable. Even though severe rationing in Britain made life difficult enough for Kokoschka and Olda, he characteristically thought of his family first, not only sending parcels of food and medicine to Vienna and Prague but encouraging others to do the same. When Alma Mahler contacted him again shortly after the war ended he immediately asked her to send a care package to his brother Bohuslav which she did. His reply to New York, where Alma Mahler had been living for some time, provides evidence that he had long since come to terms with the hurt she had inflicted upon him thirty years before. He now regarded her as a friend. When he heard that she was growing deaf, was drinking heavily and was unwell, he wrote her warm, comforting letters. She needed his sympathy and he was strong enough to provide it.

In 1947 the first post-war exhibition of Kokoschka's work was held in Basle at the Kunsthalle, a museum with one of the greatest collections of modern art in the world. For Kokoschka the exhibition was a symbolic event. It reassured him that his reputation was intact and that most of the works he feared lost or destroyed had been preserved. Many of the early portraits were on show, as was *The Tempest* which had been confiscated from the Hamburg museum and was now permanently in Basle. The Kunsthalle had bought it at the Lucerne auction of works plundered by the Nazis.

Another large exhibition was staged in America in 1948 and 1949. Organized by James S. Plaut of the Institute of Contemporary Art in Boston, it toured to four other cities, including Washington, New York and San Francisco. It was the first substantial showing of the artist's work outside Europe even though, as Plaut admitted in the catalogue, almost a hundred of Kokoschka's paintings had by then found their way into American public and private collections.

A letter from Kokoschka to Plaut was printed as a preface to the catalogue and it returns to the artist's recurrent obsession with his historical position. 'Paris', he reminded his readers 'was not the only Mecca of modern art.' The letter also answers the criticisms which had been multiplying since the late 1920s that Kokoschka had been prepared for too long to rest on his laurels and had not been brave enough to allow his art to change.

Some visitors, well acquainted with modern art movements, may be puzzled to find that in my work there is none of the experimenting with all the different phases, from impressionism, pointillism, cubism to non-objective art, which they are used to. The explanation is simple enough: I never intended to entertain my contemporaries with the tricks of a juggler, in the hope of being recognized as an original. I simply wanted to create around me a world of my own in which I could survive the progressive disruption going on all over the world.

Whether continuous change in an artist's work is necessary or even desirable is a question best left to the art theorists. Kokoschka's statement is none the less profoundly conservative and coexists uneasily with the claims he continued to make about the originality and even the revolutionary influence of the work he produced as a young man.

Those revolutionary years were far behind him. He had long since matured and, in spite of all the external crises, his art had mellowed. For many years he continued to paint similar subjects in a similar style. His favourite motifs were the portrait and the landscape, and in 1947, remaining for several months in Switzerland after the Basle exhibition, he produced a portrait of the industrialist and art patron Werner Reinhart as well as a series of mountain views, including two of the Matterhorn.

Since 1946 had been a relatively unproductive year (there were few oils but many watercolours) 1947 marked something of a new beginning and there is no doubt that the Basle retrospective gave him new energy and determination. He was buoyed up by the proof that his reputation had survived the war unscathed. He was also relieved to discover that the exhibition's organizers had been able to track down several of the paintings he feared had been destroyed by the Nazis.

The Basle exhibition demonstrated that he had not been forgotten and the American show the following year promised that his fame would now extend across the Atlantic. Nor was that all. While 126 of his works were touring in the United States, a further sixteen were shown at the 23rd Venice Biennale.

Out walking in Venice one day, Kokoschka was surprised to be addressed by a stranger who proudly announced that he was the owner of the landscape *View of the Dents du Midi* as well as a number of other Kokoschka paintings which had been removed from German museums by the Nazis and were feared lost. The collector had simply suggested to some prominent Nazi that he exchange objects from his collection for some of the modern masterpieces which had been confiscated. In this way he acquired an important collection of modern German art.

Kokoschka might have been annoyed by the story but delight at the recovery of several of his paintings was his only reaction. Almost immediately after the chance meeting with the collector, Kokoschka excitedly told the story to Walter Feilchenfeldt, once Cassirer's partner and Kokoschka's dealer before the war. Feilchenfeldt quickly travelled to the Tyrol where the collector lived and bought the *Dents du Midi* for his personal collection.

So it was that the past came to be reconstructed little by little. Less had been irretrievably lost than Kokoschka had first feared and, as the Basle exhibition and the Venice Biennale demonstrated, even his reputation on the Continent appeared to be undamaged; indeed it appeared to have been enhanced by the enthusiasm of everyone for anything unsullied by the Nazi poison.

Only in England where Kokoschka and Olda continued to live in their small but comfortable flat on the Finchley Road was the pleasure of real fame denied him. In England the greatest attention he received was from the Inland Revenue which plagued him with tax demands.

EIGHTEEN

In 1949 Kokoschka had another thirty-one years to live. Already over sixty years old and continuing intermittently to suffer from the effects of the injuries sustained during the First World War, Kokoschka did not allow his pace to lessen. On the contrary, relishing the freedom to travel which had been denied him until 1945, he eagerly grasped every opportunity to work wherever commissions took him.

He undertook no fewer than three major trips in 1949: to Vienna, where he painted a portrait of the mayor, to Rome and, for the first time, to the United States, where he saw the exhibition which had begun its tour the year before and did some teaching in Boston.

Although portraits and landscapes remained his major subjects,

Kokoschka now extended his range to include classical mythology. He had tackled mythological themes before, of course, above all in print cycles such as *Orpheus and Eurydice* and *Columbus Bound*, but he had rarely employed such subjects in paintings and never on such a large scale as he did now. It was almost as though, in his old age, he wished to stake a final claim to greatness by returning to the kind of motifs and monumental formats which in the past had been regarded as the touchstones of artistic excellence.

The first of these classical paintings was *The Myth of Prometheus* on which Kokoschka worked for the first seven months of 1950. The medium – tempera – was consciously traditional, so too were the triptych format and the purpose of the work: it had been commissioned by the Austrian collector Count Antoine Seilern to decorate the ceiling of one of his rooms in his splendid house in South Kensington.

The Myth of Prometheus is a complex composition in which scores of figures are incorporated into a deep illusionistic space. In its brilliant orchestration of colour and atmosphere and its bravura handling it recalls Baroque decorative schemes and was thus entirely appropriate to the interests of the patron. At the University of Vienna Count von Seilern wrote his doctoral thesis on late Venetian illusionistic fresco painting.

Kokoschka returned to classical themes repeatedly during the next thirty years. His next monumental project was another triptych and deals with the battle of Thermopylae. It was begun in 1953 and now hangs in a lecture theatre in the University of Hamburg.

These two paintings were merely the most visible evidence of a growing fascination for the ancient world which characterizes the rest of Kokoschka's career. He began to travel regularly to Greece, to collect ancient Greek coins and to read more and more Greek literature in translation. Kokoschka now believed more passionately than ever that the only bulwark against what he saw to be contemporary barbarism was a return to the principles of classical humanism. As he wrote to a friend in 1971:

The collapse of Graeco-Roman culture as a result of Platonic illusionism and oriental ideologies; the great migration of peoples which injected into Christian beliefs the philosophy of the Celts . . . especially; the French Revolution which put an end to the individual and preached égalité in an age become mechanistic, a belief on which Marx set the seal as God was dethroned – these are the stopping points on the rails of progress. These, for Europe critical times become visible in the documents of the visual arts and the youth of the west must become aware of them if Europe is not to degenerate again into an oriental slave society. In art what human history is is made visible.

The Prometheus triptych was completed at the end of July 1950 when Kokoschka left London to spend the summer in Salzburg. This trip to Austria was immediately followed by an extended visit to Germany and marks the beginning of a new and more sympathetic attitude to Kokoschka's homeland.

While staying in Salzburg, painting views of the city and regularly attending concerts and the opera, Kokoschka was encouraged to think of ways in which he might directly contribute to the cultural life of the city and to the strengthening of its international ties. The result, in 1953, was a summer art school located in Salzburg castle and open to fee-paying students of any age and any background. The idea for the school may well have come from Kokoschka's experience of teaching at a summer school at Tanglewood, outside Boston, during his first visit to the USA in 1949 where music was an important part of the course. Until 1962 Kokoschka spent every summer in Salzburg teaching at the school. He greatly enjoyed the opportunity to influence enthusiastic amateurs unaffected by what he considered to be the baleful results of a conventional artistic training, and he loved working in such congenial surroundings. He taught during the day and every evening he went to the concerts and recitals which were part of the Salzburg Festival.

Kokoschka called his school the *Schule des Sehens* – the School of Seeing – a name intended to convey the idea that the emphasis of the instruction would fall less on the acquisition of technical skill than on the stimulation of the imagination which, Kokoschka had always been convinced, made everyone a potential artist. He was not the only teacher. Several sculptors assisted him, including his old friend Uli Nimptsch and, at various times, Manzu and Greco.

The *Schule des Sehens* remained a major part of Kokoschka's life for almost ten years; it continued after he was no longer strong enough to teach and remains a permanent summer fixture in Salzburg. Critics see the school as a pleasant indulgence for both teachers and students, as a scarcely serious enterprise intended for the children of the wealthy with time on their hands and for leisured middle-aged amateurs prepared to pay for the privilege of meeting famous artists and the opportunity to dabble in painting and drawing for a few weeks in a fairy-tale castle in one of Europe's most attractive cities.

Whatever the motives of Kokoschka's students and whatever the quality of the work they produced, the artist himself took the enterprise very seriously. Reports of his teaching make it clear that he had not lost his ability to be critical and encouraging at the same time. Part of a conversation he had with a student in his final year at the school was recorded and it reveals that his methods had not changed much since his time as a professor in Dresden: 'You ought to go to the museum again, look at something', he told the student.

A later Frans Hals, the faces of the old people . . . they hold the attention from close to, also from a distance. Art: to achieve increasing richness and at the same time increasing simplicity. . . . How poor Cézanne tormented himself with a peach: or Chardin – Cézanne was tiny by comparison. Don't lose that first vision. . . . Don't talk about technique, that is academy, school lessons. One must only love. No one forces you to paint. . . . School is crippling because it trains people to think of purpose. Paris has a beauty industry and painting is part of it. But painting has nothing to do with the beauty industry. Everything is permitted except compromise.

The writer Robert Jungk had the opportunity to observe Koko-schka in action at the *Schule des Sehens* and remembered that the artist advised students:

Let your eyes ring like a tuning-fork. Look suddenly at some object or a form, quickly and full of surprise. Record the sight within you and close your eyes. Then you will never forget the colours. Remember, and refresh yourselves with the memory. Only then look at the object again. You will see so much in it that you did not notice the first time.

Jungk also remembered the faces of some of the students:

The large, heavy head of a man in his mid-forties, a professor of chemistry, the astonished look of a fashion designer, the relieved smile of a grey-haired Dutch lady, the expression – changing from shyness to confidence – of a nun. Without embarrassment the master put his arm round her shoulder and explained: "Here, here in the back of your head and there in your heart – that is where the picture is created. Only what the spirit creates is real. But what reality is is something which not even the physicists know any more. Therefore they must become metaphysicians. But you, sister, you know it from your own experience. You must know it."

Jungk was writing in 1957 when Kokoschka was already seventy-one years of age, but his energy appeared to be unquenchable. Most evenings were devoted to concerts and Kokoschka would often drink and talk far into the night with conductors and performers. At breakfast the next day there would be meetings, with a dealer perhaps or with the director of an opera planned for next year's festival who wanted the artist to design the costumes and sets. Then at about nine o'clock he would go back to the castle to begin that day's teaching. He would return home at about three in the afternoon for a light meal and a rest. Then, before going into the town again, he would receive visitors.

Jungk also noticed something which had characterized Kokoschka's teaching from the moment he took his first life class at the Vienna School of Arts and Crafts: free from prescription of any kind, it was designed to bring out the ability latent in every student.

'What emerges from this unusual instruction,' Jungk wrote, 'is not "little Kokoschkas" but personalities who were given something which they basically always possessed without knowing it.'

The School of Seeing marked Kokoschka's reconciliation with Austria and at the same time he once again established close links with Germany, the country which had first recognized his genius. In 1950 he was commissioned to paint the President of the Federal Republic, Theodor Heuss, and from then on he travelled almost annually to Germany and especially to Hamburg, producing landscapes and portraits of the famous and influential. In 1951, for example, he was commissioned by the Hamburg Kunsthalle to paint Max Brauer, the first post-war mayor of the city. The portrait is one of the best of Kokoschka's later portraits, far more convincing a likeness of a powerful personality than most of the other paintings of public figures which the artist produced during an artistically difficult period. Kokoschka had great respect for Brauer and for his vision of a city rebuilt after almost total devastation. In 1956, the year of his seventieth birthday, he was awarded Germany's highest honour, the *Pour le Mérite*.

Kokoschka relished the attention he received from politicians, cities and museums. But the reconciliation with both Germany and Austria was more important for both countries than it was for him. Germany and Austria were anxious to win the public recognition of important artists and writers untainted by the Nazi past. To have been declared 'degenerate' was enough to ensure a cascade of honours and commissions.

But Kokoschka, more than any of the other victims of Nazi cultural policy, became the object of enthusiastic official attention. He became the unofficial court painter to the Federal Republic. He had painted Heuss and in 1966 he painted the Chancellor Konrad Adenauer. He painted other national politicians and he painted the mayors of great cities. German museums competed for examples of his work.

This elevation was observed with a variety of emotions by other artists. In 1954 Kokoschka's old adversary George Grosz visited Germany again after almost two decades of exile in the United States. After seeing an exhibition in Munich at which Kokoschka's work was represented, Grosz wrote to a friend that Kokoschka had become 'the semi-official painter of the Federal Republic'.

Grosz, whose own work had long since lost the bite and satirical edge that so distinguished it in the 1920s, also criticized Kokoschka's style.

He is entirely an 'Impressionist', he doesn't build up his oils, 'composing' isn't important to him, nor where the fingers end, or whether they're half cut off by the frame; he obviously doesn't know about the discoveries of the modern painters, neither pattern, design nor textures; the scandlapes [sic] make one think – at some remove of course – of the Englishman Turner, of the older Turner, see *The Fighting Temeraire*, etc.

The grudging comparison with Turner 'at some remove' does not disguise the harshness of Grosz's criticism which was motivated more by a dislike of all official or semi-official art than by envy of Kokoschka's obvious fame and financial success. In one point at least Grosz was wrong. Kokoschka knew everything about the discoveries of the modern painters, but he was not interested in them. Most of them indeed provided proof of the barbarism which, he was convinced, was threatening to engulf the world. The more extreme the experiments of his contemporaries, the more strident the claims made for them by the critics and cultural mandarins, the more conservative Kokoschka's attitudes became. Commenting in 1959 on recent claims for the artistic abilities of some chimpanzees, Kokoschka noted that 'art is used as propaganda in Russia but in West Germany a number of bad boys have succeeded in making society so stupid that, forgetting the classical heritage, it looks for the spiritual in daubings and forces not only painters to produce them but also the apes caged up in zoos.'

Time has demonstrated the justice of Kokoschka's scepticism. His attitudes to art had become conservative but they remained as individualistic as ever. As his reference to 'poor Cézanne' to his student in Salzburg revealed, he was never prepared slavishly to follow received opinion even of artists commonly held to number among the giants of world painting. What he said about the painters of the past as well as his contemporaries was almost always controversial and invariably intelligent. Mondrian for example was a kind of architect of a world lost to man rather than a great painter. He is too exclusively concerned with only one aspect of art, with the problem of proportions. He is a Puritan, a Calvinist, an Iconoclast. The subjective world that he communicates to us appears, in my eyes, tragically dull and uninteresting.

From the moment he set foot on the Continent again after the end of the Second World War Kokoschka thought about returning to some part of it to live. In 1951, in a Volkswagen, the first car they had ever owned, Olda and he explored the Valais in Switzerland looking for attractive places. Most of the houses were either too small or too expensive, too remote or situated at too great an altitude to permit easy access to someone of advancing years.

Forsaking the Vallais, they inspected the area around the north-eastern shores of Lake Geneva in the canton of Vaud. It was an area which Kokoschka had known well ever since his first trip abroad with Loos in 1909. Blonay, the village where he had lived for part of 1923, was also close by. The Kokoschkas eventually found a plot of land for sale on the outskirts of Villeneuve close to the Castle of Chillon and not far from Montreux. The price of land in that part of Switzerland was still reasonable at the time and after teaching in the United States Kokoschka had enough money to buy the plot and think about the kind of house he and Olda wanted to build on it.

The house was ready in 1953 when the Kokoschkas finally left England and moved to Villeneuve. The house is of modest size; even the studio, the biggest room, is not very large. The garden, however, is spacious and overlooks the lake. The Kokoschkas' house is a quiet and friendly place, obviously designed for a couple wanting privacy rather than the opportunity to entertain in style.

1953 was also the year in which Kokoschka began to teach at the *Schule des Sehens*, so for ten years Olda and he spent part of each summer at Salzburg. They also travelled for part of every spring. Essentially therefore they were in Villeneuve only for the autumn and winter. But the winters in the area are seldom harsh and the light is generally good at that time so Kokoschka was able to paint. He tried to make a point of beginning a new canvas on 1 January of each year.

At Villeneuve Kokoschka concentrated on his work. He went to bed and rose late, painting or drawing while the light held and writing once it had grown dark. He read a great deal, too, and liked listening to records played on his gramophone. During the last ten years of his life he wrote his autobiography and worked on an edition of his collected writings. He began to collect copies of his letters which had ended up in private and public collections throughout the world. He also concerned himself with identifying forgeries of his paintings and drawings which appeared on the market with increasing regularity and which provided unwelcome evidence of his fame and of the prices his works were fetching at auction.

When Kokoschka left England to live in Switzerland he did not turn his back on the country completely. He remained a British subject and was gratified by the signs that his achievement was gradually being recognized even in Britain. In 1959 he was created a Commander of the British Empire and in 1963 the University of Oxford awarded him an honorary doctorate.

The Kokoschkas travelled to London almost every year where so many of the friends they had made during the war continued to live. London was also the location of Kokoschka's most important dealer, Marlborough Fine Art. In 1960 the Marlborough staged an exhibition of Kokoschka's work executed in England and Scotland. Since its foundation after the war by two Austrian refugees, Frank Lloyd and Harry Fischer, the Marlborough had become the leading gallery specializing in contemporary art in London.

It was Fischer who took a special interest in Kokoschka's work and who, together with his son Wolfgang, was largely responsible for introducing the British public to modern German and Austrian art in general. The Marlborough staged the first English exhibitions of Kirchner and Nolde and of Klimt and Schiele for example.

Kokoschka did not have a contract with the Marlborough; he had refused all offers of written agreements since his last contract with Cassirer; but his association with the Marlborough was relatively untroubled and of great benefit to both parties. Thanks mostly to the energies of Harry Fischer the British Arts Council staged a large Kokoschka retrospective at the Tate Gallery in 1962. It was Kokoschka's first important exhibition in Britain and consisted of 291 paintings, drawings and prints.

The event was of the greatest significance for the artist who felt that the country which had given him refuge had now finally also given him his due. The reaction to the exhibition was warm, a mixture of delight and astonishment that such a major artist should have remained hidden from the general gaze for so long even though he had lived in Britain for no less than fifteen years. A critic writing in a German-language newspaper in New York described the exhibition's reception as one of embarrassment at the late discovery of an artist who, unknown and unrecognized, lived and worked in this country for so long and who only now and at last is being publicly honoured. In the *Guardian* Eric Newton feels like Cortez who was struck dumb on the mountain-top because he was overpowered by the colour and majesty of the view.

The new enthusiasm for Kokoschka in Britain was not unqualified, however. For several years the great portrait of Herwarth Walden was on loan to the Tate Gallery from a private British collection. When it was not in the basement it was usually badly hung on the stairs leading down to the restaurant and nothing could persuade the director to move the portrait to a better position. Although the owner had originally intended to bequeath it to the Tate, he was angered by the museum's lack of enthusiasm for one of the most important twentieth-century portraits, withdrew the picture and sold it to a museum in Germany.

In spite of the Tate's casual attitude to the Walden portrait, since bitterly regretted, the 1962 retrospective was enough to make Kokoschka feel that the reputation in Britain which he had for so long desired was now secure. There too he was finally regarded as the greatest modern Austrian artist.

Kokoschka continued to travel every spring until his ninetieth year. Not until then did he yield to the inevitable pressures of old age and especially failing sight. Already in 1972 he suspected that he would not be able to continue working for much longer and painted *Time Gentlemen Please*, a full-length nude self-portrait, its title ironically alluding to the call at closing-time of every pub landlord in Britain.

But Kokoschka did continue to paint for another five years. In view of the serious injuries he had sustained during the First World War it was something of a miracle that he had lived in relatively good health for so long. He had never quite recovered from the damage to his inner ear and had problems with balance until the end of his life. He also had difficulty walking because heavy smoking had caused a narrowing in his leg arteries. But it was his eyes which caused him the greatest difficulties.

In 1975, in his ninetieth year, he had an operation which failed to improve his sight; but the depression this caused was as nothing in comparison with the grief he experienced when, on 12 January 1976, his younger brother Bohuslav died. Somehow he managed to continue to paint and draw. One of his last portraits was of the German playwright Carl Zuckmayer whose wife had been a student in Kokoschka's art class at Eugenie Schwarzwald's school in Vienna.

Kokoschka's final years were marked by events which set the seal on his career. Numerous exhibitions throughout Europe celebrated his ninetieth birthday; an *œuvre* catalogue of his graphic work was published; the house in which he was born in Pöchlarn became a Kokoschka museum and archive.

Kokoschka died on 22 February 1980, a week before his ninety-fourth birthday, in a hospital in Montreux. He is buried in the cemetery at Clarens.

Almost the first posthumous honour was the announcement that the Austrian government had decided to fund an 'Oskar Kokoschka Prize' to be awarded every other year for outstanding achievement in the visual arts. Given Kokoschka's complicated feelings about the country of his birth and his lifelong opposition to non-figurative art there is something ironic about the first recipient of the prize: it was Hans Hartung, a German painter of abstract compositions. But if the Austrians were ignorant of, or had forgotten Kokoschka's implacable hostility to abstract art, one official action taken soon after the artist's death did much to make up for the years of hostility and neglect. When, in 1980, *The Tigon*, the great painting Kokoschka had made at the London Zoo, was put up for sale in New York, the Austrian Chancellor Bruno Kreisky immediately ordered that money should be made available for its purchase for the nation. For that Oskar Kokoschka the Austrian would have been grateful.

NINETEEN

We know a great deal about Kokoschka the artist. In spite of the lack of juvenilia, of the loss at the hands of the Nazis of some thirty paintings (of which photographs exist in any case) and some crucial problems of dating the earliest known work, we can follow his development in detail throughout an unusually long and productive life.

We know considerably less about Kokoschka the man. In spite of the autobiography, three biographies, countless reminiscences and memoirs and an edition of his collected writings, his personality remains elusive. In all the accounts of the artist's life it is not so much Kokoschka himself as the people around him who emerge with the greatest clarity: Loos, Kraus, Walden and Alma Mahler all appear as figures in the round while Kokoschka seems shadowy, contradictory.

Kokoschka never kept a diary and his autobiographical writings are an intentional mixture of fact and fantasy. He was an enthusiastic correspondent however, and his letters not only reveal much factual information but also provide valuable insights into his personality. Only one volume of letters, ending with 1919, has as yet been published and the definitive biography must wait until the remaining three volumes have appeared. Even then, however, important questions will remain unanswered. Alma Mahler's letters to Kokoschka were destroyed and the artist's letters to Loos and Käthe Richter will remain inaccessible for the foreseeable future. Without them any picture of the early, crucial period of Kokoschka's life must remain incomplete.

Time and time again Kokoschka's biographer, struggling to perceive the substance which casts the shadow, is confronted by the image which the artist himself created and assiduously cultivated from the start of his career. It is the image of an unusually gifted man fated to be an outsider: misunderstood and rejected as a young man and, as a mature successful artist, denied the greatest fame because he refused to follow the dictates of fashion.

It is a romantic image; it is also very modern inasmuch as many of Kokoschka's contemporaries did their best to create a similar mythology for themselves. Some of them went to even greater lengths than Kokoschka. Ernst Ludwig Kirchner for example, reconstructed his early career to support his own exaggerated claims to originality. He also became his own critic, inventing the French writer Louis de Marsalle to give his work the kind of attention denied him.

One of the most important elements in Kokoschka's image of himself is the real or pretended existence of supernatural powers. Romana Kokoschka, her son tells us, was gifted with second sight. Kokoschka himself was also able on occasion to see into the future and from time to time was visited by supernatural experiences, some of which have been described already.

The earliest such experience occurred in the park near Kokoschka's home on the outskirts of Vienna when, as a small boy, he blew up an ants' nest and nearly died. Some years later, walking home with Ernst Reinhold after the first performance of *Murderer, the Hope of Women*, Kokoschka had the experience of levitation:

I had an eerie sensation of floating in mid-air. I still vividly remember hanging sideways three feet above the pavement. I was slanted downwards to the left, my legs in the air, the back of my head perilously close to the ground, my arms flailing, trying to get hold of something.

Later still, on this occasion in London, but also (and curiously) with Reinhold, Kokoschka had his vision of two people from the past, a governess and a little girl who disappeared into a miniature landscape.

Such experiences complement accounts of Kokoschka's uncanny abilities as a painter of portraits. According to some of his sitters he was able to see into their past as well as their future, to reveal in his paintings of them aspects of their past known only to themselves. There is also evidence that he also had occasional flashes of intuition about his own future. In several of the posters, drawings and paintings executed before the First World War, Kokoschka portrays himself as a wounded figure, occasionally even as a wounded warrior. The wound to which the figure frequently and dramatically draws attention, is always in the general area of the wound which Kokoschka in fact sustained while fighting on the eastern front in 1915.

The rationalist will find it difficult to accept such evidence at face value. Reinhold himself did not see either the levitation or the little girl in London, and it is easy enough to explain Kokoschka's supernatural experiences as the momentary effects of a mental crisis. The claims of second sight made for at least one of the portraits are also open to doubt.

Kokoschka says that his portrait of Forel shows a man suffering from the effects of a stroke: the professor's left side appears in the picture to be partially paralysed. Yet Forel, according to Kokoschka, did not have a stroke until some time after the painting was finished. Forel's autobiography implies a rather different course of events. Although the scientist was generally unhappy with the painting, he did approve of 'one eye and the left disabled hand' which were 'particularly good and expressive'. Had the hand not been paralysed when Forel was sitting for the portrait he could not have failed to comment on the artist's extraordinary, prophetic powers.

More important than the authenticity of the gifts with which Kokoschka credited himself is the weight he places on them in accounts of his life. They are a vital part of his self-image and also reveal how he wished his work to be judged. In his biography as in his painting, superficial, mundane facts must yield to an inner and higher truth, that of the imagination.

That is why fact and fantasy are inextricably intertwined in all Kokoschka's autobiographical writings; why episodes in the allegedly fictional *A Sea Ringed with Visions* are interchangeable with episodes in the allegedly factual *My Life*. All truth for Kokoschka was subjective: the external world was a projection of an inner vision and the only valid art was that in which the vision was preserved.

As vital as the image of the artist as visionary is, equally vital is the image of the artist as victim. He was the victim of blind and savage critics in Vienna, of a hostile public, and of dealers and artists like Oppenheimer and Schiele who sought to profit from travesties of his own unique achievement.

There is no doubt that Vienna was and remained largely hostile to Kokoschka for decades after he made his début, just as there is no doubt that several artists, and most notably Oppenheimer and Schiele, were influenced by his work. Equally clear, however, is that Kokoschka exaggerated his persecution at the hands of critics and mistakenly saw a conspiracy at work.

It is almost as though Kokoschka required evidence of persecution as proof of his own genius and from time to time invited adverse comment as a means of drawing attention to himself. In 1909 he had his head shaved and began to dress in suits made by the court tailor. The contrast between the shaven head of a convict and the clothes of a gentleman was ostentatious and intended to provoke interest and surprise. Kokoschka was neither a convict nor an aristocrat. As an artist, he felt like an aristocrat; as a man, he knew he came from an unexceptional background. Blessed with a high degree of natural intelligence, he knew that in the Vienna of the time the key to success lay more in artifice than art. Even a painter had to become something of an actor in order to make his way. Notoriety is also a kind of fame.

'Mad Kokoschka' – *Der tolle Kokoschka* – was a figure of his own making and he continued to work upon it until the 1920s when his artistic success seemed assured. In Dresden it was the doll in the image of Alma Mahler which provided proof that the painter was deranged, yet even that bizarre episode is ambiguous enough to suggest that it was part of an elaborate process of self-advertisement.

Intensely private feelings may well have inspired the doll's making, but once the fetish was finished Kokoschka seems to have been determined to publicize his strange behaviour. He not only paraded the doll in public. In 1925 he allowed a selection of his letters to Hermine Moos to be published. Those who had not already been scandalized by the sight of the doll in restaurants or at the opera were now to know about the artist's unconventional private life.

Once he had been accepted by German critics and admitted to the canon of great contemporary artists, Kokoschka shifted his sights elsewhere. He needed to be recognized not only in Central Europe but in Paris, the artistic capital of the world. Now he became the victim of the French 'beauty industry', an artist rejected firstly because he was an Austrian and secondly because he refused to experiment, to yield to the standards dictated by the arbiters of the avant-garde.

The earlier self-image as a rebel was no longer enough. Unconventional behaviour gave way to an increasing conservatism. He had once been a revolutionary artist, proud to assert that he was the first to work in what was manifestly a new way. Now he sought to preserve everything that was solid and valuable from the past. The image changed but it did not entirely yield to reality.

The truth is usually less remarkable than fiction. In Kokoschka's case the fiction lies close to the heart of the truth and his personality only begins to emerge with any clarity when his need for a personal mythology is understood. That need has everything to do with his background. The child of an inadequate father and a strong, ambitious mother, Kokoschka must early have acquired a belief in the importance of his own destiny. At the end as in the beginning he was dominated by a sense of history and of his own part in it.

Kokoschka's cultivation of his own myth does not diminish his achievement as an artist in any way. By revealing what drove him on, it rather enhances it. His own estimation of his gifts is well-founded, especially in the case of the work of his early maturity and middle years. As both painter and writer he redefined the limits of his craft, and if one measure of artistic greatness is provided by the influence it exerts, then Kokoschka's contribution to the art of this century is major and unassailable.

ACKNOWLEDGMENTS

As I implied in Chapter Nineteen, this biography which marks the hundredth anniversary of Kokoschka's birth, cannot claim to be definitive. The moment for a more comprehensive and detailed life will come only with the publication of all the artist's letters, with the gathering of more documentary evidence about his friends and colleagues and with the completion of a thoroughly revised catalogue of the artist's complete *œuvre*.

I hope none the less that this book does contribute to our knowledge and understanding of one of the most important figures of the twentieth century and clears away at least some of the confusion which is so prominent a feature of most of the publications about Kokoschka's life and art which have appeared thus far.

If this book does indeed succeed in this, it is in no small measure due to the assistance I have received from several quarters. As many of the quotations make clear, I have drawn heavily for my account of the artist's early life on Werner J. Schweiger's excellent documentary study *Der junge Kokoschka* and the many scholarly publications by Heinz Spielmann have also provided much valuable information.

I have also benefited greatly from conversations with Dr Wolfgang Fischer, who knew the artist and is an outstanding scholar of the culture and history of Vienna. Richard Calvocoressi of the Tate Gallery, London, read the typescript and suggested many corrections and additions. I have not been able to acknowledge his contribution in the source notes and am anxious to do so here, especially since he selflessly gave me the benefit of his extensive knowledge at a time when he was preparing the catalogue of the Kokoschka exhibition to be held in London, Zurich and New York in 1986. Others would have been less generous in their sharing of information. I am also most grateful to Elizabeth Drury, who applied her critical and editorial skills to the typescript to its great benefit, and to Annette Smith, who typed the final draft.

I am most grateful of all to the artist's widow, Olda Kokoschka, whose willingness to assist in every way possible was of immeasurable help at every stage of the writing. She allowed me to inspect hundreds of letters and postcards and patiently worked her way through the typescript correcting factual errors and chronological inaccuracies. She did not interfere; she has allowed me to provide an account of her late husband's life which in some important respects differs substantially from her own.

She feels that my picture of her husband is too sentimental, flawed by my habit of seeing events too negatively and of looking for, and finding, too much misery everywhere. Kokoschka, she says, 'was warmhearted and kind and required sympathy from others. Later his best moments were in front of great works of art, they talked to him and he to them often with much greater intensity than people did . . . He was highly strung and emotional but not sentimental; that he criticized in people.'

I cannot thank Olda Kokoschka enough for her help, understanding and the benefit of her knowledge of Kokoschka's art and life both before and after she met him. I hope that she feels this book does a little justice to her husband's memory even though she may find it difficult at some points to recognize the man and the artist in what I have written.

F.P.W. Great Wilbraham, 1985

SOVRCES OF QVOTATIONS

The following abbreviations are used:
B   Oskar Kokoschka, *Briefe*, ed.
Olda Kokoschka and Heinz
Spielmann, Vol. I, 1905–1919,
Düsseldorf 1984
F   *Die Fackel*
JK   Werner J. Schweiger, *Der junge
Kokoschka*, Vienna and Munich 1983
ML   Oskar Kokoschka, *My Life*,
trans. David Britt, London 1974

Where no source for a letter is given,
the original or a transcript can be
found in the Kokoschka Archive,
Villeneuve.

All translations are by the author
except where otherwise indicated.

Chapter One

4 'through a dreadful accident'
letter to Erwin Lang, Vienna,
Feb–March 1908. B, p. 9
6 'Everything in our almost' Stefan
Zweig, *Die Welt von Gestern*,
Frankfurt am Main 1970, p. 14
6 'On the streets at night' Zweig,
p. 14
7 'world which . . . consisted' H.
M. Wingler (ed), *Oskar
Kokoschka, Schriften 1907–1955*,
Munich 1956, p. 11
7 'Drinking water was brought'
Wingler p. 12
7 'the childhood Eden of my
dreams' ML, p. 70
'on a heap of filth' ML, p. 71
8 'The schoolboys, unobserved'
Wingler, p. 37
9 'because the teachers' J. P.
Hodin, *Oskar Kokoschka, The
artist and his time*, London 1966,
p. 61
9 'We never even heard of Byron'
Hodin, p. 61
9 'Comenius was a humanist' ML,
p. 11

Chapter Two

12 'Then Oskar rushed beaming'
Berta Patočkova-Kokoschka,
'Kindheitserinnerungen der
Schwester' in H. M. Wingler,
Oskar Kokoschka. Ein Lebensbild,
Frankfurt am Main and Berlin
1966 p. 18
13 'no one could have expected'
Karl Baedeker, *Oesterreich-
Ungarn. Handbuch für Reisende*,
Leipzig 1892, in G. Wunberg
(ed), *Die Wiener Moderne*,
Stuttgart 1981, p. 102
16 'being sick when the professor'
ML, p. 43
16 'because there was not a trace' C.
O. Czeschka, letter to Hans
Ankwicz-Kleehoven, Hamburg
11 Sept. 1952, in JK, p. 25
16 'neither saw' JK, p. 25
17 'In October I gave Kokoschka'
JK, p. 25
19 'the basis of my' Letter to
Johannes Spalt, Villeneuve? 23
Feb. 1976

Chapter Three

22 'in archetypal symbols' Carl E.
Schorske, *Fin-de-Siècle* Vienna,
London 1980, pp. 329–30
22 'My unbridled body' Oskar

Kokoschka, *Die Träumenden Knaben*, trans. Schorske, p. 332

22 'and i reeled' Oskar Kokoschka, *Die Träumenden Knaben*, Salzburg 1959, p. 26

22 'first love letter' ML, p. 20

23 'because I haven't got' letter to Erwin Lang, Vienna, end of 1907, B, p. 7

23 'Dear God' letter to Erwin Lang, Vienna, winter 1907–8

24 'the teacher of my children' letter to C. O. Czeschka, Vienna, 4 Feb. 1908, in JK, p. 60

24 'to print it at [their] expense' letter to C. O. Czeschka, Vienna, 4 March 1908, in JK, p. 60

25 'Here is the most perfect' in Werner J. Schweiger, *Wiener Werkstätte*, trans. Alexander Lieven, London 1984, pp. 138–9

25 'there has long been a debate' Karl Kraus, 'Eine Kulturtat', in F, 1907, No. 236, 18 Nov. 1907, p. 4

26 'Only a few people came' Max Mell in JK, p. 44

27 'He lacks the most important' Christian M. Nebehay, *Klimt Dokumentation*, Vienna 1969, p. 422, note 5b

28 'We have the responsibility' Nebehay, p. 397

28 'a review of the strength' JK, pp. 64–5

28 'I am finally able to write' letter to C. O. Czeschka, Vienna, 5 June 1908, JK, p.76

29 'the chief savage' JK, p.63

29 'the *enfant terrible*' JK, p. 74

31 'He had made the poster' Adolf Loos, *Sämtliche Schriften*, Vol. I, Vienna and Munich 1962, p. 443

32 'the last apotheosis' Werner Hofmann in 'Experiment Weltuntergang; Wien um 1900', exhibition catalogue, Hamburg,
Kunsthalle 1981, p. 64

33 'This taste' Otto Stoessl, 'Kunstschau' in F, 1908, No. 259–60, 13 July 1908, p. 28

33 'districts of misery and crime' in 'Experiment Weltuntergang', p. 256

Chapter Four

35 'certainly the strongest talent' JK, p. 83

35 'undeniable gifts' JK, p. 83

35 'This Oskar Kokoschka' quoted after L. E. Tesar 'Oscar Kokoschka und die Gesellschaft' in F 1911, No. 319–20, 31 March 1911, pp. 31–32

38 'a dreadful row with poor Kokoschka' letter to C. O. Czeschka, 14 Sept. 1909, in 'Oskar Kokoschka: Themen', exhibition catalogue, Albstadt, Städtische Galerie, 1979, p. 72

39 'Naturally Kokoschka's hopes' in 'Oskar Kokoschka: Themen', p. 72

39 'Philippole [i.e., Plovdiv, a small town in Bulgaria]' quoted after Ludwig Münz and Gustav Künstler, *Adolf Loos, Pioneer of Modern Architecture*, London 1966, p. 18

39 'the time will come' quoted after Münz and Künstler, p. 17

40 'mentally very hard work' quoted after Werner J. Schweiger, *Wiener Werkstätte*, p. 90

40 'a young architect' Robert Scheu, 'Adolf Loos' in F, 1909, No. 283–4, 26 June 1909, p. 26

41 'Adolf Loos dedicates his life's work' Scheu, p. 28

41 'The aim of a work of art' quoted after Münz and Künstler, p. 20

42 'Austria . . . is threatening' Karl

Kraus in F, 1899, No. 1, beginning of April 1899, p. 1

42 'Adolf Loos and I' quoted after Edith Hoffmann, *Kokoschka, Life and Work*, London 1947, p. 42

42 'They have the dirt' Karl Kraus 'Der Löwenkopf' in F, 1913, Nos 384–5, 13 Oct. 1913, p. 4

43 'the wild men to be' F, No. 1, p. 1

43 'only a painter' ML, p. 40

44 'His eyes flashed feverishly' ML, p. 39

44 'those who know me will not recognize' Karl Kraus, 'Pro Domo et Mundo', in F, 1910, No. 300, 9 April 1910, p. 25

45 'I no longer have' Karl Kraus, 'Pro Domo et Mundo' in F, 1911, Nos. 336–7, 23 Nov. 1911, p. 40

45 'the kind of enthusiastic applause' Elias Canetti, *Die Fackel im Ohr*, Frankfurt am Main 1982 pp. 69–70

45 A snob is unreliable' F 1908, Nos. 267–8. 17 Dec. 1908, p. 41

45 'If you lack ability' F, 17 Dec. 1908, p. 42

45 'Emancipated women' F, 17 Dec. 1908, p. 43

45 'A lightning conductor' F, 1909, Nos. 272–3, 15 Feb. 1909, P. 43

45 'I do not trust the printer' F. 15 Feb. 1909, p. 43

46 'Education is what most people' F, 1909, Nos. 277–8, 31 Mar. 1909, p. 60 'The devil is' ibid.

46 'What the painter of pictures' F, 1911, No. 333, 16 Oct. 1911, p. 7

46 'In a true portrait' F, 16 Oct. 1911, p. 7

48 'I was left alone' ML, p. 45

48 'The colours look' Werner Hofmann in 'Experiment Weltuntergang; Wien um 1900', exhibition catalogue, Hamburg, Kunsthalle, 1981, p. 71

Chapter Five

52 'Every evening Forel' Hodin, *Oskar Kokoschka*, pp. 96–7

52 'had never read any of his work' Hodin, p. 97

52 'this man Loos is who' Edith Hoffmann, *Kokoschka, Life and Work*, London 1947, p. 62

53 'I could work' Auguste Forel, *Out of My Life and Work*, trans. Bernard Miall, London 1937, p. 273

53 'knew very well that he was one' Karin Michaelis, 'Ein Blick genügte' in H. M. Wingler, *Oskar Kokoschka, ein Lebensbild* p. 29

53 'devoted to [Bessie] from the first' ML, p. 49

54 'and she introduced me' Oskar Kokoschka, *Das schriftliche Werk*, Vol. II, p. 85

56 'The painter Oskar Kokoschka' Georg Brühl, *Herwarth Walden und Der Sturm*, Cologne 1983, p. 33

57 'It's all only Thuringia' Nell Walden, *Herwarth Walden Ein Lebensbild*, Mainz 1963 p. 16

58 'in a red velvet jacket' quoted after Brühl, p. 18

58 'Truly I say unto you' F, 1911, Nos. 326–8, 8 July 1911, p. 40

59 'like a network of underground' ML, p. 64

60 'the more hungry' Peter Scher, 'Als Kokoschka mich malte' in Wingler, p. 32

61 'In the doorway stands' quoted after Paul Raabe (ed.), *The Era of German Expressionism*, trans. J. M. Ritchie, London 1974, p. 309

61 'must have presented' ML, p. 59

Chapter Six

66 'unless I follow his moral advice' letter to the Folkwang Museum,

Berlin, 28 November 1910,
quoted after JK, p. 157

66 'I believe Herr Kokoschka' letter
to Walter Serner published in
Karlsbader Zeitung, 2 July 1911,
quoted after JK, p. 158

67 'On a large sheet of ordinary'
Peter Scher in Wingler, *Oskar
Kokoschka, ein Lebensbild*,
pp. 32–3

69 'me quietly starve' letter of 10
April 1912, quoted after JK,
p. 133

69 'Please, you have to help me'
letter of 24 July 1914, quoted
after JK, p. 134

69 'I should like to escape from'
Vienna, 7 April 1914, B, p. 157

69 'My heavy debts' Vienna, 28
April 1914, B, p. 158

71 'entire life is hell' Berlin, 24
December 1911, B, p. 15

Chapter Seven

73 'He brews up his paints' Arthur
Roessler, *Kritische Fragmente*,
Vienna 1918, p. 97

74 'look as though they had
suffered' Franz Grüner, 'Oskar
Kokoschka' in F, 1911, Nos.
317–8, 28 Feb. 1911, pp. 18–19

75 'a shadow who copies' Vienna,
May–June 1911, B, p. 19

75 'my entire development' Vienna,
May–June 1911, B, p. 20

76 'booked up, so that my friend
Oppenheimer' letter to Lotte
Franzos, Munich, March 1911,
B, p. 16

76 'I have also heard from
Sch[oenberg]' Vienna, 13
November 1911, quoted after
JK, p. 203

76 'One doesn't need to call
someone' quoted after JK, 203

77 'Dear Max O' Else Lasker-
Schüler:'Brief an einen

Nachahmer' in Wingler, *Oskar
Kokoschka, ein Lebensbild*, p. 34

77 'Sir On the day' Else Lasker-
Schüler 'Briefe nach Norwegen'
in *Der Sturm* 1912, No 94, Jan.
1912, p. 752

78 'the first Viennese painter'
quoted after Edith Hoffmann,
p. 110

78 'The artist who starved' quoted
after Wingler pp. 41–2

80 'for Kenner's academic kind' JK,
pp. 254–5

80 'he did not correct our drawings'
JK, p. 254

80 'full of good humour and
energy' JK, p. 254

80 'I spoke to Roller' Vienna, 20
May 1913, B, pp. 110–111

81 'so quiet that those' Eugenie
Schwarzwald, 'Der
Gesprächspartner' in Wingler,
p. 25

81 'tall, blond, thin, upright' JK,
pp. 240–1

82 'With a magical touch' JK,
p. 243

82 'and rather unexpectedly' JK,
p. 244

82 'he had the girls draw' ibid.

83 'lecture about his' JK, p. 247

83 'One tree left alive' Oskar
Kokoschka, 'On the Nature of
Visions' trans. Hedi Medlinger
and John Thwaites in Edith
Hoffman, pp. 285–7

Chapter Eight

88 'When will the time come'
Vienna, probably early Sept.
1910, quoted after Reginald R.
Isaacs, *Walter Gropius, Der
Mensch und sein Werk*, Vol. I,
Berlin 1983, p. 103

88 'wait and hunger for you'
Vienna, probably mid-August
1911, quoted after Isaacs, p. 112

89 'young genius' Alma Mahler-
Werfel, *Mein Leben*, Frankfurt
am Main and Hamburg, 1963,
p. 47
89 'He had brought some rough
paper' Mahler-Werfel, p. 48
90 'Every Friday evening' JK,
p. 255
91 'poor family has to suffer'
Vienna, 29 April 1912, B, p. 34
91 'a single, violent lover's quarrel'
Mahler-Werfel, p. 49
92 'How am I living' Vienna, 6
May 1914, Isaacs, p. 115
93 'May *the* time come' Semmering,
31 Dec. 1914, Isaacs, p. 139
93 'When you get leave' Berlin,
probably June 1915, Isaacs,
p. 142
95 'The awakening to death'
Werner Hofmann in 'Experiment
Weltuntergan; Wien um 1900'
exhibition catalogue, Hamburg,
Kunsthalle 1981, pp. 256–7
95 'The picture is slowly being
finished' Vienna, April 1913 B,
p. 94
96 'in our top hats and tailcoats'
ML, p. 86

Chapter Nine

97 'the very last critical' Stefan
Zweig, *Die Welt von Gestern*,
p. 164
98 'The first fears about' Zweig,
p. 165
98 'The woman who went' Vienna,
end of July 1914, B, p. 176
99 'these little, starving' Vienna, 30
August 1914, B, p. 179
99 'If I were to get' Vienna, end of
Sept. 1914, B, pp. 182–3
99 'now going secretly' Vienna,
Oct. 1914, B, p. 184
99 'We talked about his artistic' B,
footnote, p. 354
101 'waiting, waiting in a tight'

Wiener Neustadt, 1st Day of
Exile, 3 Jan. 1915, B, p. 190
101 'I don't like to go' Wiener
Neustadt, 3rd Day of Exile, 5
Jan. 1915, B, p. 191
101 'And then exercise' Wiener
Neustadt, mid-Jan. 1915, B,
p. 193
102 'because I am not stupid' Wiener
Neustadt, end of Jan. 1915, B,
p. 194
102 'The infantry is beyond' Wiener
Neustadt, first half of February
1915, B, p. 201
'as long as the war' Wiener
Neustadt, Hotel Central, end of
Feb. 1915, B, p. 204
103 'had learned from the Japanese'
ML, p. 85
103 'ten divisions, drawn up'
Norman Stone, *The Eastern Front
1914–1917*, London 1975, p. 89
104 'In the endless forest' Galicia, 6
Aug. 1915, B, p. 226
104 'My wounds' Vienna, 27 Oct.
1915, B, p. 230
105 'I had actually set eyes on' ML,
p. 13
105 'My horse had been killed' Oskar
Kokoschka, 'In letzter Stunde'
quoted after Diether Schmidt
(ed), '*In letzter Stunde*', Dresden
1964, pp. 94–5
107 'dashing general still in the
prime' Oskar Kokoschka, *A Sea
Ringed with Visions*, trans. Eithne
Wilkins and Ernst Kaiser,
London 1962, p. 47
107 'I *never* want to see this person'
Vienna, probably end of Aug.
1915, quoted after Reginald R.
Isaacs, *Walter Gropius*, Der
Mensch und sein Werk, Vol. 1,
Berlin 1983, p. 146
108 'The thing you know about'
Klosterneuburg or Vienna, end
of June 1916, B, p. 240
108 'the most famous' Klagenfurt, 17

July 1916, B, p. 242

108 'Now I've been in the field' Isonzo front, 5 Aug. 1916, B, p. 245

108 'Today I received' Isonzo front, 30 July 1916, B, p. 244

Chapter Ten

111 'world production of petrol and coal' Eugenie Schwarzwald, 'Der Gesprächspartner' in H. M. Wingler, Oskar Kokoschka, p. 36

112 'At thirty years of age' Berlin, 23 Oct. 1916, B, p. 256

113 'had, as you know' Dresden, Weisser Hirsch, 21 Nov. 1917, B, pp. 278–9

114 'to go to a sanatorium' Berlin, 26 Nov. 1916, B, p. 259

115 'Katja, thank God' Dresden, Weisser Hirsch, 21 Nov. 1916, B, p. 260

116 'worse than ever' Stockholm, 24 Oct. 1917, B, p. 276

117 'I will not take part' Dresden, Weisser Hirsch, 6 Jan. 1918, B, p. 281

Chapter Eleven

119 'should not be made' Dresden, Weisser Hirsch, 22 July 1918, B, p. 291

119 'Yesterday I sent . . . a life-sized drawing' Dresden, Weisser Hirsch, 20 Aug. 1918, B, pp. 293–4

120 'absolutely astounded' Berlin, 10 Dec. 1918, B, pp. 299–300

121 'the news from you' Dresden, Weisser Hirsch, 15 Jan. 1919, B, p. 304

121 'I was honestly shocked by your doll' Dresden, Weisser Hirsch, 6 April 1919, B, p. 312

123 'whom no man had ever seen' Oskar Kokoschka, A Sea Ringed with Visions, p. 109

124 'the birds outside your window' Dresden, 24 April 1923

125 'The dustcart came in the grey' ML, p. 118

125 'the first Viennese painter' quoted after H. M. Wingler, Oskar Kokoschka, ein Lebensbild, p. 168

125 'Hans Posse, the director' P. F. Schmidt, 'Erinnerungen an Dresden' in Wingler, pp. 54–5

126 'The play was performed' Hugo Ball, Flight out of Time. A Dada Diary, trans. Anne Raimes and ed. John Elderfield, New York 1974, p. 106

Chapter Twelve

128 'cried for poor Klimt' Dresden, Weisser Hirsch, 11 Feb. 1918, B, p. 284

129 'You needed a pass' ML, p. 109

129 'The revolutionaries' Dresden, Weisser Hirsch, 9 Mar. 1919, B, p. 310

129 'both banks of the Elbe' ML, p. 110

130 'What initially surprised us' Hans Meyboden, 'Kokoschka der Lehrer' in H. M. Wingler, Oskar Kokoschka, p. 78

131 'the week with Kokoschka' F. K. Gotsch, 'Kokoschka als Lehrer' in J. P. Hodin, Bekenntnis zu Kokoschka, Berlin & Mainz 1963, pp. 96–7

132 'All romanticizing painting' Gotsch in Hodin, p. 102

132 'How did the master act' Gotsch in Hodin, pp. 102–3

133 'I direct the most urgent plea' Oskar Kokoschka, 'An die Einwohnerschaft Dresdens' in Das Schriftliche Werk, ed. Heinz Spielmann, Vol. IV, Politische

Äusserungen, Hamburg 1976, pp. 31–2

133 'We urge everyone' John Heartfield and George Grosz: 'Der Kunstlump', quoted after Walter Fähnders and Martin Rector (eds.), *Literatur im Klassenkampf*, Frankfurt am Main 1974, p. 51

134 'I thought it was' Dresden, early 1921

136 'fallen in love' Dresden, early 1921

136 'mother will forgive me' Dresden, 27 May 1921

136 'I am sitting' Dresden 27 May 1921

137 'been engaged in a kind of fight' Dresden, not dated

138 'The exhibition is very striking' Dresden, May 1922

138 'In one month' Dresden, May 1922

138 'he has something' Alma Mahler-Werfel, *Mein Leben*, p. 133

Chapter Thirteen

142 'I . . . found doctors' ML, pp. 121–2

144 'wanted Kokoschka to have dinner' J. P. Hodin, pp. 75–6

146 'We in Vienna' London, Savoy Hotel, 1925

146 'We were all sitting round' Tilla Durieux, *Eine Tür steht offen*, Berlin 1954, p. 275

147 'It was not so easy to arrange' J. P. Hodin, p. 226, note 14

149 'As I painted him' quoted after 'Oskar Kokoschka zum 85. Geburtstag', exhibition catalogue, Vienna, Galerie im oberen Belvedere, 1971, No. 48

149 'was startled by something' ML, p. 131

149 'On a bench' ML, pp. 131–2

Chapter Fourteen

152 'Kokoschka's studio' Julius Meier-Graefe, 'Besuch im Wiener Atelier' in H. M. Wingler, *Oskar Kokoschka, Ein Lebensbild*, Frankfurt am Main und Berlin, 1966 p. 81

152 'Seen through alien spectacles' quoted after Wingler, p. 88

154 'It was commissioned' Meier-Graefe in Wingler, p. 82

154 'first picture with' Edith Hoffmann, p. 197

156 'Throughout my long life' *Centralvereins-Zeitung*, Berlin 11 May 1933, quoted after Joseph Wulf, *Die bildenden Künste im Dritten Reich*, Reinbek bei Hamburg, 1966, p. 35

156 'My life is only half over' *Frankfurter Zeitung*, 8 June 1933, quoted after Diether Schmidt (ed.) *In letzter Stunde*, Dresden 1964, p. 42

157 'paintings representative' Hans Hinkel, 'Kunst dem Volke', in Wingler, p. 89

Chapter Fifteen

160 'During the fateful years' Heinrich Mann, *Ein Zeitalter wird besichtigt*, Berlin 1947, p. 467

160 'not getting on very well' J. P. Hodin, p. 178

161 'was collected every morning' ML, p. 155

162 'To distinguish oneself' quoted after 'Entartete Kunst', exhibition catalogue, Munich, Haus der Kunst, 1937, p. 30

164 'You have been lost' quoted after Edith Hoffmann, p. 198

164 'had [she] not, obviously' JK, p. 239

166 'as long as there' Prague, winter 1937–8

167 'I was stupid' quoted after J. P. Hodin, p. 226, note 14

168 'German art suffers' anonymous reviewer, *Apollo*, August 1938, Vol. XXVIII, No. 164, pp. 94–5

168 'I paid 2s 6d for seeing the exhibition' Fred Uhlman, 'A Personal Memoir' in exhibition catalogue, *Hampstead in the Thirties*, London, Camden Arts Centre 1974–5, p. 29

169 'at first worked' letter to Ehrenstein, Prague, no date

169 'left the realm' Peter Thoene, *Modern German Art*, Harmondsworth 1938, pp. 55–6

169 'you would put me' Prague, 17 May 1938

Chapter Sixteen

172 'were allowed to take only' London, c/o Korner, Reddington Road, Hampstead, 20 Oct. 1938

175 'Somehow we raised' Diana Uhlman, 'Hampstead in the Thirties and Forties', in exhibition catalogue, *Hampstead in the Thirties*, p. 30

175 'arranged to give square meals' Diana Uhlman, p. 31

176 'The theme was hospitality' J. P. Hodin, pp. 25–6

178 'I must admit' Hodin, pp. 226–7, note 14

179 'was the one' ML, p. 165

181 'a big quiet room' Hodin, p. 1

Chapter Seventeen

183 'The world to which' quoted after *Das Kunstwerk*, 1948, Nos. 1–2, p. 36

184 'In Vienna' letter to Gitta Perl-Wallerstein, London 21 Oct. 1946

185 'In spite of their better' in Edith Hoffmann, pp. 253–82

185 'the only country' ibid.

186 'causing great excitement' letter to Paul Westheim, Park Lane, London, 24 Jan. 1946

187 'during a blizzard' ML, p. 170

189 'Paris . . . was not the only' London, 13 May 1948

Chapter Eighteen

192 'The collapse of Graeco-Roman' letter to Heinz Spielmann of 27 Dec. 1971, quoted after *Oskar Kokoschka Themen*, exhibition catalogue, Albstadt, Städtische Galerie, 1979, pp. 80–1

194 'You ought to go' transcript of a conversation with an anonymous student, 10 Aug. 1962, W. G. Fischer Archive, London.

194 'Let your eyes ring' Robert Jungk, 'Kokoschka lehrt das Sehen', in H. M. Wingler, *Oskar Kokoschka*, pp. 102–3

195 'What emerges' Jungk, p. 104

196 'He is entirely an "Impressionist" ' George Grosz, *Briefe 1913–1959*, Hamburg 1979, p. 483

196 'art is used' letter to Paul Westheim, 29 June 1959, quoted after *Oskar Kokoschka Themen*, p. 69

197 'a kind of architect' Edouard Roditi, *Dialogues on Art*, London 1960, p. 80

199 'the late discovery' quoted after Wingler, p. 122

Chapter Nineteen

202 'I had an eerie' ML, pp. 30–1

203 'one eye and the left' Auguste Forel, *Out of My Life and Work*, trans. Bernard Miall, London 1937, p. 273

Acknowledgements

207 'was warmhearted and kind' letter to the author, Villeneuve 30 April 1985

INDEX

Illustration numbers are in bold type.